THE ECONOMY
IN THE REAGAN
YEARS

THE ECONOMY IN THE REAGAN YEARS

The Economic Consequences of the Reagan Administrations

Anthony S. Campagna

Contributions in Economics and Economic History,
Number 150

GREENWOOD PRESS
Westport, Connecticut • London

338.973
C18e

Library of Congress Cataloging-in-Publication Data

Campagna, Anthony S.
    The economy in the Reagan years : the economic consequences of the
Reagan administrations / Anthony S. Campagna.
      p. cm. — (Contributions in economics and economic history,
ISSN 0084-9235 ; no. 150)
    Includes bibliographical references and index.
    ISBN 0-313-28866-6 (alk. paper)
    1. United States—Economic policy—1981–1993. 2. United States—
Economic conditions—1981–   I. Title. II. Series.
HC106.8.C34   1994
338.973′009′048—dc20   93–14125

British Library Cataloguing in Publication Data is available.

Library of Congress Catalog Card Number: 93-14125
ISBN: 0-313-28866-6
ISSN: 0084-9235

First published in 1994

Greenwood Press, 88 Post Road West, Westport, CT 06881
An imprint of Greenwood Publishing Group, Inc.

Printed in the United States of America

The paper used in this book complies with the
Permanent Paper Standard issued by the National
Information Standards Organization (Z39.48-1984).

10 9 8 7 6 5 4 3 2 1

FOR
RUTH
OF LA JOLLA

Contents

Tables

Preface

Under Ronald Reagan, economics was, for a time at least, no longer the dismal science. He, along with whom Ayn Rand called "capitalist hippies," rode the wave of disenchantment with the Carter administration to foist on the American public a "revolution" in the approach to the management of the economy. Armed with simple answers, a straightforward economic program, and a religious zeal, they proceeded to apply their prescription for a struggling economy.

It is not our purpose to examine the emergence of Ronald Reagan on the national scene. Others will have to undertake that intriguing task. Whether he benefited from the conservative swing in the nation (from Nixon to Ford to Carter), or whether he benefited from an antipolitician mood (read anti-Washington), or simply whether his personal appeal allowed him to take advantage of a willingness to take a risk by the voting public, Reagan was able to capitalize on these trends to win election and be granted the chance to try out his economic program and philosophy. Cynics might add that power brokers saw a chance to use an innocent person for private gain in the name of conservatism.

Whatever the explanation for the phenomenon of Ronald Reagan, he was given most of what he wanted of his economic program. In fact, he eventually received more than most presidents in this regard. This is a major theme of this book, and one that allows for the examination of rather clear promises against results; the success or failure cannot really be blamed on others if the program received a reasonable chance to operate.

This book, then, is concerned with the evaluation of that economic program. It is composed of three parts. They ask three direct questions: What was planned? What happened? What are we left with?

Therefore, Part I sets out the aims of the program. After examining the legacy of Vietnam and the first half of the 1970s in Chapter 1, the Carter years are covered both as a forerunner of Reaganomics and for the state of the economy when he left office. Chapter 3 sets out the Reagan agenda so that the record of what he hoped to accomplish is made clear. Finally the role of ideology, so important in the Reagan administrations, is discussed in Chapter 4.

Part II deals with the results of the economic plan. Fiscal policy is covered in Chapter 5 and monetary policy in Chapter 6. The regulatory policy is examined in Chapter 7, whereas all other results of the economic plan are discussed in Chapter 8.

Part III is concerned with the legacy of the Reagan administrations' economic policies. Fiscal policy and role of government is covered in Chapter 9; monetary policy and the banking system occupies the concern of Chapter 10; and international trade and the U.S. position in the world economy follows in Chapter 11. Chapters 12 and 13 deal with the changing structure of society: Chapter 12 with the economic structure and Chapter 13 with the social structure. Finally I ask, What if Reagan had been allowed to be Reagan? in Chapter 14 and conclude with Chapter 15.

I have concluded that the economic program was basically a failure. This essentially untested and unexamined program contained too many inconsistencies for it to have worked as billed and was based on economic responses that were simply too fanciful. In my view, the program itself was flawed and attempts to blame others for its failures are not justified.

Some may argue that it is too soon to make such judgments. The disagreements over Reagan's economic policies are continuing and are likely to continue for some time with proponents of every view expressing their opinions. Over time, a consensus may be reached, but in the near term, not much agreement can be expected. Still it is necessary, in books like this one, to begin to formulate some conclusions, however tentative. Future scholars will benefit from the views of contemporaries who wrote with events fresh in mind and with enough results at hand to begin to make some judgments. Accordingly in this book, I have expressed mine. In addition, it should be noted that I did not back the Reagan economic program right from the beginning. So I belong to the professional, intellectual types that Reagan so disparaged when criticisms of his policies were made. So my bias is apparent at the outset. However, I have tried to compensate for whatever bias emerges by carefully considering all sides in the assessment of the Reagan years and by consulting as many sources as possible before redundancy set in.

In any case, no one book can hope to cover the entire period, particularly one so rich in controversial policies. Moreover, the usual space limitations were imposed by the publisher that often dictated the depth of coverage of the material. For example, there remains the intriguing question of what happened to macroeconomic theories and their ability to explain the events in this period? The monetarist explanation was found lacking when large increases in the money supply failed to induce inflation, and in the inability to adequately explain the changes in velocity. Keynesians might ponder why huge deficits did not create inflation or abnormally high interest rates. Supply-siders need to explain why saving and investment did not behave as predicted. Finally, new classical economists and neo-Keynesians still must fit the experience of the 1980s into their models. These topics would take us far afield and double the size of this book; in fact, the reassessment of our macroeconomic models would require a separate book.

Fortunately, there are many books on the *policy* topic that cover various aspects of the Reagan years in more or less detail. I have benefited from them enormously, and they have influenced me in many ways, often not adequately acknowledged. I urge the reading of as many of them as possible. The problem for me is that I may not have acknowledged my debt to the authors sufficiently, or have not attributed to them their ideas that inadvertently will be seen to be mine. I apologize for any of these omissions.

I also want to thank all those who helped me at the University of Vermont and, on sabbatical, at the University of California at San Diego. I have benefited from discussions with my colleagues at both institutions. An unknown reviewer made several suggestions that I tried to follow, but I alone am responsible for any errors that remain.

Finally, I would like to thank my wife, who once again had to suffer through two readings of the manuscript, and who once again made valuable suggestions for its improvement. But her assistance went far beyond mere editing, as she bore with me through the long writing process. My dedication of the book to her is but a trifling recognition of her support.

Part I

The Plan

Chapter 1

The Legacy of Vietnam and the First Half of the 1970s

The economy in the 1970s dealt a severe blow to followers of complacency. The decade began in the middle of a recession and the Vietnam conflict, and inherited all the problems created by both unfortunate experiences. When the war ended, the Arab members of OPEC declared war on the inflation-ridden U.S. economy by withholding their oil. This episode, along with other supply-side shocks, created stagflation—that inelegant marriage of stagnation and inflation—and made the trade-off between price stability and unemployment appear obsolete. The decade ended with the prospect of another recession, forecast with regularity in 1978 and 1979, but not finally arriving until 1980.

Events in this decade included: the political scandals of Watergate and the downfall of Richard Nixon who resigned in the face of impending impeachment; the elevation of unelected public officials to the highest offices in the land; the foreign policy reversals in Iran and Afghanistan; the food embargoes and food shortages; the revivals of wage and price controls; and the deterioration in foreign trade balances.

Clearly, all of these events, and more, added up to a thoroughly confusing period, both for the economy and for the political structure. Policy makers were either paralyzed or overactive with results that were equally schizophrenic. In retrospect, it is easy to condemn the actions of those who sought to govern, but it should be no comfort to those who sought to advise; the decade was characterized by wild swings in conditions and disturbing events, and equally wild reactions to them.

In the remainder of this chapter, some attempt will be made to sift through these events to justify the claim that the 1970s was a strange but interesting decade. Events in the economic and political worlds were remarkably upsetting; there were no real modern precedents for either the economic or political upheavals that occurred. Of course, that left policy makers free to blunder and advisors free to offer conflicting advice.

Our aim, of course, is not to rummage through the 1970s looking for situations to investigate to prove some point or other but to select those events that were to have substantial influence on the economic, political, and social conditions of the 1980s. It is my contention that without the experiences of the 1970s, the 1980s would have been far different. In fact, many of the concerns and policies of the 1980s were in reaction to what happened in the 1970s.[1]

So it is proper to start with the decade of the seventies to understand the following decade. The argument that the events of one period influence subsequent periods is trivial, of course, and obvious, and needs no further justification. However, the argument made here is that the 1980s represented such a radical departure from recent past experience that a more profound look at the preceding period is not only necessary but crucial. Whenever sharp breaks are made from past behavior, there are likely to be identifiable causes that help explain them. If our premise of the crucial importance of the 1970s is valid, the reactions to them in the 1980s will not be as sharp as claimed nor as surprising. This then is the purpose of this chapter.

THE LEGACY OF THE VIETNAM WAR

Any real understanding of the 1970s must begin with the hangover created by the Vietnam War. It is not the cost of the war that is essential here, although it was substantial, ranging from the official estimate of $140 billion to well over $500 billion, but the funding of it that caused some major problems.[2] In addition, reactions to the managing of this unpopular and divisive war really transformed the functioning of the U.S. economy to such an extent that it would never be the same again. Similar responses would be elicited in the political arena. These structural changes were not fully recognized as the 1970s began (and some would deny them still), but they were to have a profound impact on the functioning of the U.S. society.

Everyone acknowledges that the expenditures on the Vietnam War overheated the economy and caused inflation. Wars and inflation are familiar bedfellows, and this conflict once again verified that observation. The yearly inflation rates can be seen in Table 1.1 along with the unemployment rate. The record is clear, although how much of the inflation can be attributed to the Vietnam War may be debatable. The CPI rose at the start of the buildup for the war in 1965 and the rate continued to grow until wage and price controls were instituted in 1971; in 1973 the controls became voluntary, and inflation began to respond, until the system was dismantled in April 1974.

The unemployment rate, often used to gauge economic conditions, declined steadily as the war escalated, reaching a low of 3.3% in February 1969. The recession year, 1970, broke that record and the rate returned to more normal magnitudes.

As inflation continued and the Federal Government took almost no action to combat it, forecasts of continued inflationary pressures were easy to make, and soon those who could began to build in an inflationary premium in their economic affairs. This inflationary psychology, once allowed to develop, is difficult to treat. The temporary income tax surcharge of 1968 was too little and too late to do the job of signaling the administration's resolve to combat the problem. So, regardless of how much of the inflationary pressures can be attributed to the war and how much to administration errors, inflation was allowed to proceed virtually unchecked as the economy boomed.

Table 1.1
Inflation and Unemployment during the Vietnam Era

Year	% Change in CPI	% Unemployment
1964	1.0	5.0
1965	1.9	4.4
1966	3.5	3.7
1967	3.0	3.7
1968	4.7	3.5
1969	6.2	3.4
1970	5.6	4.8
1971	3.3	5.8
1972	3.4	5.5
1973	8.7	4.8
1974	12.3	5.5
1975	6.9	8.3

Note: The Vietnam War buildup began in late 1965 and the war ended in March 1975. Wage and price controls were instituted in August 1971 and ended April 30, 1974.

Source: Council of Economic Advisors, *Economic Report of the President, 1991.*

The administration's failure to counteract inflation through monetary and fiscal policies was only the most glaring of its mistakes in this period. Other actions or nonactions were to set the stage for the economy in the 1970s. Consider some of these. Keynesian-type policies that promised to compensate for cyclical variations in the economy failed the second test to which it was put. The Kennedy–Johnson tax cut in 1964, the first test, stimulated the economy as predicted and earned the "new economists," the liberal group who wanted to control the economy by altering monetary and fiscal policies, high marks for its success. They showed the means to stimulate an economy when needed and promised to restrain it when the opposite conditions warranted.

They were wrong, or at best overly optimistic. They simply forgot that politics plays a major role in policy making, and Lyndon Baines Johnson was a master politician. He would not support the imposition of a war tax nor would he sacrifice the Great Society programs, or lose the other war—on poverty.

How much time was required for people to observe the lack of symmetry of public policy? It is easy to stimulate an economy; it is difficult to restrain it. The former creates boom times, and the latter recessions. This simple lesson was slowly grasped by politicians, and at each realization, the interventionist government lost some adherents. Or rather, what was learned was the political benefits of prosperity and the pain of hard times; one wins votes and one wins retirement. The economic principles behind the application of the tools of monetary and fiscal policies appropriately applied were relegated to background noise as the politicians heard only what they wanted to hear.[3]

The liberal philosophy, typically identified with an active government, became tarnished as well. The slow erosion of what was known as Keynesian economics prepared the way for acceptance of alternative approaches. The critics were not long in coming. Conservatives who had been chafing under liberal regimes and all those opposed to government actions for whatever reasons, were eager to disclose the flaws in liberal thought and policies.[4]

Long a critic of interventionist governments in economic affairs, Milton Friedman's economic theories were gaining adherents. Friedman led a ''new'' school of thought, called monetarism, that brought into question the ability of policy makers to stabilize an economic system. Stressing the importance of money to the economy, monetarists discounted fiscal policy as being able to influence the economy beyond a very short period; even monetary policy was limited in effectiveness, and in the long run, neither fiscal or monetary was effective. So much for stabilization policies. Any government that ignored this advice, no matter how well meaning its intentions, would likely make things worse. The assault was perfectly timed to gain acceptance, as the nation looked on at an economy in disarray.

There were more disconcerting developments in the period. The economic problems might have been rationalized, as is generally the case, except for the fact that there was a growing distrust in government anyway. The failure to manage the economy properly was nothing compared to the mistrust generated by the deceptions, distortions, and miscalculations emanating from the Pentagon and the White House over the conduct of the Vietnam war. Politicians in the United States have always been subject to great skepticism as a matter of course, and, hence, trust in government has always been difficult to obtain. Moreover, once the basic trust is lost beyond normal bounds, the resulting distrust and skepticism spreads to all areas of government activity, even to those areas not affected, including managing the economy.

Trust in government is also partly conditioned by trust in governmental leaders. This obvious fact is clearly illustrated by the experience of President Johnson. He squandered that trust as he deceived the public about his crusade in Vietnam. The good will he was given after the death of President Kennedy was quickly surrendered as he blundered into Vietnam and paved the road to his own personal downfall in the playing out of some curious Greek tragedy. Johnson's fate is not the issue, however, and the point is that distrust in political leadership lingers, and, although always latent in the American public, deepens in periods like this when suspicions turn into fact. Gradually, the public paints all politicians the same color, and no amount of red, white, and blue can remove the stain.

In the economic world, the loss of confidence in the government's ability to control the economy led to changes in the economy itself. People began to take steps to protect or insulate themselves from the vagaries and uncertainties of both the political and economic systems. As they did so, they transformed the economy in ways that ensured that no return to the past would ever be possible;

the economic system would be permanently altered. Only a few of these changes will illustrate the trend.

The voluntary incomes policy, called guideposts, was a quick victim of the overheated economy. The Kennedy Administration's Council of Economic Advisors tried to use this informal, sanctionless, system of controls to educate labor, management, and the public about the relationships among labor productivity, wage rates, costs of production, and inflation. If wage increases could be related more closely to the growth in labor productivity, costs could be stabilized and inflation could be kept in check. Everyone would benefit, and the endless conflict between labor and management would be less confrontational. Some claimed that this voluntary program worked to curtail exorbitant wage claims (when if granted, were passed on to consumers in the form of higher prices) and strengthen firms' resolve to resist them, but, again, the guideposts program failed the test when economic conditions became less stable and more uncertain. Of course, this is when they are needed most.

What was lost was not just an attempt at an incomes policy, although that loss served as another example of the failure of economic controls, but, even more serious, the loss of respect for a government-sponsored program that could be easily complied with when it was convenient to do so, and just as easily ignored when it was not. After all, imposing voluntary controls without legal sanctions and asking economic agents to act in the national interest are not prescriptions for success in the long term anyway. But the gradual and hard-won cooperation of labor and management that had been built up with great effort in the early 1960s was now to be gradually eroded.

Nowhere are the subtle structural shifts more evident than in the financial community. The process of self-protection from government rules, regulations, and policies began in the late 1960s and continued through the 1980s. Always adept at finding ways around the rules and regulations anyway, the financial sector had the incentive to be even more imaginative in this period.

In an effort to combat inflation, the economy was forced to endure two credit crunches, one in 1966 and one in 1969. The monetary authorities, lacking any real fiscal restraint, were given the unwelcome task of applying the brakes to the economy. The credit crunches sent everyone scrambling around for funds, producing several liquidity crises. With the demand for funds in a booming economy greatly exceeding the supply, predictable results followed: The economy veered toward recession in both periods.

The Federal Reserve was subject to much criticism for its actions and soon retreated, in both instances, to a more accommodating posture. But the credit crunch experiences were not lost on those who suffered from their consequences. As might be expected, all who could do so took steps to protect themselves from future repetitions. Banks created new negotiable instruments, for example, CDs, pursued liability management techniques, raised interest rates, and so forth, and, over the longer run, began to deal in Eurodollar markets, resorted to off-shore banking establishments, turned to one-bank holding companies, engaged in repurchase agreements, forced the deregulation of interest rate ceilings, established real estate affiliations (REITs), and, in general, pursued every avenue to avoid the influence of the Federal Reserve. Thrift institutions, facing huge losses of funds to other institutions, clamored for help and found some in the tampering of interest rate ceilings, floating interest rates on mortgages, and in new negotiable instruments rivaling the commercial sector.

These developments in the financial sector encouraged more risk-taking on the part of these institutions. As interest rates rose, more risky ventures were funded to make profits. Thus, these credit crunches, designed to reduce lending, may well have encouraged more lending activity in riskier areas.[5] In brief, innovations in the financial sector reduced the power of the Federal Reserve to control monetary conditions by its usual means and encouraged the growth of speculation, if not outright gambling. The Federal Reserve fostered this more adventurous spirit when it continually backed down in the confrontations with the larger banks when interest rate regulations threatened to cause problems for them, thus letting the banks take the lead in deciding financial conditions. When the Federal Reserve rescued the financial community in the Penn Central case and when the Franklin National Bank failed, the lessons were not lost on the financial community: The Fed would not allow any large bank to fail or allow any serious disturbance in financial markets. The caution sign was removed.

Another disturbing development that surfaced in this period was the decline in the rate of growth of labor productivity. In the late 1960s, the trend was not pronounced and was, therefore, ignored. Later, when the downward trend took a sharp turn in the 1970s, concern over this important measure rose dramatically. Still largely unexplained, and in some cases denied, the decline in the rate of growth of labor productivity would become one explanation in the analysis of falling living standards and reappear as an explanation for the decline in competitiveness with other nations. Both of these arguments will warrant further discussion in subsequent periods.

The turbulent sixties transformed the society in many ways too numerous even to enumerate here. For example, the war on poverty, the other war, was lost before its first major battle; black ghettos erupted in flames and violence as rising expectations and hope were dashed; women began entering the labor force in larger numbers, creating problems for the nuclear family. These and other trends all would reappear to transform the society in later decades.

THE ECONOMY IN THE 1970s

Richard M. Nixon won the presidential campaign of 1968, promising peace with honor as he patted his breast pocket for the nonexistent plan to end the war. The law-and-order campaigner, the speaker for the silent majority, and the leader who would restore pride in America, Nixon promised also to return stability to the economic system. It was not immediately clear how this was to be achieved, however.

The Nixon administration inherited an economy in disarray, but it promised nothing new to straighten it out aside from more reliance on the private sector. As the new administration assumed responsibility for the economy in 1969, the unemployment rate was 4.5% and the inflation rate as measured by the Consumer Price Index (CPI) was 3.6%. Ever mindful that adverse economic conditions cost him the 1960 presidential election, Nixon wanted to restore price stability without exacerbating the unemployment rate beyond the socially acceptable rate of 4%. The restoration of stability to the economy would also allow Nixon to concentrate on foreign affairs, his real interest. Accordingly, he was willing throughout his tenure to delegate the responsibility for economic affairs to his advisors.

His advisors devised the plan of attack that came to be known as "gradualism," referring to the hope that inflation could be reduced over a longer run period without aggravating the unemployment rate excessively. True to conservative ideology, this plan was to be implemented using monetary policy with much less emphasis on fiscal policy. This is not to infer that his advisors were monetarists, believing only in the efficacy of monetary policy, but in the words of Herbert Stein, one of the advisors, they were "Friedmanesque." True, they placed greater faith in monetary policy over fiscal policy but were much more pragmatic than the dogmatic monetarists. They were also, as others have noted, liberals masquerading as conservatives.[6]

Good intentions aside, the policy of gradualism did not work and was abandoned at the first sign of trouble. The tight money policy that was supposed to curb inflation drove interest rates up to their highest level since the Civil War as, for example, the 3-month treasury bill rate rose to 7.7% in December, up from 5.9% a year earlier. Fiscal policy, meanwhile, was also restrictive as government expenditures were cut by $7.5 billion, and the budget for 1969 registered a small surplus of $3.2 billion, the last budget surplus to date. This surplus was actually due to the Tax Reform Act of 1969, which the administrations opposed, that removed the investment tax credit, reduced accelerated depreciation, curtailed depletion allowances, and increased the tax on capital gains. The administration regarded these measures as discouraging to private fixed investment and economic growth but was unsuccessful in blocking passage of the Act.

The tight monetary policy caused the second credit crunch in the 1960s. Again the results were predictable as the financial community scrambled around for funds and created the institutional changes in the financial world that were described earlier. To reiterate, their actions, designed to protect themselves against future repetitions of crunches, ultimately would lead to making monetary policy less effective in the future, or to be made effective, would require the policy to be stronger or applied longer.

The immediate result, however, was to push the economy into a recession, halting the longest expansion up to that time. The recession began in December 1969 and lasted until November 1970, a rather brief downturn in which the inflation rate rose to 5.4%, unemployment fell slightly to 3.5%, and the growth rate of the GNP fell to 2.8% from 4.9%. In real terms, however, the GNP fell by 3.9%. Clearly, these were not the hoped-for results, and the policy of gradualism through monetary restraint was quickly abandoned. Monetary ease brought some reduction to interest rates, but other events were disturbing the financial markets as well as the society as a whole. Financial markets were shaken by the invasion of Cambodia, the shootings at Kent State, the Vietnam War jitters, and by the collapse of Penn Central Railroad.

Penn Central, as did many other corporations, was raising funds by selling commercial paper since the credit crunch of 1966 forced it to seek funds in nontraditional ways. When the commercial paper became due, the corporations simply rolled them over—that is until 1969–70. The second credit crunch severely restricted the raising of funds in this manner and a genuine liquidity crisis was at hand. The near demise of Chrysler and Lockheed did not help the situation either as the financial markets, starved for liquidity, were near panic.

The Federal Reserve responded by reducing the discount rate and encouraging banks to borrow. The panic was averted, but the goal of reducing inflation had to be sacrificed. Throughout these latter years of the 1960s the lessons to be learned from credit crunches were mastered by the financial community.

WAGE AND PRICE CONTROLS

The Nixon Administration was clearly not achieving its goals of reducing inflation to more socially acceptable rates while keeping unemployment from exceeding its socially acceptable rate of 4%. With the presidential election just around the corner and not wanting to be accused of manipulating the economy just to win reelection, the secretary of the treasury, John Connally, conceived a plan to win reelection for the president and reduce inflation. So at a secret meeting at Camp David, a few trusted advisors devised a policy of wage and price controls to accomplish what traditional monetary and fiscal policies were not. The Kennedy–Johnson guideposts were now history, and despite Nixon's disavowal of controls of any kind (a lesson he presumably learned in helping to administering them in WWII), some quick actions had to be taken to show the country that steps were being taken to get the economy under control and to display the president as a forceful, courageous leader.[7]

Never mind that controls are one of the most anticapitalist policies that can be devised (free markets are supposed to determine wages and prices), and never mind that this was presumed to be a conservative Republican Administration, the public was asked to accept this swift and surprising shift in policy as necessary for the health of the economy. At first, the controls were greeted with approval by the public; management wanted to curb wage demands; and labor wanted to curtail price increases. After the initial euphoria, the support for controls dwindled the longer they were in effect.

In general, the controls worked at first, and then ran into various problems normally solved through market decisions. However, it is not our purpose to evaluate the wage and price controls experience; how the controls actually worked is not the issue here. Suffice it to say that failure was embodied in them at the outset; they were inflexible, poorly conceived and administered, regarded as *temporary*, and regularly denounced by those entrusted to enforce them. Of course, bureaucratic blundering added to their downfall.

Judged on economic grounds, the control system was not very successful domestically, and after they were removed, prices resumed their upward spiral. Judged on political and international trade grounds, the policy was a huge success. After the controls were instituted, the administration was free to pump up the economy so that it would be booming at election time. Both fiscal and monetary policy became expansive, stimulating the economy without having to worry about inflation—just what Nixon and Connally wanted.[8] On the international scene, the administration eventually won what it could not win by persuasion—flexible exchange rates. By unilaterally declaring the Bretton Woods system void, by closing the gold window in the United States, and by threatening to raise import duties, the administration forced the rest of the world to comply with its wishes.

The question is whether this cynical attempt at manipulating the economy for political reasons had any repercussions in ensuing years. What is important now is not whether controls were necessary, effective, or efficient; what matters now is their role in the transformation of the economic and political system. The controls left a legacy that included the following:

1. A disdain for institutions that permitted the blatant manipulation of the economic system for political ends. Both the Federal Reserve and the executive branch were condemned.
2. The loss of confidence in the United States by the international community over its tactics in forcing changes in international monetary conditions.
3. A severe blow to the efficacy of direct wage and price controls. Even though this experience would be an inappropriate guide for their future use, another control system would not likely be attempted for a long time.
4. More distrust, cynicism, or uncertainty over the government's ability to manage the economy for the general good, and more distrust of government leadership in general.

NIXON'S DOWNFALL AND ECONOMIC LEGACY

After the controls were lifted, the economy was once again in trouble. No longer needed for political purposes, the controls gave way to traditional monetary and fiscal policies. Both types of policies quickly turned restrictive; with the election over, it was time to turn to more traditional ways of fighting inflation—recessions. The rate of monetary growth slowed, interest rates rose, and discretionary spending was curtailed. The economy dutifully responded and produced a recession that began in late 1973 and lasted until March 1975.

Long before the recession bottomed out, Nixon lost whatever concern he had for the state of the economy. He had larger worries as the Watergate scandal began to unfold. In August 1974, facing impeachment, he resigned, leaving Mr. Ford to deal with the economy.

The Ford administration was handed an economy in shambles. All prices were increasing by double digits in 1974, both in the CPI (11%) and the WPI (19%), with fuel prices rising by over 33%. The unemployment rate rose to over 7% in 1974, and real wages fell by 5%. As the economy sank into the recession, stagflation was becoming painfully evident.[9]

The recession was caused partly by the reversals of monetary and fiscal policies in 1973 after the election was won. The devaluation of the dollar in 1973 might have contributed to the decline as well. Incorrect macroeconomic policies, ill-conceived changes in the controls program, and incorrect forecasts of economic conditions all contributed to the downturn. But the whole picture is complicated by the emerging energy problem. In October 1973, several Arab members of OPEC decided to place an embargo on oil to the United States and other developed nations. The embargo, in part, reflected the objection to the U.S. support of Israel in the Arab–Israeli war. Some punishment was deemed appropriate, and some reminder of how vital OPEC was to the United States had to be demonstrated.

Equally, if not more important to these Arab countries, was their concern over inflation in the United States. From 1950 to 1970, oil prices were stable or falling, but import prices to the Arab nations rose steadily. Oil-producing countries stood by and watched inflation erode the purchasing power of revenue collected from their precious commodity. Oil revenues were used as the principle means to finance economic development. Now those revenues were falling rapidly in real terms. To make matters worse, oil prices were denoted in dollars, and as the dollar depreciated, imports from other western nations were also more costly. The oil embargo was imposed as a protest to these developments.

The removal of imported oil to the United States while hardly devastating, did cause severe disruptions to the economy. The shortage of energy forced prices up and forced curtailment of consumption by households and firms alike. As consumers reallocated their budgets and spent less on other goods, firms reduced output and employment or were forced to cut back production for lack of energy. Together with domestic macroeconomic policies, a recession was assured.

Given these conditions, what was done about them? As far as the recession goes, the answer is easy—not much. In the face of the most severe economic downturn since the 1930s, the record of fiscal and monetary policies is baffling.

Concern for inflation prompted the administration to request a ceiling on government expenditures and a tax increase! Only later, when the recovery had begun, did the administration reverse itself and call for a temporary tax decrease. As Blinder put it, "It is hard to find much good to say about fiscal policy during the period of the Great Stagflation." [10] Monetary policy was no better, resorting to tight money or stable money growth to fight inflation. It would appear that macroeconomic policies were not only not helpful in this recession but actually made it worse.

The response to the energy crisis was equally dismal. The administration did create the Federal Energy Administration (FEA) to regulate oil supplies and prices. The FEA did attempt to allocate the scarce oil supply and did propose a windfall profits tax on old oil. Other schemes included conservation advice, tax incentives to foster conservation, the 55-mile-per-hour speed limit, and the requirement that automobile producers must meet some minimum gas mileage per gallon. The FEA operated in a climate of mistrust, for there were always reports of oil being plentiful and that various parts of the country were experiencing shortages while other parts were not.

SOCIETAL REACTIONS

The last half of the 1960s and the first half of the 1970s offers us an opportunity to observe some fundamental shifts in the perception of the society by its members. The political, economic, and social worlds were profoundly shaken by events in this period, and the reactions to them would influence future periods in ways that may never be fully documented.

1. The 1970s began with a recession in the midst of which a system of wage and price controls was instituted. Given the credit crunch of 1969, the unsuccessful experiment with gradualism, and finally a wage and price control scheme, the public would be forgiven if it concluded that the management of the economy was out of control.

As we have seen, the credit crunches of 1966 and 1969 set off a revolution in banking practices that forever changed the financial sector and caused the Federal Reserve to lose some measure of control over the economy. The reactions to these crunches accelerated the tendency, always present, to find means to avoid the regulatory aspects of the central bank. Monetary policy would henceforth be less effective and less efficient in carrying out its main functions of monetary control. In effect, more power was transferred to major banks in the economy with the Federal Reserve being the loser. If banks could avoid or circumvent the controls, the Fed would have to listen and pay heed to what the major banks found acceptable.

Wage and price controls have always been advocated by the public, regardless of actual experience with them. Apparently, everyone thinks that other people's prices will be controlled, or firms feel that wages will be controlled; their own rewards will continue unabated, of course. The experience of the controls in the 1971–74 period should have disillusioned people in that the administration of them was incredible, the political nature of them was cynical, and the results of them were questionable at best. This was not the case, for the public continually expressed the desire, according to Gallup polls, to have even stricter controls while they were in effect and wanted to bring them back in the latter part of the 1970s when they were not in effect.[11]

What accounts for the public's faith in controls when economists probably reject them by a wide margin? I believe this is a manifestation of disillusionment with traditional policies designed to fight inflation. In the past, all too often, recessions have been engineered to stabilize prices, and the public has some difficulty with this method—the old time religion. The desire to avoid the painful effects of recessions (not borne by economists) is understandable and leads to the search for a better way. Wage and price controls offer one such avenue, particularly when they are viewed as affecting the other fellow more than the advocate.

But there is more than just this desire to avoid the pain of recessions. *Many more people, particularly the most disadvantaged, are hurt more by recessions than by inflation.*[12] They realize that the fight to subdue inflation will benefit higher-income groups, the wealthy with financial assets receiving high real interest rates, creditors in general, and those with portfolios to protect themselves from price changes, and will do little to help those who lose their employment. The inflation fighters seem to be always at the bottom of the economics scale, but without employment and income, prices become irrelevant.

Thus, economists who are baffled by the public's support of wage and price controls would do well to reconsider the distributional effects of inflation versus unemployment before dismissing the public's acceptance of controls as stemming from ignorance.

2. The economic response to the recession that began in 1973 would seem to confirm that traditional policies cannot be trusted to correct matters. Never mind that traditional policies were not utilized correctly; the perception was that the economy was mismanaged. Some faith in the ability to manage the economy was surely sacrificed in this episode. I am not referring to conservative economists, monetarists, and others, who were maintaining that traditional monetary and fiscal policies were ineffective anyway and who were actively advocating less government intervention into the economy. These economists may have had some influence at the time in convincing others of the veracity of their views, but the general public was hardly interested in esoteric debates among economists. The public saw only confusion and irresolution in policy making.

The question was: Did economists know what they were doing? Recent experience would suggest a negative answer. Policy makers seemed less certain of how to proceed, economists seemed to be equivocating in their advice and offering conflicting views, and economic agents were unsure of which policies would be followed. Altogether, this was a rather unsettling period for economists and policy makers as some of the confidence in the ability to manage the economic system was eroded and more criticisms of political leaders developed.

3. Recessions were not new to the U.S. economy, but the oil embargo was. The fact that the shortage of such a vital resource was a new problem requires a different, perhaps tempered, evaluation. Caught unawares, in the midst of a recession, some confusion on the part of policy makers could be expected. In retrospect, however, the response to this crisis was not praiseworthy. The reaction to this supply shock was ambiguous, vacillating, and tentative. A price shock of this kind can be met in a variety of ways. It could be regarded as a one-time price shock, and adjustments made to it slowly over time; or it can be allowed to permeate the economy through a wage price spiral in an effort to make up for losses in real income that followed. The inflationary spiral combined with the recession already underway (caused by cutbacks in production because of energy shortages), resulted in the worst of all worlds—stagflation.

The recession went untreated, as we have seen, and now worry over inflation prevented any policy actions that might have addressed it. Instead, the price of oil was allowed to move through the system as we stood helplessly by, apparently willing to pay any price. There was no energy policy. There was no call for sacrifice, nor ready measures to encourage conservation. The measures taken seem insignificant in hindsight.

The trouble is that little has been learned from this experience. A similar occurrence would probably result in similar responses. But the American public learned a lot about the ineptness of public policy. They learned fear, anger, resentment, and worry over the course of the embargo. Events seemed to be getting out of control, and leaders were no match for the problems created. Policy makers were not able or willing to deal with the recession, the oil problem, or economic stagnation. Events seemed to be controlling the economy, not rational people controlling events.

4. With these events in mind, consider the impact of the Nixon administration and Watergate. If faith in the leadership was shaken by economic turmoil, then faith in politicians was really devastated by the Nixon administration. The cynical manipulation of the economy for political purposes with its ill-conceived system of controls, the exploitation of government agencies, and all else involved in the Watergate scandal, and the total disregard for the law and all conduct of decency were sufficient to destroy all faith in government.

When Nixon resigned, after his vice-president Spiro Agnew before him, the nation now had two appointed leaders to the two highest posts in the land. When President Ford pardoned Nixon for all offenses, the disenchantment with political leaders was almost complete. Despite all the analyses of these events, it is still difficult to estimate just how the distrust of political leaders really was affected. Intellectuals can react quickly and can express their dismay in various forums. Others do not have the means or avenues to express their views. Hence, how deeply affected the public might have been must be inferred by later manifestations. Much of the discontent is registered, if at all, in the ballot box, and not much can be readily observed. We will return to this theme again.

5. It is an understatement to suggest that the Vietnam War tore the nation apart in many ways. Never entirely justified, or even explained, for a large part of the American public, the war never had the legitimacy of, say, WWII. The Korean War was never accepted either, but by 1965, that experience was too remote to affect thought about the current conflict. Divisions over the war emanated not only from questions over its purpose but also from its conduct in terms of weapons used, its determination of who should fight it, its public relations—reporting via body counts, and so on. Every aspect of the war engendered some controversy.

Everyone agrees that the war generated opinions that sharply divided the society, and to continue to justify that conclusion would be kicking at an open door. Rather, it is to the legacy of the war that more attention is required. *The fact is that to a large part of the public, we lost the war!* Never mind the questions over whether the United States should have been involved. There would remain the bitter question of whether we could have won the war if different weapons were used, if the military were not hampered by the home front, if political pressures were not so interfering, and so on.

The aftermath of the war would witness the loss of pride and patriotism. Distrust in the military and anxiety over the diminution of American power and its uses would add to the confusion over the position of the United States in the world. The Vietnam syndrome was born.

What these propositions add up to is an anxious society, confused and bewildered by events that seemed uncontrollable, at least by the current leaders. We seemed to have lost control over our own destiny in a world in which the problems confronting us appeared to be getting more and more complex; we could neither understand nor cope with the changes. Confidence in ourselves and the nation was one casualty, optimism was another. Fear and worry took their place.

The nation was staggering during the first half of the 1970s like a surprised champion at the hands of a newcomer. That much is evident by the scorecard. But before attempting an assessment of the entire decade, let us see if the latter half of the seventies offered any possibility of a comeback.

NOTES

1. In the analysis of the economy and macroeconomic policies of the 1970s, I have drawn heavily from my book *U.S. National Economic Policy, 1917–1985* (New York: Praeger, 1987). There, of course, the analysis is much more detailed than are the summaries provided here.

2. For more details on the cost of the war see my book *The Economic Consequences of the Vietnam War* (New York: Praeger, 1991).

3. Arthur M. Okun, *The Political Economy of Prosperity*, (Washington, DC: The Brookings Institution, 1970), 71.

4. E. J. Dionne, Jr., in *Why Americans Hate Politics* (New York: Simon & Schuster, 1991), has written a penetrating analysis of liberalism's decline that includes social as well as economic factors. One summary is worth quoting in full:

The moralism of the left blinded it to the legitimate sources of middle-class anger. The revolt of the middle class against a growing tax burden was not an expression of selfishness but a reaction to the difficulties of maintaining a middle-class standard of living. Anger at rising crime rates was not a covert form of racism but an expression of genuine fear that society seemed to be veering out of control. Impatience with welfare programs was sometimes the result of racial prejudices, but it was just as often a demand that certain basic rules about the value of work be made to apply to all. Those who spoke of "traditional family values" were not necessarily bigots opposed to "alternative lifestyles." As often as not, they were parents worried about how new family arrangements and shifting moral standards would affect their children. And those who complained about the inefficiency of government programs were not always antigovernment reactionaries; in many cases, the programs really did stop working and the bureaucracies really were unresponsive. (330–331)

5. For an excellent review of these events see Albert M. Wojnilower, "The Central Role of Credit Crunches in Recent Financial History," in *Brookings Papers on Economic Activity* 2 (1980): 277–339; also in the same source, Donald D. Hester, "Innovations and Monetary Control," 1 (1981): 141–199.

6. See, for instance, A. James Reichley, *Conservatives of Change: The Nixon and Ford Administrations* (Washington, DC: The Brookings Institution, 1981), 1–37.

7. For a description of the events surrounding this policy, see Herbert Stein, *Presidential Economics* (New York: Simon & Schuster, 1984).

8. Douglas A. Hibbs, *The American Political Economy: Macroeconomics and Electoral Politics* (Cambridge, MA: Harvard University Press, 1987), 271.

9. For an excellent analysis of this period, see Alan S. Blinder, *Economic Policy and the Great Stagflation* (New York: Academic Press, 1979).

10. Ibid. 155–166.

11. Ibid. 110–111.

12. See the discussion in Hibbs, *The American Political Economy*, 77–89.

Chapter 2

The Second Half of the 1970s: Carter, the Precursor

As suggested earlier, the Ford administration did little to combat the recession and, as late as October 1974, was calling for tax increases to combat inflation. In January 1975, in a total reversal, Ford called for tax reductions to fight the now obvious recession. The tax rate reductions for individuals and corporations were not enacted in time to affect the downturn, as the economy began to turn around in March 1975. By that time, the GNP had fallen by some 6.6% and unemployment had risen to 8.5% in what was really a sharp recession. Still, consumer prices continued to rise, by 14.7% over the course of the downturn. Stagflation was still painfully evident.

The tax cuts did not help in the downturn but did help in the recovery period. The problem was that these tax reductions were billed as temporary. Temporary tax reductions are believed to be less effective than permanent ones because consumers are expected to develop their consumption plans on the basis of their permanent incomes. Temporary changes in their current incomes do not affect consumption as much as permanent changes are thought to do. Blinder estimates that little of the tax reduction was spent in 1975 (which would have provided the desired short-run stimulus) and more was spent in 1976. In any case, he found that temporary tax changes are less effective than permanent ones.[1] These temporary changes were extended into 1976 as a type of indexing, whereby consumers were compensated for the rise in their money incomes due in large part to inflation caused by energy prices. Throughout the period, the Ford administration insisted on keeping a lid on government spending to avoid budget deficits, which according to the administration caused inflation.

Energy problems were not solved either as the Congress and the President battled over decontrol of domestic oil prices. The administration wanted to decontrol oil prices quickly, whereas Congress wanted to decontrol oil prices gradually to avoid another price shock. The administration also imposed a $1 per barrel import fee, later increased to $2, and an excise tax on domestic oil. A compromise was eventually reached with Congress, and in December 1975, the Energy Policy and Conservation Act was passed which phased out all controls by 1979, eliminated the import fees, and included fuel-efficiency standards for automobiles and trucks.

The monetary authorities came under much criticism in this period from all quarters. Some thought that the rate of monetary growth was too slow; others criticized the underlying model that the Fed used to predict the necessary growth rate. Without elaborating on this debate, it is clear in retrospect that the Federal Reserve kept monetary growth fairly constant and did not support the recovery in a vigorous manner.

The recovery faltered, however, and in the second quarter of 1976, the economy began to stall. The rate of growth of the real GNP fell sharply in this quarter, to 4.5% from 9.2% in the first quarter, and unemployment rates were still high at around 7.5%. Critics charged the administration with cutting back on government spending just when the recovery needed the stimulus. At any rate, the timing of the slowdown could not have been worse for Ford who was running for president, trying to win the post in his own right. He lost, and part of explanation must be attributed to the state of the economy.

THE CARTER ADMINISTRATION

James Earl Carter, former governor of Georgia, won by a slim margin in what was an uninspiring campaign. Despite the clear distinction in party positions, the conservatives wrote the Republican platform and the liberals wrote the Democratic one, the voter turnout (53.5%) was the lowest since 1948. Carter won partly by stressing that he was a Washington outsider, able to see problems from a different perspective and free of the taint of past mistakes, and by promising to return morality to public life; he emphasized justice, peace and love, and the preservation of human rights.

The slowdown in the economy helped Mr. Carter win the election, and now his responses to it helped to label him a liberal. A 2-year fiscal stimulus package was proposed that included a one-time tax rebate, an increase in personal deductions, a reduction in business taxes, increases in jobs programs, including public service jobs (Comprehensive Employment and Training Act or CETA), public works spending increases, and increases in grants to states. The package was estimated to be worth $31 billion. The 2-year plan was devised to allow for flexibility, for changes could be made if economic conditions changed.

Unfortunately for the Carter administration, economic changes were to occur too rapidly. The first one saw a sharp turnaround in the economy as consumption spending stimulated GNP growth in the first quarter of 1977. With prices rising, and unemployment stable, the administration did not see the need for further stimulus and accordingly revised its fiscal package by withdrawing the tax rebate for households and the business tax reductions. The result was a reduction in the package to $14 billion from the original $31 billion. In the second quarter, the trend was again reversed and private spending began to fall, along with net exports. Luckily for the administration, government purchases increased to make up for the loss, and some positive effects of the tax reductions helped.

Meanwhile, monetary policy was erratic. The authorities were trying to fight inflation without stopping the recovery. The Federal Reserve was having trouble managing the rate of growth in the money supply as NOW accounts and money market funds were playing havoc with the definition of money, and the velocity of money was proving unstable. Interest rates rose, as did the price level; the rate of growth of labor productivity was falling, labor costs were rising, and money wages were rising, but real wages were falling as workers saw their money wages eroded by price increases in food and energy costs.

Clearly, 1978 was not going to be a comfortable one. Accordingly, the administration fashioned another tax package to stimulate the economy and provide some tax relief to those who were pushed into higher tax brackets as a result of inflation. Reductions in personal and corporate tax rates (effective in October 1978) and repeal of the tax on telephones were supposed to yield $25 billion in stimulus. When it became clear that inflation was continuing at a pace of around 8% and unemployment was holding steady at over 6%, the administration postponed the tax reductions until January 1979 and reduced it to $20 billion. Moreover, the budget moved to fiscal restraint as expenditures were reduced by over $12 billion. Inflation was now receiving more and more attention from the administration.

Monetary policy was also restrictive as the rate of growth of the money supply was reduced and interest rates were allowed to rise. The discount rate was altered several times during the year to signal the Fed's intention and rose from 6.25% at the beginning of the year to 9.25% at the end.

With the move toward fiscal and monetary restraint, the decline in investment spending, the continued fall in real wages, the rise in prices, and so on, forecasts of another recession were becoming more frequent. The administration concluded that the economy was not responding to traditional monetary and fiscal policies. Prices and wages were not declining as predicted, even in the face of slack demand.

So the administration proposed a voluntary system of wage and price controls. In October 1978, it offered a system which allowed wages and fringe benefits to rise by 7% and prices to rise by 0.5% below the average annual rate of price increases in the period 1976–77. It also proposed to allow workers to recoup up to 3% in tax credits if the rate of inflation exceeded the wage standard; Congress never approved this portion of the proposal.

Another voluntary wage and price control system appeared to many to signal an administration reaching for straws in an attempt to regain some control over the economy. Many were losing faith in the ability of the administration to manage economic affairs in a rapidly changing world. Economists added to the confusion as they argued over the effectiveness of traditional monetary and fiscal policies. Monetarists claimed that fiscal policy was relatively useless and monetary policy almost as ineffective. The rational expectations school was insisting that the public would learn somehow to anticipate macroeconomic policy actions and economic agents would take steps to protect themselves against them and thereby thwart the actions and render them useless. Others were insisting that the traditional policies were still viable and should be used, if more judiciously.

Administration economists found no comfort in the debates because they would be criticized no matter what they did. In reality, they were liberal in tax policy and conservative in spending policy, but basically leaned toward traditional approaches. Moreover, despite the experience with the Nixon wage and price control system, they were willing to resurrect a Kennedy-like system, perhaps in desperation, in order to appear to be actively engaged in bold approaches to stagflation.

The forecasts for 1979, as for 1978, were for another recession. The forecasts were close to becoming reality, but the recession did not actually appear. Despite the forecasts, the administration continued its policy of restraint. As the CPI rose by over 11% with unemployment falling to around 5.8%, and with the wage and price control system in existence, the administration saw no need to provide any stimulus to the economy. Falling investment and consumer spending should have signaled eventual problems, but inflation was now considered the number one problem.

The monetary authorities also continued to regard inflation as the foremost problem facing the economy and so pursued a policy of restraint as well. The Fed tried to restrict the rate of growth of the money supply, but beyond the first quarter of 1979 was not able to do so. Changes in the banking structure, new types of accounts, and so on made managing the money supply more difficult. The definitions of money were revised to recognize these changes but still control was another matter. In October, the Fed gave up and embraced monetarism in an attempt to better control the monetary aggregates. In the last quarter of 1979, the Fed was able to manage the growth of monetary aggregates better but, in the process, abandoned control over interest rates. Because the Fed cannot control both the money supply and interest rates simultaneously, focusing on one lets the other find its own rates. Accordingly, interest rates shot up so high that usury laws had to be suspended. Of course, interest-rate-sensitive industries, such as construction, and small firms suffered immediate adverse consequences.

FOREIGN AFFAIRS

If 1979 was a stagnant period for the U.S. economy, it was not in foreign affairs. The Shah of Iran was overthrown, and later in the year the revolutionary government stormed the U.S. embassy and held 52 U.S. citizens hostage until January 1981. The United States appeared helpless in this situation but did manage to freeze Iranian assets in the United States and suspend oil imports from Iran. Although oil imports from Iran were not very great, this action combined with those of other oil-producing countries produced oil shortages in the United States. Various rationing schemes had to be employed by the states to cope with the excess demand. Of course, prices rose as well, adding about 2.5 points to the CPI in 1979 alone.

President Carter suffered enormously from this episode. The lack of an effective response to this affront to U.S. citizens angered the American public; with all its might, the United States was unable to act, and this humiliation burrowed through the society. When a rescue attempt was unsuccessful, the mortification ran deep.

Whatever else the Carter administration accomplished in foreign affairs, the Panama Canal Treaty, the mediation of talks between Egypt and Israel, and the elevation of human rights considerations in foreign affairs, were now effaced from the record and all that remained was this incident. But Mr. Carter's foreign policy tribulations did not end there because the USSR decided to invade Afghanistan to support its government. The cold war revived as the United States, in retaliation, placed an embargo on grains and corn sales to the Soviet Union and limited the trade in technical equipment. U.S. farmers and manufacturers ended up being the losers as a result of these trade restrictions; at the time, however, the embargo was questioned but did not seem unreasonable. The refusal to participate in the Olympic games in Moscow by contrast seemed only petulant.

These foreign policy setbacks made 1979 a troubled year, but domestic events made it even worse. The near disaster at the nuclear power plant at Three Mile Island in Pennsylvania called into question nuclear power as a way to solve the energy problem for the United States. The safety issue, largely esoteric up to this point, now surfaced and alarmed the general public. The nuclear power industry never did recover from this incident. On a less dramatic scale, the bailout of Chrysler Corporation by the federal government generated a great deal of controversy. It seemed both unwarranted and precedent setting.

THE 1980 RECESSION

The forecasted recession for 1978 and 1979 finally arrived in 1980. Once again, the administration did little to combat it; both monetary and fiscal policy were restrictive. The administration wanted to remove government's contribution to inflation by reducing spending. Accordingly, it reduced planned expenditures on social programs—mass transit, revenue sharing, federal civilian employment—while increasing expenditures on national defense. National defense increases could be blamed on outside forces, whereas social program cuts could be blamed on inflationary forces. No one was happy with the result, conservatives wanted even more national defense spending and liberals wanted to restore the cuts in social programs.

Monetary policy was meant to be restrictive as well. The Fed succeeded in the first half of the year in restricting the growth of monetary aggregates but failed to keep to its targets in the second half. This was partly due to the state of the economy as the economy revived in the second half, and partly due to the Fed's program of credit controls from March to July. Both responses were underestimated. Interest rates followed this erratic path, rising in the first quarter, falling in the second, and rebounding in the latter half. By year's end, the adherence to monetarism resulted in record highs for interest rates as they reached 20% for the prime rate and 19% for the federal funds rate.

Of course, these high interest rates caused havoc in the economy. All interest-rate-sensitive industries were affected as usual, but these high rates were even more damaging than in previous periods of tight money. Banks responded by dropping out of the Federal Reserve System to avoid tying up funds in non-interest-bearing reserves, creating variable interest rate mortgages, introducing new deposits, and so on. Something had to be done about the states' usury laws now in conflict with regulation Q that established interest rate ceilings on savings accounts. These and other problems led to the passage of the Depository Institutional Decontrol and Monetary Control Act of 1980 in which regulation Q was phased out; usury ceilings were repealed on mortgage rates and relaxed on other loans; NOW accounts were permitted in all banks; and thrift institutions were allowed to grant consumer and business loans, in return for joining the Federal Reserve System with its reserve requirements. At the time, few saw any problems with this Act; later, many would.

Meanwhile, the wage and price control system was still in effect, and the administration claimed success for it in 1979. Controls did not stop inflation, however, as firms opted to use the alternative profit margin standard and pass on higher prices. Thus, prices rose by 12.5% while wages rose by 8%, resulting in a decline in real wages of 4.5%. Prices of food, energy, and housing rose rapidly in this period and workers suffered. Still the administration wished to continue with the program; it revised the wage and price standards upward, that is, wages could rise between 7.5 and 9.5% and prices by 5% over a 2-year period, but few had any faith in these controls, and critics were numerous.

So this brief recession—it ended in July—was allowed to run its course without governmental interference. For the year, the GNP fell only 0.2% in real terms, but unemployment rose to 7.4% at year end. Prices continued to rise, even in the recession, as the CPI rose by over 12% for the year. The economy seemed to be getting out of control, and no one seemed to be in charge.

THE PERSISTENT ENERGY PROBLEM

The Carter administration's approach to the energy problem was to encourage conservation. If sacrifices had to be made, the American people should be willing to make them because they had developed a distorted sense of values over the years anyway. He chided the nation in his warning that "our decision about energy will test the character of the American people and the ability of the president and the Congress to govern the nation. This difficult effort will be the 'moral equivalent of war' except that we will be uniting our efforts to build and not to destroy." [2]

In addition to conservation, Carter did propose a series of measures contained in the National Energy Plan (NEP). Chief among the measures proposed was a tax on domestic oil to bring it up to the world price, but the plan also called for tax credits for conversions from oil to coal by firms, greater use of nuclear power, a "gas guzzler" tax on fuel inefficient cars, and tax credits for home insulation and solar devices. Congress did not go along with him and produced an Act that essentially included only the gas guzzler feature and limited tax credits for conservation.

Carter continued to press for a windfall profits tax and the decontrol of domestic oil prices. Congress finally did pass a measure that included these issues and agreed to use the proceeds of the tax to establish the Energy Security Corporation which would use the funds to encourage alternative fuel sources. There were other approaches that were adopted, including a petroleum reserve scheme, but, in the end, not much was accomplished for the long-run problem, certainly not measuring up to the moral equivalent of war rhetoric.

Special interests, a largely apathetic public grown accustomed to wasteful practices, and the artificial nature of fuel shortages made a coherent approach to energy problems extremely difficult. If Americans had grown selfish and spoiled, as Carter maintained, they simply did not want to hear about it and certainly did not want to be preached to either.

THE CARTER LEGACY

Mr. Carter took office as a Southern populist. In his words, "The Southern brand of populism was to help the poor and the aged, to improve education, and to provide jobs. At the same time, the populists tried not to waste money, having almost an obsession about the burden of the excessive debt. These same political beliefs—some of them creating inherent conflicts—were to guide me in the Oval Office." [3] The trouble was that his administration never did overcome those inherent conflicts. They called for liberal policies with conservative constraints. It would be extremely difficult to reconcile these conflicts in any period, and nearly impossible in the latter half of the 1970s. Mr. Carter, thus, could not maintain allegiance to his philosophy, but in attempting to reconcile the contradictions he was called indecisive and weak.

It is easy to find examples of this behavior. Upon taking office, his administration embarked upon a course to fight recession with tax cuts. These tax cuts were reduced shortly thereafter when restraint became necessary, then further tax cuts were proposed, and so on. Social programs were part of the initial stimulus package, but it was not long before cuts in these programs were deemed necessary. Inflation came to preoccupy this administration and, in the process, it surrendered its populist ideology. Tax reductions, cuts in social programs, inflation fighting, deregulation of industry, and increases in national defense spending all look like conservative ideas and unlikely to "help the poor."

Similarly, bringing morality to government is certainly a desirable aim. But perhaps the public was not prepared for its introduction in reality. Calling for sacrifices in energy usage earned him only scorn; calling for human rights considerations in foreign affairs earned him the label of naïveté as did calling for an embargo of grain to the USSR; calling off the participation in the Olympic games earned him derision for making symbolic gestures to no avail.

Few would argue with the contention that the latter half of the 1970s was not a propitious time to lead the nation. Mr. Carter was forced to take the blame for events and conditions for which he was not responsible and could not control. The energy crisis was not of his making, but his proposed solutions found few takers. The structure of the economy was changing, and economists were struggling to explain what was happening. Their contentious debates and opposite conclusions over what to do left politicians free to select that economic advice with which they were predisposed to agree as the proper course to follow. Economic problems seemed to be ganging up in this period—stagflation, the decline in the rate of growth of labor productivity, energy usage and pollution concerns, the changing composition of the labor force, and so on; if economists could not reach agreements over how to proceed, what can be expected of politicians?

The public, of course, did not know or care about these esoteric debates. People were worried over inflation, high interest rates, energy shortages, the reemergence of the cold war, and the floundering of government in confronting these problems. Impatience turned to criticism, and criticism turned to scorn, and scorn turned to rejection of this administration and its moralistic president. It was held responsible for all the ills facing the nation. Perhaps the nation would have been more forgiving of failures in the economic sphere if the setbacks in foreign affairs had been less dramatic. Even here, the Russian invasion of Afghanistan might have been tolerated, with the usual bluster, of course, but the Iranian hostage crisis could not. The traumatic defiance of Iran, coupled with the dismal rescue failure, was more than the public was willing to overlook. The image of the helpless giant, steadily losing face in the world, together with the constant harangue of the press counting the days of the hostages, cost the administration the last ounce of indulgence the impatient American public had to offer.

In the end, facing a reelection battle, unable to employ traditional policies to combat the problems effectively, and unable to devise alternative solutions to rectify their shortcomings, the administration retreated into more conservative patterns. Unable to reconcile the contradictions of philosophy and actions, the administration lost its rudder and was drifting. Its initial energy turned to caution, but it was perceived as weakness by the generation that was unable to subscribe to the notions of self-denial, cooperation, and brotherly love.

What kind of society did he bequeath to his successor? Here in outline form are the major elements of that world that his successor would inherit.

1. A public grown accustomed to tax reductions. Throughout the 1970s, tax cuts were used to provide stimulus to the economy as well as to assuage the public ire as inflation pushed people into higher tax brackets—a form of indexing. The Carter administration merely continued the trend of his predecessors.

Adding to this tendency was the beginning of the tax revolt as evidenced by

Proposition 13 in California that limited property tax rates. Also the Kemp–Roth supply-side tax reduction proposal was initiated in 1978. The society was receptive to tax reductions for whatever reason.

2. The clamor for additional social programs had almost ended. Few social programs were initiated, and those in existence suffered cutbacks when inflation threatened (e.g., CETA, mass transit). Government was not the problem solver that it was characterized as being in the 1960s. Only Social Security was sacrosanct. The Carter administration, by its own admission, was forced to "strike a balance" among competing demands on the federal budget. The other major competing demand was national defense.

3. The cold war revival made national defense expenditures necessary once more and, of course, were easily justified on that score. The Carter administration began the budgetary shifts to national defense and away from domestic social concerns. The increase in national defense spending in real terms in the Carter years was 10%, and projected to 1983 would have shown increases of 22%. In term of outlays, defense spending would have risen from 24.4% in 1977 to 25.6% in 1983.

4. American industry was allegedly overregulated and, thus, was held to be less flexible. Some industries were deregulated in the Carter years—banking and airlines—while regulatory rules for others—trucking, railroads—were relaxed. Other federal regulatory agencies (FCC, ICC, CAB) were asked to reduce the burden of regulation where possible.

5. Inflation gained prominence as the most important problem, and price stability replaced full employment as the number one goal.

6. To fight inflation, monetary policy was given the major role. In the Carter years, some form of monetarism—control over monetary aggregates—was invoked to do the job.

Just a glance at this partial list is sufficient to conclude that the swing to conservatism was well under way in the 1970s, and particularly with the gradual shift of the Carter administration. *A longer look would reveal that this shift formed the Reagan agenda, and, thus, Carter can be viewed as a precursor of Reagan.* The much heralded Reagan revolution was a continuation of what was already happening and does not represent a major break with the past.[4] Of course, there were other elements of the Carter administration programs and proposals that would not fit into the conservative mold, such as its flirtation with another type of incomes policy called TIP for tax-based incomes policy. Still the basic thrust of the administration was toward programs that any conservative would gladly have accepted.

OTHER TRENDS IN THE 1970s

In addition to the factors mentioned in the foregoing that made the 1970s so troubling, there were still others that would have profound effects on the economy and society. A brief enumeration of them is necessary before moving into the 1980s.

1. The changes in the composition of the labor force were dramatic. The rate of population increase was slowing down and, hence, the median age was increasing. However, the baby boomers were now entering the labor force, and the economy had to provide jobs for this group. Moreover, female labor market participation rates were increasing as this group sought to augment family incomes, sought careers in a new sense of liberation, and so on. In the process, the entire nature of the family and internal relations among members had to be reexamined. Maternity leaves, child care, and glass ceilings became problems to be solved by the changing structure of the family and the labor force.

Unemployment rates drifted upward in the 1970s perhaps because of the changing composition of the labor force. There were other explanations in this period of stagflation, but they are not of concern at this point. Equally puzzling was the sharp decline in the rate of growth of the productivity of labor. It began in the mid-1960s but took a severe drop in 1973 and continued throughout the 1970s. Explanations were many, too many, and no consensus developed on the major causes.

2. Another shift that began in this period was the movement of employment out of manufacturing into the service industries. Again explanations were many, but the more thoughtful analyses had to await the 1980s. In the meantime, there were fears that the United States was losing its industrial base to other nations and failing to meet foreign competition. The Carter administration rejected any government interference in the form of an industrial policy that, like Japan, would aid industries in difficulty or promote those with potential.

With these trends, even the nature of work was changing. The less educated, less skilled would have increasing difficulty finding jobs in a world that was demanding more technical skills. New fears of automation in the form of robots and other gadgets were creeping into minds of many workers, and such developments sent chills through the labor movement as well.

3. International trade problems continued in this period. The balance of merchandise trade illustrates one element of the problem; the balance was $-9.3 billion in 1976, and rose to $-25.3 billion in 1980 as imports soared. Capital flows increased in both directions as funds flowed in from oil-producing countries, were recycled to third world countries without much regard for security, and ended up in nonperforming loans in major U.S. banks. Foreign competition was increasing from many countries but particularly Japan and other parts of Asia. Predictably, U.S. firms clamored for protection. U.S. firms were losing out to foreign firms, so many went abroad seeking lower costs and less restrictions, exporting jobs in their haste.

Freely floating exchange rates were not working as advertised as they did not eliminate balance of trade problems, nor stabilize fluctuations. Countries did not permit their exchange rates to fluctuate and cause trade problems but intervened to manipulate them for their benefit.

4. In line with the conservative shift, the annually balanced budget was suggested as a way to limit political spending profligacy. The call for a constitutional convention was urged to propose a balanced budget amendment to the constitution. A model resolution of such an amendment was passed by 30 states in the 1970s. Keynesians pointed out the fallacy of the balanced budget philosophy as being obviously procyclical—it would exacerbate the cyclical swings—but the simple and appealing arguments would not be denied; households balance their budgets, why can't government? Simplistic arguments to complex problems often gain popularity (in fact, every president in this century has taken office as a champion of balanced budgets), and matters of definition, enforcement, exceptions, restrictions, and so on would have created as many difficulties as the current system of budgetary discretion. Still, the movement attracted many adherents in political circles.

CONCLUSION

The 1970s experienced sufficient upheavals to earn the label convulsive. Some problems were new, for example, the oil embargo, and some were ongoing, for example, trade problems, but whatever their life span, there were enough of them to trouble any administration. Having to follow the disastrous Nixon administration, the difficulties for Ford and Carter were magnified because they inherited the distrust in government and politicians that ensued. Starting with Johnson, the public had become increasingly cynical about governmental leaders and about solutions to what appeared to be intractable problems.

Consider only a few of these unsettling features of the times: energy shortages, stagflation, high interest rates, declining real wages and negative real interest rates, changing composition of the labor force and the repercussions on the family, increasing foreign competition and the decline in the manufacturing sector, deterioration in foreign trade, and setbacks in foreign affairs. These and other concerns were more than enough for any administration to handle.

Vacillations in macroeconomic policies came to be viewed as incompetence rather than caution; hesitancy in managing affairs, domestic or foreign, was seen as weakness rather than deliberation. Ford could be forgiven; Carter could not. The general feeling was one of doubt that the Carter administration was up to the task of treating the nation's ills. As criticisms mounted and the election neared, Carter turned more and more to conservative modes of attack. Tax cuts, deregulation of industry, making inflation control paramount, increasing defense spending and reducing social spending, favoring monetary over fiscal policy, rejecting any industrial policy, and so on are manifestations of the turn to the right. They also serve as precursors of what Ronald Reagan was to champion as a new agenda.

Thus, at the end of the decade, the mood of the public can only be described as insecure. The Vietnam War, the hostage crisis in Iran, the Russian invasion of Afghanistan, and revolutions in Latin America all combined to decrease pride and strain patriotism and to create skepticism of American power. America was no longer in charge of its destiny, no longer number one.

The energy crisis showed us to be helpless, blackmailed by third world countries. No real solutions to the crisis emerged, and future recurrences could not be ruled out. Inflation bothered everyone, even those who benefited by it, and again no real solutions were offered to fight it; stagflation bewildered economists and policy makers as well as an unstable economy worried business and consumers alike. Again the mood was one of worry and fear. Events seemed to be controlling us and not the other way around.

Real wages declined for many, and the loss of good manufacturing jobs caused increasing concern. The economy appeared to be floundering and losing out to foreign competitors.

In brief, people were either perplexed, insecure, or angry at the state of the nation as the decade ended. So when Ronald Reagan asked during the campaign of 1980 if people thought they were better off after four years of Carter, many could answer no. It did not matter whether they were truly worse off or not; it did not matter even if they were in reality better off, as many of them were. *All that mattered was that they felt worse off.* But this feeling was the result of numerous factors, some of them mentioned above, and Mr. Carter could hardly be blamed for all of them. Nevertheless, this clever campaign rhetorical question was well designed to ferret out the vague feelings of insecurity and give voice and expression to the latent apprehensions and dissatisfactions of a troubled populace.

NOTES

1. Alan S. Blinder, *Economic Policy and the Great Stagflation* (New York: Academic Press, 1979), 155–177.

2. Carter's speech to the nation on April 18, 1977.

3. Jimmy Carter, *Keeping Faith* (New York: Bantam Books, 1982), 74.

4. William A. Niskanen, a member of the Council of Economic Advisors in the Reagan Administration, also acknowledged the influence of Carter when he stated "most of economic policies of the new administration represented an acceleration rather than a reversal of policy trends initiated during the late 1970s. There was substantial precedent for each of the four key elements of the initial Reagan program in the prior decade." *Reaganomics: An Insider's Account of the Policies and the People* (New York: Oxford University Press, 1988), 20.

Chapter 3

The Reagan Agenda

If Carter anticipated most of the major elements of what was to become the Reagan agenda, why did he lose the election? No doubt Mr. Carter has though of this often since 1980 and may still be at a loss to explain fully the reasons.

Clearly, it is easy to demonstrate, as was done in the last chapter, the frustration, anxiety, and apprehension of the American public at the close of the Carter administration; the lack of confidence in his administration's ability to confront the issues of the day was evident. The economy was in a recession, foreign policy setbacks were fresh in the minds of the public, and fears over high interest rates, energy shortages, and so on worked against him. When the hostages were seized by Iran, his popularity plummeted, it rose again for a time, and then fell when the rescue attempt failed.

Still, Carter did manage to defeat the challenges from within his own party, so there must be more to his decline and Reagan's rise than just the vague feeling that the administration was not capable of governing the nation. The public was well aware, even if it did not always articulate it, that the problems facing the country were complex and not always of our own doing. Still, someone had to pay for our unhappiness, and that someone was Jimmy Carter who became the lightning rod for all the ills that had befallen the nation. Yet, curiously, according to the Gallup poll that asked those who voted for Reagan, 22% said they were dissatisfied with Carter, 21% said it was time for a change, and only 12% said Reagan would make a better leader; moreover, only 17% said they liked Reagan's economic policies.[1]

Mr. Reagan told the nation what it wanted to hear. His message was upbeat and optimistic just as he himself had always been; it was not a phony stance nor was it perceived as such. The public wanted hope, the restoration of pride of country, and it wanted to dream. Reagan was determined to provide them and set out on a course designed to harvest these underlying and often unspoken yearnings.

He had a simple program, easily understood, and he surrounded it with one-liners, anecdotes, quips, and self-deprecating humor. He seemed warm, friendly, and trustworthy, a fellow who would be nice to know. It was the same image he projected as a movie actor, and he learned how to make the best use of his experience from that occupation. He was always prepared (with those 4×6 cards from which he read or that he used to remind him of the subject at hand), knew his lines, knew how to reach an audience, and understood just how he would be perceived by others. He also surrounded himself with people who knew just how to capitalize on his strengths and minimize his weaknesses. It was a well-run campaign, well financed and managed. The campaign brought in all of those groups that previously felt disenfranchised, such as the religious right, the antiabortionists, anticommunists, antigovernments, and so on. All of these personal attributes and campaign strategies served him well, and by this time they are well known and well documented.[2] True as these analyses are, I still think most observers miss a major point. The American public had grown so disillusioned with politics and, of course, politicians that they permitted whatever reservations they had about Reagan to be overcome by cynicism. A what-the-hell's-the-difference attitude was allowed to overrule normal caution and restraint. People were not just voting against Carter; they were voting against the status quo and willing to replace it with anything that promised novelty and reassurance. Reagan represented that promise, and Carter promised still more prosaic directions. But one wonders whether other programs might have filled the bill as well. What other paths for the nation might have been accepted in the same way that Reagan's were? What other schemes for revamping the American society might have found favor? With a vengeful and contemptuous public casting ballots, the possible answers are intriguing to contemplate, even now.

Of course, people also took whatever part of his program that appealed to them and dismissed the rest as irrelevant. How can I benefit, not what is good for the country, became the rallying cry around the affable Reagan, ushering in the era of greed as a national virtue. Those who stood to gain from his program naturally backed him, often without regard for the effects of the total agenda. This will become more evident and discernible when the program is described below.

As demonstrated in the last chapter, the program itself was not a particularly radical departure from the past. There were unmistakable trends that developed in the 1970s, and these trends were accentuated by the Reagan agenda. The Reagan administration was willing to pursue its program to degrees that previous administrations would have balked at and retreated. What is also different is the fervor with which the program was supported, the strategies employed to achieve it, the defense of it when it was questioned, and the adherence to it when it seemed to be going awry. The belief in the free markets, in government-created problems, and in supply-side solutions amounted to religious dogma, and all who questioned them were dismissed as hopelessly passé. Keynesians particularly were subject to derision, along with their demand-side solutions. Government was the problem, Reagan was fond of saying, not the solver of them.

In 1980, many could agree, having witnessed the macroeconomic policies in the 1970s, the welfare mess, the energy crises, and the farm problems. So

Reagan struck the chord of discontent on his harp and sounded the call for a new vision. In his presidential nomination acceptance speech in Detroit, he made it quite clear:

They [Democrats] say that the United States has had its day in the sun, that our nation has passed its zenith. They expect you to tell your children that the American people no longer have the will to cope with their problems, that the future will be one of sacrifice and few opportunities. My fellow citizens, I utterly reject that view. The American people, the most generous people on earth, who created the highest standard of living, are not going to accept the notion that we can only make a better world for others by moving backwards ourselves. And those who believe we can have no business leading the nation.

THE REAGAN AGENDA

In the speeches he made during his transformation from a liberal Democrat to a conservative Republican, largely as an after-dinner speaker growing out of his tenure on a television show sponsored by General Electric, and throughout his campaigns for the presidency, Reagan kept harping on three themes: taxes should be cut, government spending and involvement in private affairs should be reduced, and national defense spending should be increased to ensure that the United States was strong enough to meet any challenge. He was ever faithful to these beliefs, right up to the time he left office. He would not be budged from these positions no matter how eloquent the arguments made to the contrary.

This then is basically the Reagan agenda, and although others added elements to it that came to be known as Reaganomics, he would remain loyal only to the three basic themes. This was characteristic of Reagan who resisted all attempts to move him away from his basic biases, leaving much of the remainder of the agenda to others. He had no grand designs, no conception of how best to achieve these ends, and no interest in many of the programs that were initiated in his name. He knew what he wanted to achieve and delegated much of everything else to his aides. His was not an analytical mind, and he did not think in the abstract. His management style was called passive, detached, and disinterested, and although many, inside and outside government, questioned his intellectual ability, he demonstrated a faculty to stick with what interested him and leave the rest to others.[3] His knowledge of economics was minimal, and complicated arguments of any kind went beyond him. He simply was unprepared for the job and did not wish to engage in the type of study that would have remedied the matter. Still, he was unwavering in his desire to achieve his lifelong goals, and when these goals were not achieved or were compromised, he refused to acknowledge error or defeat.

During the campaign, Reagan kept hammering away on his favorite themes, punctuated by anecdotes about welfare cheats and the costs of government regulations. After the election, the campaign pledges, promises, and the usual political rhetoric were finally codified in the presidential message to Congress issued on February 18, 1981 called *A Program for Economic Recovery*. The plan for economic recovery included four parts: the reduction in the growth of federal spending but an *increase* in national defense spending; the reduction in tax rates; the reduction in government regulations; and a monetary policy consistent with the other elements of the program. Three of these components were the themes emphasized by Reagan, and the fourth was added to complete the plan. A closer look at each part, however, reveals other subsidiary goals as well and should have alerted everyone to the inherent contradictions in the overall plan.[4]

First, the reduction in government expenditures during the campaign were only supposed to eliminate waste in government spending. Who could be opposed to that? After the election, the cuts in government spending went far beyond cutting out waste to slashing spending on a wide variety of social programs. Only the "truly needy" (the poor, elderly, unemployed, veterans) would be protected and supported by government. All other entitlement programs, subsidy programs, and public sector investment programs, were up for review, as were the number of government personnel and federal grants to states and localities. These reductions in the growth of federal expenditures were to lead to a *balanced budget* by 1984 (1983 during the campaign) and a surplus by 1985.

The reduction in federal income tax rates was supposed to provide the necessary incentive for economic agents to begin to invest and produce more. Greater investment would provide more jobs, increase labor productivity, encourage economic growth, and, in the end, the greater economic activity would bring in more tax revenue, some said enough to cover the revenue loss of the tax rate reduction. If the tax reductions did not cause an increase in the federal deficit, there was no need to worry about cuts in government spending if that should prove a problem. If taxes could be cut without worrying about increasing the budget deficit, and without worrying about government spending, what politician could resist this siren's song?

This was the same song sung by Andrew Mellon in the 1920s when he fought to reduce taxes for the same reason—high taxes discourage productive use of resources. This precedent for supply-side economics was not empirically based then and, when reinvented by Arthur Laffer, was not empirically based then either. Laffer, as did Mellon, persuaded a small but vocal group that tax revenues vary with the tax rate! Using a parabolic (bell-shaped) curve, he was able to demonstrate that tax revenues rise with the tax rates until some optimal rate was reached; thereafter, as tax rates rose, revenues fell. It follows that tax rates beyond the optimal one were undesirable for they hinder productive investment without bringing in more revenue. It also follows that a reduction in tax rates would *increase* revenues if the tax rate were beyond the optimal one. So far, this Laffer curve was nothing but a tautology and added nothing to our knowledge. Supply-siders, however, were convinced, without the benefit of empirical analysis, that tax rates in the United States were beyond the optimal ones and that reductions in tax rates would stimulate productive activity and increase tax revenues.

Many economists would have favored tax reductions for a variety of reasons, but few would have professed to know anything about optimal tax rates, or would have been willing to predict what would occur to productive effort if rates were cut. To supply-side economists, such reservations were the result of past faulty thinking, and supply-side predictions became a matter of dogma—of faith. So the Kemp–Roth tax bill of reducing tax rates by 30% became part of the Reagan agenda; it fit into his pattern of thinking and verified his own experience of high taxes and reduced effort when he was in Hollywood. High tax rates discouraged making more than four pictures a year back in World War II.[5]

The relaxation of government regulations was designed to reduce the costs of compliance by industry and reduce the administrative costs of the bureaucracy created by them. Get the government off our backs was the campaign cry, and let industry compete. U.S. industry must not be shackled if it was to meet the growing competitive threat from abroad. Moreover, burdensome regulations affected economic growth because they discouraged research and development, reduced investment, raised labor costs, and reduced competition. Again, no evidence was supplied to support these contentions.

Monetary policy was to be the restraining force to bring down inflation. By restricting the rate of growth of the money supply, the economy should be able to expand without inflation. In the long run it was predicted that interest rates would come down as well.

Finally, one element of the plan that is frequently underemphasized was the change in expectations that the whole program was supposed to bring. In *A Program for Economic Recovery,* the importance of this feature is clearly stated:

The ultimate importance of this program for sustained economic growth will arise not only from the positive effects of the individual components, important as they are. Rather, it will be the dramatic improvement in the underlying economic environment and outlook that will set a new and more positive direction to economic decisions throughout the economy.[6]

PROSPECTS FOR THE PLAN

Omitting the details, this is the outline of the plan for economic recovery.[7] Most economists, even those sympathetic to the aims of the administration, would have some difficulty believing in a proposal that promised to cut taxes, balance the budget, increase spending on national defense, reduce inflation, cut government spending, and change expectations simultaneously! Clearly, elements of the plan were contradictory and mutually exclusive. Pursuing an expansionary fiscal policy and a contractionary monetary policy is alone sufficient cause for skepticism. How could such a program be taken seriously?

During the campaign, George Bush, a rival presidential candidate, labeled it "voodoo economics." There were internal conflicts as well, as traditional Republicans battled the new comers—the supply-siders. Consider that the administration brought to Washington three (and probably more) groups who were bound to disagree. The supply-siders wanted a tax cut for economic stimulation; the monetarists wanted tight money to fight inflation; and the budget balancers wanted to eliminate the deficit and balance the budget annually. If the tax cuts were passed, would not the expansion be limited by high interest rates caused by tight money? If the tax cuts were passed without significant reductions in government expenditures, would that not increase the deficit? Should not government expenditures be reduced before taxes are cut, as conservatives had maintained since Goldwater expressed their aims? These debates raged within the administration and in Congress as soon as the groups began to press their views.[8]

Where was Reagan in all this? According to Cannon,

. . . [Reagan] was far more interested in economic recovery than he was concerned about the deficits that would be the by-products of his policies. The quarrel between supply-siders and traditionalists completely bored him. Reagan wanted both tax cuts and spending reductions. He believed that he would get more of each if he did not choose between the competing policies.[9]

This is typical Reagan who always found it difficult to choose sides when his aides differed, and either asked them to find a compromise or split the difference (often resulting in ludicrous policies) or failed to offer any direction giving his aides control over policy or leaving them confused as to the direction the president wanted to take.[10]

Of all Reagan's advisors, perhaps the one most familiar with the entire economic program was David Stockman, the head of the Office of Budget and Management (OMB). To Stockman was given the task of translating the overall plan into numbers. He also found that "The broad policy architecture of the plan was riddled with potential contradictions."[11] Stockman really mastered the budget numbers and became the administration's authority on the economic plan. Later, he was to admit that

"None of us really understands what's going on with all these numbers . . . the defense numbers got out of control and we were doing the whole budget-cutting exercise so frenetically . . . And it didn't quite mesh . . . Kemp–Roth was always a Trojan Horse to bring down the top rate . . . Supply-side is "trickle-down-theory."[12]

Without belaboring the point, it is clear that there were contradictions in the program, that they were recognized by those in charge of the policy, and that nothing was done to amend the basic thrust of the economic plan. On a more technical level, it was pointed out to the administration that the monetary policy was inconsistent with the economic growth forecasted. The growth in the nominal GNP for 1981 was predicted to be about 11%, with the rise in the CPI predicted at about 11%. However, the rate of growth in the money supply was to be about 5%. How, then, could the economic growth be financed? Unless the velocity of money increased phenomenally, not very likely unless interest rates *fell* or spending patterns changed dramatically, there would not be sufficient means to finance the expansion. The administration simply refused to deal with this glaring contradiction, less it upset the alleged favorable expectations that were being created.

So at the start of the alleged economic revolution, we have a president with a few long-held biases against taxes and government spending and a conviction that America was weak militarily. We are told that he had no grand designs for how best to achieve these vague desires nor what the effects on the country would be if they were enacted. He did not think in the abstract and was continually surprised to learn of possible adverse effects of proposals being made in his name. Biases cannot substitute for objective analysis and detachment cannot substitute for leadership. Therefore, when the policies did not seem coherent and the numbers did not add up, those around him, his loyal advisors, had to contend with a president who did not care to contemplate options or revise his thinking; hence, they did not tell him of the problems! They had to proceed with plans that were contradictory, turning aside all criticisms with a fallback position that amounted to religious dogma. And in the case of a major architect of the economic plan, David Stockman, even that was not sufficient once he lost the faith and resorted to deception to please his superiors.

So the economic plan was built on deception, on illusion, on hope, and on biases. These are hardly the foundations for a genuine revolution. Yet, Ronald Reagan was probably the only kind of president able to carry it off. A leader who knew what he wanted and who would not be deterred from it sent the right signals to everyone in the administration; a leader who did not know very much about the details of how to get what he wanted but who knew enough to surround himself with loyal aides who did certainly warrants some claim to being an effective, if accidental, strategist.

Reagan was aided in this by a desperate public willing to risk stability for change, in aides who were willing to protect the president from challenges to his knowledge and biases, and in Congress which was willing to be led into policies it frequently was suspicious of but was afraid of the popular president. In addition, the administration pursued the agenda with an incredibly effective strategy and zeal not seen in Washington since the New Deal.[13] Tip O'Neill, Speaker of the House, put it this way,

Another reason Reagan was so successful in getting his legislation passed was that he had strong capable people around him, including Michael Deaver, Ed Meese, Jim Baker, and David Stockman, among them. I didn't like their mean-spirited philosophy, but they knew where they were going and they knew how to get there. They put one legislative ball in play at a time, and they kept their eye on it all the way through.[14]

O'Neill was a severe critic of the administration's economic plans and was continuously at odds with the president and his aides. Finally, the pressure from the public became so great that he gave in: "As Speaker, I could have refused to play ball with the Reagan administration by holding up the president's legislation in the Rules Committee. But in my view, this wasn't a politically wise thing to do. Despite my strong opposition to the president's program, I decided to give it a chance to be voted on by the nation's representatives."[15] Because Congress was rather reluctant initially to follow the Reagan administration's lead in charting new avenues, one wonders also of the extent of the sympathy effect following the assassination attempt in March 1981.

THE PUBLIC REACTION

The path of the Reagan revolution was surely a strange phenomenon in American politics. The American public, not especially known for its economic knowledge, generally favored the economic plan of the Reagan administration. It is always difficult to gauge the mood of the public, and even more difficult to ascertain how it feels about specific issues. Public opinion polls have well-known shortcomings, but they are at present the only way to measure the perceptions of the public. In general, the public received the Reagan economic plans with approval. Here is a sampling of opinion in the early part of the plan's disclosure. On spending cuts, 34% of the public felt they were too high, 12% too low, and 46% about right; and as will be observed many times later, on specific spending cuts, 48% disapproved of one or more of them, with Social Security heading the list. In May 1981, 60% of respondents believed that the administration would be able to reduce inflation; in August only 50% thought so; 48% said it would be able to reduce unemployment, in August only 40% thought so; and 41% said it would be able to balance the budget, in August only 37% thought so. One interpretation of these results is that the public was very hopeful in the beginning as it responded to the administration's forecasts; later, the public viewed them with some reservations.[16]

On the tax rate reductions, 59% approved of them in August 1981 even though 69% said that the tax cuts would not affect them very much or not at all! Interestingly, 51% said they would save the tax reductions and 40% said they would spend them. As might be expected, those who said they would save the reductions were in the highest income groups. Finally, a year after the election was won, the question was asked about what the respondent's financial situation would be under the Reagan administration's economic policies: 5% said much better, 29% said somewhat better, 30% said somewhat worse, 15% said much worse, 15% said the same, and 6% had no opinion. Clearly, the initial stages of the recession were causing some reassessments.[17]

It is clear that the public bought into the cheerful optimism generated by the Reagan administration, but reality soon made it question the rosy forecasts. Where support was strong in the beginning, it faded as time went on and split the nation into several camps. This theme will occupy us in later chapters, but it is apparent that the divisions started early in the administration and not after the economic results were all in, and before everyone could make an individual accounting.

ECONOMISTS' REACTIONS

The public's reaction to the Reagan economic plans can be expected to vary by a number of variables such as income, education, race, and geography. A more detailed discussion of the public opinion polls would reveal some of these differences. Also the degree of economic sophistication would affect the responses of individuals. To explore these nuances would be interesting but unnecessary for the purposes at hand. Instead, we turn to professional opinions on the administration's economic plans. With professional views, none of the problems associated with the public's lack of knowledge of economics or motivations apply. This is not to state that economists are objective in their analyses, only that their views are more coherent and less self-centered than the general public's.

Of course, we seek their views after the economic plans were announced but before the results were tabulated; in this way, their assessments were given before their opinions were affected by reality. Moreover, some of these economists may have changed their minds in some manner after their initial reactions and, consequently, there is no intention here of holding them to their first reactions nor is there any intent to measure their success or failure as forecasters. All we are after here is a spectrum of views by professional economists as they considered the Reagan administration's economic plans.

In its December 15, 1980 issue, *U.S. News and World Report* published interviews with four Nobel prize winners on the economic prospects for the nation.[18] Here is a summary of their remarks:

Milton Friedman

To get out of this situation [of the late 1970s], the steps that must be taken are clear. They are ones that President-elect Reagan committed himself to during the campaign. First, the Kemp–Roth tax recommendations. . . . Second, an immediate revision of the U.S. budget, with a lower ceiling on total expenditures. . . . Third, a reduction of the regulatory burden on industry. . . . Fourth, presidential support for a policy of stable and steady monetary growth.

Lawrence R. Klein

What is required is greater capital formation, a larger proportion of expenditures for research and development, more generous support of basic research and further industry deregulation. These are all elements of a developing consensus on U.S. industrial policy. . . . Our efforts should be oriented toward business tax cuts rather than personal. . . . I don't like the Kemp–Roth proposal, because it cuts tax rates across the board . . . Furthermore we don't need to stimulate individuals' demand. . . .

Kenneth J. Arrow

The most important thing is a steadiness of policy. A great effort should be made to stabilize the operation of both the money supply and the government fiscal system . . . A tax cut should be one of the first items of business in 1981. The 10 percent cut being discussed sounds about right. Beyond that, the idea of cutting taxes 10 percent a year for three years sounds absurd. It will produce deficits [and may] reduc[e] private investment . . .

Paul A. Samuelson

Tax cuts alone won't bring us lower inflation and steadier growth. There is a great deal of supply-side moonshine for which there is no scientific basis. The talk of repeated tax cuts . . . means a more expansionary fiscal policy and bigger deficits unless there are cuts in nonmilitary spending. Interest rates will be rising. . . .

Other economists' views on the economic outlook would include all shades of opinion beyond these representative ones. Sidney Weintraub, writing in *The New Leader,* maintained that

The federal budget balloons as a consequence of spiraling prices, it does not cause them. . . . The quest for a balanced budget will collide with the new administration's tax cutting objectives, too. If the Kemp–Roth recommendations are enacted, the three annual 10 per cent tax cuts will devastate government income. There has been much brave talk about how they will eventually foster greater tax revenues. Not in a stagflation economy it won't. . . . Reagan would have us believe that "unleashing" business will spur plant modernization, lift productivity and thus slow the rate of inflation. Such dreams should be taken with a full sack of salt.[19]

Lester Thurow wrote

"President Reagan wants both dramatic tax cuts to encourage investment and an even more extensive military buildup. But he cannot have both without wrecking the economy . . . If his current program is carried out, he too [like president Johnson] will wreck the economy."[20]

Walter W. Heller, architect of the Kennedy–Johnson tax cuts, concluded,

If the administration and Congress decide to go ahead with the full Kemp–Roth tax plan, other tax cuts and big defense boosts, the country will have to swallow the bitter medicine of gargantuan budget cuts or drum-tight money.[21]

The architects or ardent spokesmen of the administration's economic plans have not been quoted here because their ideas have been incorporated in the Reagan proposals. Their views will be more appropriately included when the results of the program are measured against what was supposed to be happen. Those interested in their views before comparisons are made should consult one or more of these sources.[22]

It is clear that ideology played an enormous role in the determination of economic policy in this administration. Although ideology and value judgments are always present in making policy, their roles in devising theory are seldom as obvious as in this instance. For this reason, a review of the ideological content that formed the basis for both the theory and policies of this administration is imperative if there is to be a full evaluation of its attempt at "revolution." These issues are the subject of the next chapter.

APPENDIX: THE PROGRAM FOR ECONOMIC RECOVERY

The administration proposed to cut government spending by $49 billion in Fiscal Year (FY) 1982, and it used a set of nine specific guidelines to determine where the reductions should be made. They are worth reproducing in some detail:

1. Preserve the "social safety net." The social safety net was supposed to protect the elderly, the poor, the veterans, and the unemployed from major budget cuts. The programs affecting these groups were Medicare, unemployment benefits, Social Security, AFDC, SSI, and veterans' payments and health care.

2. Revise entitlements to eliminate unintended benefits. Because the administration regarded the growth of entitlement programs in the 1970s as a major contributor to excessive government spending, it sought to reverse the trend in its first budget. Budget reductions in this area included Medicaid, food and nutrition, extended unemployment aid, housing assistance, and other non-safety-net programs. Reductions in these programs would permit more aid to be focused on the "truly needy."

3. Reduce subsidies to middle- and upper-income groups. Programs such as school lunches, student aid, and housing finance, which benefited groups not requiring government aid, should be reduced or eliminated.

4. Impose fiscal restraint on other national-interest programs. Programs considered of low priority or of low merit fell under this general category. Examples are arts and humanities and science and technology programs.

5. Recover costs that can be clearly allocated to users. User fees were to be imposed on those who benefited from federal programs. Among those identified as receiving direct economic benefits included users of inland waterways, airports, and Coast Guard services.

6. Stretch out and retarget public-sector capital-investment programs. These

programs for water-resource projects, waste-treatment plants, highways, mass transit, and airport projects would face restraints or reductions.

7. Reduce overhead and personnel costs of the federal government. The administration hoped to reduce inefficiencies in the management of the federal government. Cost savings were to be made in such areas as surplus property disposal, employee travel, and federal employment practices.

8. Apply sound economic criteria to subsidy programs. Free-market principles dictated that subsidies were harmful to the economy and, thus, should be eliminated. Programs for mass transit, public service, employment (CETA), community development, and subsidies for new energy development were identified as the type of program scheduled for review.

9. Consolidate categorical grant programs into block grants. Under this guideline, 77 categorical grants in the social, educational, and health areas were combined into five block grants (unrestricted). The move was designed to return greater control over federal funds to the states and localities. Later, Mr. Reagan would introduce his New Federalism, which would continue this movement and transfer specific programs to the states and localities to fund and administer.

The tax-reduction proposal clearly adopted the Kemp–Roth bill that called for a 3-year, 10% per year across-the-board reduction in individual income tax rates. For business, a new depreciation schedule for plant and equipment was introduced to promote investment spending, job creation, and industrial revitalization. Other provisions consistent with supply-side views included in the 1981 tax bill reduced the top rate of taxation to 50% from 70% making the maximum capital gains tax rate 20%. Beginning in 1985, some portions of the income tax would be indexed according to the CPI: tax brackets, standard deduction, and the personal exemption.

Wealth taxes were also reduced. Estate and gift tax rates were cut, exemptions were increased, and the inheritance tax for surviving spouses was eliminated. Clearly, these changes would benefit the higher income groups. To encourage saving, several specific incentives were included: Individual Retirement Accounts (IRAs) were extended to employees already covered by employer plans. The amount of tax deductible IRAs was $2000 per worker with some allowances for nonworking spouses. In addition, Keogh retirement plans were permitted to double their contributions to $15,000 per year. Finally, a special "all savers" account was established that excluded interest from taxation for 1 year.

After the cutbacks in government spending and the reductions in tax rates were in force, the budget totals should have resembled those shown in Table A3.1. From this table it is clear that the rate of change of government spending was expected to slow to 6% from 1981 to 1986, down from 12% in 1976–79. Revenues would grow by 10% annually, instead of the 14% rate of the recent past. The result would be a balanced budget by 1984, with surpluses thereafter.

Table A3.1
Estimated Budget Outlook, 1981–86 (billions of dollars)

	1981	1982	1983	1984	1985	1986
Outlays	654.7	695.5	733.1	771.6	844.0	912.1
Receipts	600.2	650.5	710.2	772.1	840.9	942.0
Deficit(1) or						
surplus	-54.5	-45.0	-22.9	+0.5	+6.9	+29.9
Share of GNP						
Outlays	23.0	21.8	20.4	19.3	19.2	19.0
Receipts	21.1	20.4	19.7	19.3	19.3	19.6

Source: A Program For Economic Recovery, a White House
Report, p.9.

Moreover, the share of the federal budget as a percent of GNP would drop to 19% in 1986, from 23% in 1981.

The totals, however, mask the shift in spending priorities. By 1984, the Department of Defense would see its budget increased to account for 32.4% of the total budget (from 24.1% in 1981) while the growth in social programs would fall. The administration insisted that the "truly needy" would still be provided for, but others, apparently not needy, would find their benefits reduced. The social safety net was to grow to account for 40.6% of the budget in 1984, from 36.6% in 1981, and this growth was deemed sufficient to catch the truly needy while letting the others fall through the net.

These budget forecasts rested on economic assumptions, of course, and not everyone agreed with the rosy forecasts of the real rate of growth of the GNP of 5.2% for 1981 and over 4% per year to 1986. Interest rates (treasury bills) were expected to fall to 8.9% in 1981 and eventually to 5.6% in 1986, and unemployment rates would decline to 5.6% in 1986 and the CPI to 4.2%.

The critics who presented more "realistic" assumptions consistently came up with much different estimates for receipts, outlays, deficits, and so on. At first, Congress was in no position to challenge the popular president and reserved judgment on this economic package. Doubts continued to grow, but voting for tax cuts is nearly irresistible for politicians, especially if they have no effect on the deficit. Defenders of social programs were bucking the tide, as their constituents, the poor or disadvantaged, had little voice, little power, and did not vote anyway.

NOTES

1. George H. Gallup, *The Gallup Poll* (Wilmington, DE: Scholarly Resources Inc., 1980), 260.

2. For more on Reagan, see the biographies by Lou Cannon, *Reagan* (New York: G.P Putnam's Sons, 1982) and *President Reagan: The Role of a Lifetime* (New York: Simon & Schuster, 1991). See also Gary Wills, *Reagan's America: Innocents at Home*

(New York: Doubleday, 1987) and Haynes Johnson, *Sleeping Through History: America in the Reagan Years* (New York: W. W. Norton, 1991).

3. For the most perceptive analysis of Ronald Reagan as a personality, see Cannon, *President Reagan,* chapters 2–10 especially. This excellent book captures the Reagan phenomenon better than any other, and the brief descriptions in this book owe a great deal to the thoughtful analysis of Mr. Cannon.

4. Presidential message to Congress, *A Program for Economic Recovery* (February 18, 1981), 2.

5. David Stockman, *The Triumph of Politics* (New York: Harper & Row, 1986), 10.

6. *A Program for Economic Recovery,* 2–3.

7. Some of the details of the economic plan are in the appendix to this chapter. Comparisons of plans with actual results will also be included in later chapters.

8. William A. Niskanen, *Reaganomics* (New York: Oxford University Press, 1988), 4–5.

9. Cannon, *President Reagan,* 239.

10. Cannon gives numerous examples of this tendency in *President Reagan,* and particularly in the chapter entitled ''Passive President.'' For example, on foreign policy: ''Reagan wanted his national security adviser or his White House staff to produce an acceptable compromise that would end the argument [on Lebanon policy]. This trait inevitably invited middle-ground solutions aimed at mending differences, even in circumstances such as Lebanon where the middle ground courted catastrophe'' (402); and ''Too often, after decisions were made for any reason, Reagan did not follow through. Too often, Reagan was a performer and presidential leadership an empty shell'' (403).

See also David Stockman, *The Triumph of Politics,* 109, for another example on the budget negotiations:

Ed Meese was protecting the President from having to choose sides among his cabinet members. He was seeing to it Reagan never had to make a disagreeable choice in front of contending factions. . . . Whenever there was an argument, Meese would step in and tell us to take our arguments to some other ad hoc forum. The President would smile and say, ''Okay, you fellas work it out.''

For a more positive view of Reagan's style of management without necessarily refuting the basic criticisms, see Martin Anderson, *Revolution* (New York: Harcourt Brace Jovanovich, 1988), 281–292.

11. Stockman, *The Triumph of Politics,* 82.

12. Taken from a series of interviews with William Grieder, ''The Education of David Stockman,'' *Atlantic Monthly* December 1981, 38–40, 46–47.

13. For details of this strategy see, Stockman, *The Triumph of Politics,* 159–179.

14. Tip O'Neill, *Man of the House* (New York: St Martin's Press, 1987), 409–410.

15. Ibid. 412.

16. *Gallup Polls,* 1981.

17. Ibid. 1981.

18. ''Prosperity Without Inflation: Interviews with four Nobel Prize Winners,'' *U.S. News & World Report,* September, 1980, 50–54.

19. Sidney Weintraub, ''The Economy According to Reagan,'' *The New Leader,* 17 November 1980, 6–7.

20. Lester Thurow, ''How to Wreck the Economy,'' *New York Review of Books,* 14 May 1981, 3–8.

21. Walter W. Heller, "Can We Afford the Costs of Kemp–Roth?" *Wall Street Journal,* 10 February 1981.

22. Michael J. Boskin, *Reagan and the Economy* (San Francisco: ICS Press, 1987); William A. Niskanen, *Reaganomics* (New York: Oxford University Press, 1988); Paul Craig Roberts, *The Supply-Side Revolution* (Cambridge, MA: Harvard University Press, 1984); Murray Weidenbaum, *Rendezvous with Reality* (New York: Basic Books, 1988). For a brief description of the philosophy of the Reagan program, see Norman B. Ture, "New Directions in Economic Policy," *Tax Review,* October 1981.

Chapter 4

The Role of Ideology

Economists like to think they are relatively free of ideological concerns particularly when they are involved in theorizing. The real world is a complicated place, and the theorist must abstract from it to study whatever is of interest. Assumptions are made and some conditions specified that lead to the creation of the world that the investigator wishes to examine; in other words, an abstract model of the real world is constructed. But in the creation of this model, the theorist has also created the world he or she wishes to study. It should not take much effort to realize that ideological beliefs, biases, prejudices, and value judgments of all kinds are likely to creep in at each stage in the construction of a theory. To think otherwise is to deny the theorist a past, all learning experience, and personal observations and turn him into a computer capable of considering only what is currently fed into it.

When it comes to policy making, economists are more likely to admit that ideology, biases, and political interference enter into policy outcomes. If politics is the art of compromise, how could it be otherwise? So it is folly to deny that outside influences enter into the analysis in either theory or policy. Objectivity in the social sciences is a myth perpetuated by those who pretend to the scientific method. Rather than deny the existence of ideology, it is preferable to admit to it at the outset so that others may evaluate the analysis with a proper perspective. It is time to apply this task to the Reagan administration's economics agenda.

REAGAN'S PHILOSOPHY

As indicated earlier, Reagan went through a slow transformation from an FDR Democrat to a Goldwater Republican. There is no need to trace the evolution of his party affiliation for his biographer maintains that Reagan more or less held the same views for over a quarter century before becoming president.[1] Nor is there any need to delve into the apparent contradictions inherent in his admiration for President Roosevelt and his "lifelong" beliefs. Suffice it to say that by the time he attained the presidency, he had determined in his own mind that he was a conservative and, judging by his beliefs, held to some intransigent views.

GOVERNMENT AND THE ECONOMY

As an economic conservative, Reagan obviously favored free markets. The marketplace would solve all problems. In fact, Reagan was fond of saying things like ''government is not the solution, it is the problem,'' or ''government does not solve problems, it subsidizes them.'' It follows that government involvement in the economy should be reduced, whether that be in the form of deregulation or elimination of programs.

However, Reagan was *not* a libertarian, and what he meant by reducing the role of government in the economy would not satisfy the libertarian view because Reagan, like other conservatives, was not averse to using government for purposes he wished to foster. Once conservatives determine the moral certainty of various issues, they do not shy away from using government to make such conclusions law. Witness such issues as abortion and prayer in schools, which are not national issues at all but were devised to permit states to adopt their own responses to these social concerns.[2] He could also claim, with some justification, that he was reaching out to ''social conservatives,'' the blue-collar workers and ethnic groups normally associated with the Democratic party.

The reduction in government that was pursued was at the national level where conservatives always feared the concentration of power. If the power was transferred to the states, where presumably knowledge of problems is greater and resources better controlled, that would be acceptable. The aim was not to dismantle government but to reallocate responsibility to the local level. This decentralization of government might result in widely different approaches and commitments to programs by the states, but that is how it should be. If the assault on the welfare state could not be accomplished, this back door approach would do just as well.

So Reagan proposed his brand of federalism by attempting to transfer responsibility for some social programs, such as Food Stamps and Aid to Families with Dependent Children (AFDC), to the states. If, as a result, such programs became ineffective or inefficient, so much the better. This is not to suggest that Reagan would not have preferred to attack and eliminate the welfare state directly, which was Stockman's aim, but all those liberal entitlement programs were so well entrenched that the probability of success was very small. Consider Reagan's fiasco in attacking Social Security. Instead, he tried to reduce the welfare state by, for instance, drawing distinctions between the deserving and nondeserving poor and providing a ''safety net'' for those truly needy.[3] By interpreting the rules for eligibility for various programs, the administration could reduce government expenditures without eliminating them entirely. Thus, it could claim to be assisting the truly needy and not the chiselers. In the end, it was not the dismantling of the welfare state but the reduction in the *cost* of government that became the focus of the administration.

Reagan, as we shall see, did not accomplish all that he set out to do in the beginning, but he did send the liberal establishment scurrying to protect its programs and he did prevent them from initiating new ones. Liberals were put on the defensive and were too busy manning the barricades to propose anything new.

Another conservative view is that the nation should have a strong commitment to defense. Ever since Adam Smith, the government has been charged with providing for national defense; it is one function of government that does not separate liberals from conservatives. Here, Reagan was much more successful in achieving his aim of restoring the United States to prominence in defense areas. He was successful at virtually militarizing the economy to close the gap he saw in defense spending versus our adversaries. Again Carter started the movement, but Reagan carried it beyond all expectations. The consequences of this shifting of priorities toward defense and away from other domestic programs were profound and, as will become apparent, long lived.

Finally, beneath the opposition to government are some assumptions and value judgments that are seldom spelled out by politicians but are necessary to complete the conservative view. The free-market superiority is based on several arguments. The hallmark of free markets is individualism; the individual is the basic unit of the social structure. The (rational) individual, making free choices, benefits society through the "invisible hand"; the free market takes the individual preferences and efficiently satisfies them.[4]

From these principles it is often asserted, but seldom demonstrated, that the public sector is less efficient than the private sector. Whatever the public sector undertakes, it is less efficient than the private sector. Even if true, there may be other goals for a society than efficiency, for example, equity and stabilization of the economy. Efficiency itself is a value judgment, for it is possible to live very happily in a society that is less efficient but more equitable, where fairness and justice are valued as ends in themselves. Similarly with the assumption of individualism, is it not possible to value group preferences and to view the group as the fundamental unit of society? Does it follow that individualism is the only way to safeguard individual liberty?

Without pursuing these arguments, it is clear that many assumptions lurk behind the conservative label. Reagan brought his value judgments to the White House, but it is doubtful if he ever considered the philosophical arguments that have surrounded the whole concept of free markets. He did manage to attract many true believers to Washington, and many were accepted on the basis of how deeply devoted they were to the dogmatic assertions that were commonplace at the time.

TAX REDUCTIONS

As indicated earlier, Reagan favored tax cuts for many years. Now, thanks largely to Arthur Laffer assisted by Jude Wanniski, Paul Craig Roberts, and others, and to the tax cut bill of Kemp–Roth, he had the justification and the means.[5] Once he grasped the notion that there was a theoretical justification for his long held bias, that is, that high tax rates discourage work, he was a convert. He never had a doubt again. According to Stockman, however, he never understood the full implications of the tax cut program and particularly its relationship to revenues.[6] Throughout his presidency, he never understood the budget process and certainly not the details of budget making; he simply engaged in single-entry bookkeeping, noting that tax cuts were good, and deficits bad, but never connecting the two.

So it is to others that one must turn for the rationale of supply-side economics. Most proponents of supply-side economics developed into high priests, extolling the virtues of the new approach with near religious fervor. In their zeal, many clearly overstated their case. We turn to Norman Ture for a more reasoned explanation. He wrote that the

Basic and distinctive attribute of supply-side economics is to be found in the way it depicts the effects of government on economic activity. . . . If the government changes taxes in such a way as to make working more rewarding—hence less costly in terms of foregone leisure—the result is likely to be an increase in employment. In turn, this is likely to result in more production; therefore more income produced. . . . The focus of policy is to eliminate or at least reduce the adverse effects of taxation on incentives to work, to increase one's productivity, to save and invest, to start new enterprises, to innovate in developing new and better products and production processes. . . ."[7]

Stated in these terms, supply-side results are plausible, if not probable. However, as others pointed out, there are too many unknowns in this scenario; too many results that economists are not at all clear about nor would be willing to predict. Herbert Stein, Chairman of the Council of Economic Advisors under Nixon, wrote, "The propositions of supply-side economics are not matters of ideology or principle. They are matters of arithmetic. So far one must say that the arithmetic of any of the 'newer' propositions is highly doubtful."[8]

More hysterical supporters of supply-side economics claimed that tax cuts, in addition to increasing incentives and promoting economic growth without inflation, would *raise* revenues, leading Walter Heller to write, "Sound the trumpets and hear the heralds: There is, after all, such a thing as a free lunch! And it's not soft-headed liberals but hard-headed conservatives that bear the glad tidings. . . . And all this happens without budget cuts, the true believers tell us. Lunch is not only free, we get a bonus for eating it. P. T. Barnum, move over."[9]

SUPPLY-SIDE ECONOMICS AS THEORY

Basically, supply-side economics is not a theory—it is a policy masquerading as science. Much work has been done on the supply side of the economy, starting most notably with Adam Smith and especially with J. B. Say who maintained that "supply created its own demand." In this famous law of markets, Say reasoned that economic agents work only so long as to furnish the income that would be sufficient to meet their demand for goods. Because work involved disutility, why would anyone work more than necessary? Hence, in supplying effort, one is simultaneously demanding goods; an oversupply of all goods is, therefore, not possible, at least in the long run.[10] Without delving into the esoteric arguments, much of this analysis was discredited by Keynes who held that saving would not be matched by investment to ensure that all income is spent by someone, or that income could be saved in such a way that it does not return to the income stream. This is the view from macroeconomics.

Supply-siders looked to microeconomics to explain where the necessary incentives were to be discovered. *Individual* economic agents would see their after-tax incomes increase with a tax cut and decide to supply more effort, invest more, produce more, and so on. The after-tax rate of return would increase, making productive effort more profitable. Despite the numerous expressions of this propensity, there is no empirical evidence to support this conclusion; it is merely an assertion. In technical terms, it means that people would substitute work for leisure now that the price of leisure has risen. But the reaction could easily be the other way around; people could work less now that their after-tax incomes had increased.

Firms too are likely to see their after-tax rate of return increased and invest more. Again, this overlooks the complete motivations of investors. More investment might occur for this reason, but the higher return is not the only governing motive. There may be excess capacity to begin with, there may be even higher returns to be had abroad, and there may not be favorable expectations of the future to warrant the current commitment of resources. Therefore, the higher after-tax incomes could easily be diverted into areas, for example, the stock market, extra dividends, foreign investment, that would not promote economic growth in the United States. The increase in jobs, productivity, and opportunity that would have followed would be denied as well.

The administration was at least partly aware of this as they hoped to influence the expectations of the business community. A new regime, demonstrably favorable to business, was supposed to create the climate for firms to project a rosy future, as did the supply-side proponents. Firms, however, were not about to adopt such a sanguine view of the future on the basis of hope, and expectations were not altered immediately, and perhaps not at all.

So at the outset, the new approach, the revolution, had a very shaky foundation. It was based more on faith than reason, but the true believers would hear of no criticisms as they carried the revolutionary banner with religious fervor. So anxious were they to see their ideas carried out that they appealed to the Kennedy–Johnson tax cut of 1964 as a precedent for their proposal. The analogy was a false one, as the earlier tax cuts were designed to influence the demand side of the economy. Walter Heller, the architect of the Kennedy–Johnson tax reductions, vehemently denied the parallel and had some sport in doing so.[11]

The real problem with supply-side economics is that it lacked the theoretical foundation that is so necessary for sound policy. The theoretical foundation was not only shaky but did not undergo the usual scrutiny that radical departures normally receive before being adopted as public policy. For example, the Keynesian model was subject to years of analysis, empirical testing, refinements, and criticisms before it was applied to the economy. There was a consensus of sorts among economists as to the nature of reality before subjecting the theoretical abstractions to actual economic conditions. If the model worked as predicted, there was considerable analyses to credit; if the model did not work, then the past analysis would offer a basis for finding out why it did not perform as predicted.

For supply-side economics, no such painstaking analysis took place. There was no time for professional discussion of its tenets; no evidence to support the predictions made; and no chance for refinements to be made to the basic model. In short, it did not receive the critical discussion that it should have to lend it legitimacy. Either one believed it would work, or one did not. This is not the proper foundation for public policy! The predicted results were so tenuous, so uncertain, that it was folly to pursue it without more research and review.

This is not to disparage new approaches in policy making. In fact, new approaches are desirable, but examples like the supply-side experiment are likely to discourage new avenues rather than promote them. Making public policy through proselytization rather than persuasion is not the method to encourage the undertaking of different courses.

DEREGULATION

The Reagan campaign promised if elected to "get government off our backs." Accordingly, providing regulatory relief became part of the program for economic recovery. The administration was not only concerned with intrusions into economic freedom, which any conservative would oppose, but it also claimed that federal regulation imposed some severe economic costs on society. In its report to Congress, *A Program for Economic Recovery* of February 1981, these costs are outlined:

The most readily identifiable of the costs are the administrative outlays of the regulatory agencies since they appear in the Federal Budget. These costs are passed on to individuals and businesses directly in the form of higher Federal taxes. Much larger than the administrative expenses are the costs of compliance, which add $100 billion per year to the costs of the goods and services we buy. The most important effects of regulation, however, are the adverse impacts on economic growth. These arise because regulations may discourage innovative research and development, reduce investment in new plant and equipment, raise unemployment by increasing labor costs, and reduce competition. Taken together, these longer run effects contribute significantly to our current economic dilemma of high unemployment and inflation.

From this assessment it would appear that federal regulations are a major cause or at least a major contributor to all the economic problems that were plaguing the economy. Overstatements of past problems can be expected by a new administration, but not to this extent. The administration moved fast in its first month to remove this thorn in the side of firms and individuals. It acted to "address the problem of excessive and inefficient regulation" as it:

1. Established a Task Force on Regulatory Relief
2. Abolished the Council on Wage and Price Stability, a holdover from the Carter years designed to control wages and prices
3. Postponed the effective dates of pending regulations until the end of March
4. Issued an Executive Order to strengthen presidential oversight of the regulatory process
5. Accelerated the decontrol of domestic oil

How well this program worked is not the concern of this chapter, but it will be examined later when the assessment of the entire Reagan economic program is undertaken. Some comments on the administration's views on regulation are necessary before that evaluation is completed.

First, the cost of regulation is at best a wild guess. The administration used a much quoted estimate of over $100 billion. The estimate was apparently obtained from a study by Murray Weidenbaum, who included the budgets of the regulatory agencies, paperwork costs to business, the cost of import quotas, the loss of productivity of workers who could be doing something more productive, and the costs of regulation using the CPI as the indicator.[12]

There are clearly several things wrong with this estimate. First, it overstates the costs by including elements that do not properly belong in this category: the budgets of regulatory agencies should be included in the costs of government; the paperwork costs include filling out forms for the IRS, Social Security, and the like but these costs are not regulatory costs at all and would not disappear if all regulatory agencies were abolished; and most damaging of all, these are just costs without any mention of *benefits*. Costs are easier to measure than benefits, true, but some recognition of the benefits of regulation should be included if an overall assessment of regulation is desired. Cost–benefit analysis, advocated by the economists who were now in command, became cost analysis.

Murray Weidenbaum recognized that "benefits should not be overlooked. To the extent that government rules result in healthier workplaces, safer products, and so forth, these benefits are very real."[13] He found it difficult, however, to find examples of benefits but had no difficulty finding examples of failures.

But the administration was not interested in an objective and balanced study of the role of regulation in the U.S. economy. It knew that regulation was bad; it had been saying so for so long that it became dogma. As the Tochlins put it:

By the late 1970s, complaints of excessive regulation had become management's all-purpose cop-out. Were profits too low? Blame regulation. Were prices too high? Blame regulation. Were inadequate funds and manpower earmarked for research and development? Blame regulation for sapping both funds and manpower. Was American industry unable to compete with foreign competitors? Blame regulation.[14]

The administration merely listened to these complaints and repeated them.

Everyone agrees that regulations and regulatory agencies must be monitored to ensure that they are doing the job correctly. It is generally recognized that often regulations are clumsy, irksome, inappropriate, and counterproductive. It is also clear that regulations impose costs on the regulated and that some of these costs can be burdensome. In addition, the regulatory agencies are often controlled by those they seek to regulate. But the Reagan administration was not content to undertake the painstaking job of real cost–benefit analysis or to engage in a long-term study that would seriously investigate the justification for each regulatory agency. It was already convinced of the answer.

However, it is likely that such an investigation would reveal more benefits than is commonly acknowledged. How else can the public be assured of the safety of food and drugs? How else can pollution be controlled? How else can the environment be protected? Can these issues be left to business? To the states? To state the questions is to bring out the major issue—what is the role of government in these areas? These are not the issues that bothered the Reagan administration. It knew the answers; there was no need for discussion.

Costs and benefits to firms and individuals are necessary for any judgments about regulation. But what of communities? If an airline moves out, what happens to the economy of the community? If a bank fails, what happens to the business climate of the community? If a firm pollutes a river, what happens to everyone who makes use of that resource? Clearly, there are neighborhood or third-party effects in many areas of regulation.[15] If so, there is a cogent argument for government intervention.

However, as an early assessment concluded, "The Reagan administration's regulatory philosophy appears to be that a generally diminished federal regulatory presence is preferable except in isolated cases. Less regulation will improve business cash flow, help break inflationary expectations, get the government out of second guessing business as well as state and local governments, and increase individual freedom."[16] Business cash flow would improve as it saved the costs of regulation; inflationary expectations would diminish because the administration believed that continued growth in regulations was contributing to inflationary expectations; and getting the federal government out of the regulatory business and transferring whatever regulations are necessary to state responsibility would improve efficiency and cut costs.

Finally, the hope of the administration was to achieve a real *change in expectations*. Here, the administration hoped that business firms would see the attempt to eliminate regulations and reduce costs as incentives to firms to invest. Together with tax concessions, business confidence in the future was supposed to increase to the extent that corporate planners would decide the time was favorable for current investment. An unabashedly probusiness administration was seen as sufficient to overcome the gloom and pessimism of the late 1970s.

MONETARY POLICY AND INFLATION

The administration recognized that a consistent monetary policy was necessary if its economic program was to succeed. But the Federal Reserve System is an independent agency, separate from the executive branch, and its cooperation was not guaranteed. Thus, in its *Program for Economic Recovery,* there is the guarded language: "Thus, it is expected that the rate of money and credit growth will be brought down to levels consistent with noninflationary expansion of the economy." What did the administration "expect" was the proper policy—"The economic scenario [of the administration] assumes that the growth rates of money and credit are steadily reduced from the 1980 levels to one-half those levels by 1986."

It went on to declare that it basically approved of the direction of monetary policy in recent years. That is, it favored controlling the rate of growth of the monetary aggregates rather than controlling interest rates. This acceptance of monetarism was in keeping with its desire to reduce the rate of inflation.

With the Federal Reserve gradually but persistently reducing the growth of money, inflation should decline at least as fast as anticipated. Moreover, if monetary growth rates are restrained, then inflationary expectations will decline. And since interest rate movements are largely a mirror of price expectations, reduction in one will produce reduction in the other.

The ability of monetary policy to reduce inflation without seriously affecting output and employment was an article of faith of the administration. There was no concern for the ability of the Fed to control monetary aggregates nor any worry over the velocity of money behaving itself. As indicated earlier, even in the face of an obvious contradiction between the declining rate of growth of money and projected increase in national output, the administration refused to alter its forecasts. The administration's monetary policy relied on the advice of Milton Friedman and Beryl Sprinkel, both monetarist leaders. When Sprinkel, undersecretary of the treasury for monetary affairs, pointed out the inconsistency to Stockman, he [Stockman] refused to alter his projections of the GNP, preferring instead not to deal with this issue.[17]

Again, we find the stubborn adherence to the economic program and outcomes despite the legitimacy of the criticisms of it and the unwillingness to heed any objections to the creed. Whenever members of the administration did deign to reply to criticisms, they were apt to rely on arguments that accused the objectors of not understanding the new theory or that the critics were not factoring in the change in expectations that was going to overcome the problems.[18]

The administration was right about one part: If expectations were to be changed, it would not do to start correcting forecasts or sacrificing any of the Reagan initiatives. If the economy was not to show significant improvement, how could expectations be positively changed? Any chipping away at the total economic program would appear to be a sign of retreat to traditional ways, and the same approach to economic problems from the past would leave businessmen skeptical and unsure of the intentions of the new administration.

The administration was also correct to perceive that inflation was a major concern of the American public. The inflation of the 1970s, caused mainly by energy costs, hit everyone's pocketbook and affected everyone's life-style so that it was cursed by everyone. However, it is curious that an administration so concerned with the supply side did not recognize that the inflation of the 1970s emanated from supply-side shocks of commodities prices. The cure for this type of inflation would not likely come from controlling the money supply because that does not get at the source of the problem and is mainly a demand-side solution anyway. Listening to monetarists, however, who maintain that inflation is always a monetary phenomenon, would limit the type of solution to adjusting the growth of monetary aggregates.

Once again, dogmatic responses act as a obstruction to policy making. Added to the other dogmatic views and value judgments, monetary policy would not, indeed could not, admit criticisms. Doctrinaire views do not invite nor can they entertain close scrutiny.

More important was the cause of inflation according to the administration: government, of course. "The most important cause of our economic problems has been the government itself. . . . In particular, excessive government spending and overly accommodative monetary policies have combined to give us a climate of continuing inflation."[19] Even more directly: "The Federal Government bears most direct responsibility for the increases in inflation and interest rates, which were due to excessive expansion of the money supply. In short, Federal economic policies bear the major responsibility for the legacy of stagflation."[20]

Thus, energy prices played only a small part in the inflation of the 1970s, and stagflation, although not fully explained, must be attributed in large part to government. The administration was also pleased to announce the demise of the trade-off between employment and prices. Inflationary expectations were acknowledged to exist and to feed on themselves, making inflation more difficult to control unless there is a concerted effort to pursue its elimination consistently and without stop and go measures. It was the world according to the Reagan administration.

Finally, among ardent conservatives, in and out of government, it was believed that inflation causes the following: government deficits, high interest rates, high taxes, less economic growth, trade imbalances, and income losses, for the poor especially. These are all bad outcomes and must be attacked. Of course, more rational economic conservatives would not necessarily agree with everything on this list and might wish to add to it based on sounder economic principles.

In its *Economic Report of the President of 1982*,[21] the Council of Economic advisors listed its costs of inflation. The CEA suggested that unanticipated inflation (it did not believe that high inflation rates could ever be anticipated!) would lead to arbitrary redistributions of income because contracts are stated in nominal terms, with or without an allowance for inflation, and inflation beyond the rates anticipated would transfer income from one group to another. Furthermore, changes in relative prices confuse the market and obscure the market signals; the result is inefficiency. This confusion, over time, can distort the decisions made and makes for inefficient allocation of resources. Inflation also causes uncertainties of various kinds, and people begin to spend more effort dealing with this kind of uncertainty and less time on productive efforts. Other distortions occur in the tax system, in insufficient depreciation allowances for example, and, in general, people spend too much effort combatting the effects of inflation.

There was no mention of anyone benefiting from inflation nor who they might be. Just how accurate these beliefs turn out to be will be explored in later chapters.

BALANCED BUDGET

A balanced budget was not part of the original economic plan, but the policies put in place by the plan were supposed to result in a balanced budget in a few years. During the campaign, the budget was to be balanced in 1983; later, the date was changed to 1984.[22] However, economic conservatives had always favored an annually balanced federal budget. Milton Friedman, for instance, had promoted the idea for many years. In fact, he drafted a constitutional amendment that would have required the federal government to balance its budget annually. Other versions circulated as well, and 34 states had passed a resolution calling for a constitutional convention to be convened to consider an amendment based on these resolutions.

The wording of such resolutions left so many loopholes and qualifications that an annually balanced budget could easily be avoided by creative accountants. So many definitions of terms could be debated, for example, how to define GNP and what rate of inflation to use, that the result could be paralysis rather than discipline. In the end, how could such an amendment be enforced? What sanctions could be imposed on the president and Congress? Would congressmen be jailed for failure to obey the law?

More important, what would be the economic effects of forcing an annually balanced budget? Conservatives argued that it would impose the discipline on government officials that they lacked. The federal government taxed and spent excessively and could not discipline itself. This outside constraint of a balanced budget would limit the ability of congressmen to continue to spend and preserve their jobs by rewarding everyone and conceding to special interests.[23] Because conservatives generally favor *rules* over discretionary acts for government officials to follow, the annually balanced budget would fill the bill, is simple to understand, and would appeal to the voter as sensible. Moreover, because the economy is basically stable, government need not step in to stabilize it through fiscal policies that often lead to incurring deficits or inventing new programs that are supposed to bolster the economy. So the self-regulating, stable economy does not require government for stabilization. Neither is it necessary for all those government programs that result in excessive spending. The annually balanced budget would curtail all unnecessary spending and reduce government's role in the economy drastically. In the final analysis, this is what the conservatives want to achieve whatever the means.

An annually balanced budget, as many have pointed out, would actually be destabilizing to the economy and would represent a rather perverse fiscal policy. When the economy is booming, tax receipts would rise; a balanced budget criteria would call for an *increase* in government spending, providing further, perhaps unnecessary, stimulus to the economy. When the economy is in a downswing, tax receipts would fall; this calls for a *decrease* in government spending to match the falling revenues. But such a policy would make the recession worse and prolong the downturn. Thus, slavish adherence to the balanced budget rule would be perverse and cause more violent swings in economic activity than would otherwise occur.

The stability that conservatives see in the economy is over the long run. Keynesian countercyclical policies were designed to manipulate the economy in the short run. Because conservatives cannot deny the existence of the business cycle, they are contending that it is better to suffer the swings in economic activity that occur in the short run because government intervention is a greater evil. In the long run, stability is restored by the marketplace without help from government.

The emphasis on the long run is an integral part of conservative models. But the long run is often seen as too sanguine an horizon by those who are impatient for action. For those who suffer in the short run, waiting for things to work themselves out in time is neglect not virtue. So although the public may well understand what a balanced budget is, it may not be willing to forgo some action when the economy is threatened. If, as a result, an unbalanced budget is tolerated in times of recessions, war, or other emergencies, then the door is open for exceptions to become the norm, and discretionary policies will creep back in again.

One wonders, then, how long a balanced budget rule would survive in reality. Those who profess to favor it, including conservatives, may well reconsider their beliefs when the economy threatens their positions.

INTERNATIONAL TRADE

There was no mention of international trade problems in the *Program for Economic Recovery*. Not until July 1981 was there a policy developed for foreign trade. Was this because external problems were not deemed serious enough to be included in the document setting out the aims of the administration? Or was it because Nixon advised the new president to concentrate on domestic affairs first, and once they were in order, then foreign affairs could be tackled?[24]

The Council of Economic Advisors did address the problems of international trade in its annual report. The administration adopted polices in the international sphere that rival those in the domestic one. The council listed five components of the administration's trade policy:

1. Restoring strong noninflationary growth at home. Presumably lower inflation rates would help American firms to "respond" to changes in domestic and international markets.
2. Reducing self-imposed trade disincentives. Reducing regulations and laws that cover trade conditions.
3. Effective and strict enforcement of U.S. trade laws and international trade agreements.
4. A more effective approach to industrial adjustment problems. Market forces, not government, would correct for dislocations of industry due to changes in market conditions.
5. Reducing government barriers to the flow of trade and investment among nations.

These policies are compatible with those governing the domestic sector. Free trade, reliance on market forces, and reducing government's role in international trade are policies designed to fit into the administration's conservative approach.

As examples of how they would be applied, the conditions in 1981 can be recalled. In 1981 (and for the next 4 years), the dollar appreciated sharply against foreign currencies. In 1981, "The new administration scaled back U.S. intervention in foreign exchange markets . . . The administration has returned to the policy of intervening only when necessary to counter conditions of severe disorder in the market." The administration viewed the rise in the value of the dollar to have "reflected a positive response to underlying economic policies of the Administration".[25]

This benign neglect of foreign trade developments is inserted here to remind us of the role of international trade in the administration's economic plans and to prepare us for the repercussions of that neglect in later years. Failure to address trade problems at the outset would result in ambivalence toward them later when they became serious and would lead to more instability than nonintervention would justify.

SUMMARY

Ronald Reagan has been called an ideologue—one committed to a specified set of views. If by ideologue one means that this commitment stemmed from an abstract, theoretical thinking, then Ronald Reagan was not an ideologue at all. Rather he seems to have formed a set of prejudices and value judgments at various stages in his life; he never went through the painstaking process of reasoning to arrive at such biases, examining theories in the abstract, weighing them, rejecting some and accepting others, and so on. Some events or episodes in his own life influenced him and judgments or general principles were formed; later when presented with ideas that conformed to his preconceptions, he was easily "convinced" of the correctness of his beliefs. Contrary evidence or conflicting ideas were not allowed to sway him from his original views.

It is not at all clear that Reagan understood the factions within the conservative movement of which he was supposed to be the leader. Battles were common among the traditionalists, new right, and those who tried to reconcile the two (and more) groups that formed the revolutionary movement.[26] According to Dionne, Reagan was able to unite the warring factions, at least in the beginning, by a clever campaign designed to appeal to the major groups of conservatives:

In the marriage of supply-side economics to "traditional moral values" lay the genius of the Reagan campaign. Through issues such as abortion and school prayer, Reagan insisted that he was the candidate of the old-fashioned virtue opposing the forces of modernism and permissiveness. Yet his program told voters that they could help the economy by agreeing to let him cut their taxes; they could help their country best by helping themselves. For Reagan's liberal critics, his economics flew in the face of all his piety on traditional values.[27]

This and other contradictions never bothered Reagan, which leads one to suspect that he never understood what the controversies within the conservatives ranks were all about. Later, these controversies would end in paralysis, and the ranks separated in Reagan's second term. Because Reagan did not understand the rifts within his party, he never took the time nor made the effort to make the coalition that elected him into a permanent force. Perhaps he was too old, or too lazy, but he let the revolution slip away and become fragmented just as the Democrats had done before him.

So we are left with a president who had a philosophy based on anecdotes, ad hoc events, or personal grievances. Because tax rates were too high once in his life and encouraged him to limit his movie-making efforts, it follows that tax rates were too high in 1980 and discouraged productive effort; because a welfare queen had been apprehended, it follows that there must be many welfare recipients who are simply chiselers, and so on. Anyone who worked with him knew that a simple story that touched his own experience was worth far more than a position paper; it would be easy to gain his approval for policies if they were couched in terms that he could understand and to which he could relate.

Thus, in this manner his main biases became public policy. The other elements of his economic program that were not based on his personal experience were inserted by his advisors. He left these parts and all the details to others as long as his main concerns were recognized. The real question for public policy is to what extent the public shared his biases, and if they did, did they emanate from the same concerns? Or did Reagan have the "right" answers for the wrong questions and, thus, win elections without generating a revolution?

NOTES

1. Lou Cannon, *President Reagan* (New York: Simon and Schuster, 1991), 90–92, 235, and elsewhere in his book.

2. This point was made by Theodore J. Lowi, in "Ronald Reagan—Revolutionary?," in *The Presidency and the Governing of America,* eds. Lester M. Salamon and Michael S. Lund (Washington, DC: The Urban Institute Press, 1984), 35–36.

3. Ibid. 42. Lowi makes the point that this distinction brings us back to the nineteenth-century notions of charity whereby local officials determined who should get public help and who should not. For additional discussion of this method of disposing charity (as well as the history of public assistance), see Michael B. Katz, *In the Shadow of the Poorhouse: A Social History of Welfare in America* (New York: Basic Books, 1986).

4. For a succinct exposition of the arguments, see Andrew Schotter, *Free Market Economics* (New York: St. Martin's Press, 1985).

5. For the rationale for tax cuts, see Jude Wanniski, *The Way the World Works* (New York: Simon & Schuster, 1978) and Paul Craig Roberts, *The Supply-Side Revolution* (Cambridge, MA: Harvard University Press, 1984). There are many books on supply-side economics and many explanations of how it was supposed to work, including many of the previously referred to books on Reaganomics. Of particular interest is the book recommended by David Stockman that allegedly portrayed the philosophy of the Reagan revolution: George Gilder, *Wealth and Poverty* (New York: Basic Books, 1981).

6. David Stockman, *The Triumph of Politics* (New York: Harper & Row, 1986), 9–10.

7. Norman B. Ture, "New Directions in Economic Policy," in *Tax Review,* October 1981, 36–37.

8. Herbert Stein, "Some 'Supply-Side' Propositions," *Wall Street Journal,* 19 March 1990, 24.

9. Walter W. Heller, "The Kemp-Roth-Laffer Free Lunch," *Wall Street Journal,* 12 July 1978, 20.

10. Say repeated his "law" in several ways, ranging from a simple truism to a

variant that showed some genuine insight. The statement in the text is a crude expression of the most readily recognized form of the law of markets, without qualifications.

11. Heller, "The Kemp-Roth-Laffer Free Lunch."

12. Robert DeFina and Murray Weidenbaum, *The Taxpayer and Government Regulations* (St. Louis, MO: Center for the Study of American Business, Washington University, 1978). For a criticism of this study, see Julius Allen, "Costs and Benefits of Federal Regulation: An Overview," *Congressional Research Service,* LOC Report no. 78-152 E, July 19, 1978, 16–17, quoted in Susan J. Tolchin and Martin Tolchin, *Dismantling America: The Rush to Deregulate* (New York: Oxford University Press, 1983), 127.

13. Murray Weidenbaum, *Rendezvous with Reality* (New York: Basic Books, 1988), 230.

14. Susan J. Tolchin and Martin Tolchin, *Dismantling America,* 4–5.

15. Ibid. 250.

16. George C. Eads and Michael Fix, "Regulatory Policy," in *The Reagan Experiment,* eds. John L. Palmer and Isabel V. Sawhill (Washington, DC: The Urban Institute Press, 1982), 131.

17. William A. Niskanen, *Reaganomics* (New York: Oxford University Press, 1988), 65. For the confusion and controversy over this issue, see David Stockman, *The Triumph of Politics,* 93.

18. In its first *Economic Report of the President in 1982,* the Council of Economic Advisors wrote:

The new policies comprise an innovative approach to reducing the rate of inflation while providing incentives to achieve sustained and vigorous economic growth. *While such a development would be somewhat unusual in light of historical experience* [emphasis added], we believe that a consistent policy of monetary restraint, combined with the Administration's spending and tax policies, and reinforced by continuing regulatory relief, will provide the policy framework for both reduced inflation and increased economic growth. (24–25).

19. *A Program for Economic Recovery,* a message to Congress dated February 18, 1981, 4.

20. *Economic Report of the President, 1982,* 22–23.

21. *Economic Report of the President, 1982,* 56–58. This economic report, the administration's first, should be read if one is interested in the philosophical foundation of the new administration.

22. For a frank discussion of the budgetary process and plans for a balanced budget, see Stockman, *The Triumph of Politics,* 165–166, 222–225, 345–350, and many other places scattered throughout the book.

23. For an early stinging attack on federal fiscal policy, see James M. Buchanan and Richard E. Wagner, *Democracy in Deficit* (New York: Academic Press, 1977).

24. Canon, *President Reagan,* 77.

25. *Economic Report of the President, 1982,* 172–173.

26. For a good discussion of these groups within the conservative movement, see E. J. Dionne, Jr., *Why Americans Hate Politics* (New York: Simon & Schuster, 1991), 227–236.

27. Ibid. 252–253.

Part II

The Results

Chapter 5

Fiscal Policy in the Reagan Years: Optimism and Reality

The Reagan economic plan, based on what was billed as "revolutionary ideas," can only be judged by the outcomes. Because theoretical objections to it went unheeded and were, in fact, denounced, the success or failure must be judged by how the plan worked in practice; because the plan incorporated so little theoretical justification, empirical results are the only way to assess the validity of the assumptions and predictions that went into it. The plan was a mixture of ideology and preconceptions, dashed with hope and belief, and served on a platter of simplicity.

The purpose of this chapter is to separate hope from fact, promise from reality. This is easier said than done. To try to distinguish the results of the plan from all other influences is a monumental task. The economic world turned before the plan, continued when the plan was initiated, and is still going on. Any attempt to measure what happened to it during any particular period, independent of what went before and after, is clearly an impossible job. It is not surprising that different investigators would find conflicting evidence if different periods or subperiods are involved in the analysis. It is also true, sad but true, that human behavior is such that investigators will tend to find what they are looking for—the evidence to support a given view or bias. It is easy to overlook contrary evidence, to select from an array of facts those which are useful for what is being maintained, and to maintain only what is shown by the evidence selected.

Again, objectivity in the social sciences is a myth. All that one can do is to strive for objectivity with any bias being acknowledged beforehand. At times, this is obvious, particularly when the writer is known, but without knowing the investigator, what passes as independent and objective research may be anything but those ideals. Some researchers come closer to this ideal than others, as will become evident once we review the results and their interpretation by those who have made some attempt at measuring the success or failure of the administration's economic plans. This caveat is inserted here, before the evidence is presented, to alert the unsuspecting of the shortcomings of empirical research. There will be ample examples to illustrate what is implied by this warning.

So the purpose of this chapter is to present the evidence, both collected by me and by others, in a manner calculated to reveal the facts as far as possible. Various interpretations of the facts will also be presented to illustrate the con-

Table 5.1

Comparison of Carter and Reagan Budgets (percentages of GNP in fiscal years)

	1980	1984	1989	Peak Yr.	Low Yr.
Outlays	22.1	23.1	22.3	24.3 (1983)	22.3 (1989)
Receipts	19.4	18.1	19.3	20.1 (1981)	18.1 (1983) & (1984)
Deficit	-2.8	-5.0	-3.0	-6.3 (1983)	-2.6 (1981)

Source: Office of Management and Budget, *Historical Tables: Budget of the United States Government, Fiscal Year 1992*, 17.

troversies that seemingly simple facts generate. Some conclusions will then be offered from my perspective.

REDUCING GOVERNMENT SPENDING

One of the main elements in the Reagan administration's economic plan was the goal of reducing federal government spending. The evidence indicates that this goal was not achieved, and, in fact, government spending was higher when Reagan left office than when he entered it. Table 5.1 tells the story.

In fiscal year 1980, the last complete year of the Carter administration, government outlays totaled 22.1% of the GNP; in fiscal year 1989, the last Reagan budget year, the percentage had risen to 22.3%. Fiscal year 1980 was chosen as the last complete budget year of the Carter administration because the Reagan administration tampered with the budget for fiscal year 1981 to such an extent that Mr. Carter can hardly be held responsible for it. The data for fiscal years are provided to show a kind of midpoint in the Reagan years and to provide some evidence that was available to the public in the election year of 1984.

Note that in the election year 1984, the unfulfilled promise to reduce government spending and to have balanced the budget by that time did not appear to influence the voters as Reagan won reelection easily. In 1984, government spending had increased dramatically as did the budget deficit. By fiscal year 1989, both spending and the budget deficit had fallen, but they were still higher than existed in the Carter years.

In dollar terms, government outlays rose steadily from $590.9 billion in 1980 to $1144.1 in 1989, an increase of 94% (but "only" 30% in 1982 dollars). Increases of these magnitudes scarcely warrant any indication of success in reducing the size and influence of the federal government. Similarly, the promise to balance the budget by 1984 appears ludicrous in retrospect. The deficit rose from approximately $73 billion in 1980 (excluding off-budget items such as Social Security Trust Funds) to $238 billion in 1986 and to over $206 billion in 1989. (If off-budget items are included, the total for 1989 would be $153 billion.) Curiously, Reagan, the budget balancer, accumulated larger deficits while in office than all his predecessors combined!

Reagan continuously blamed Congress for the budget deficits but, of course, never submitted a balanced budget while in office. Congress did restore many of the budget cuts in social programs made by the administration (to be examined later), but Congress cannot be blamed alone for the tremendous budget deficits in the 1980s. To understand the budget contests between the Reagan administration and Congress, Table 5.2 assembles the necessary information. Over the Reagan budget years, the initial budgets were increased by $186.5 billion, an increase of only 2.5%, but even this total obscures the source of the increases. Policy changes, those that were the result of administration revisions and Congressional actions, accounted for $109.7 billion or 1.5%. Congress cut $61.6 billion from defense budgets and added $170.8 billion in other areas. Of the net $109 billion in policy changes, *discretionary changes came to only $38.1 billion;* these changes represented additions by Congress not included in the original budgets.

The failure of Congress to go along with the cuts in entitlement and other social programs resulted in an increase in the original budgets of some $42 billion. Congress refused to cut many programs that the Reagan administration had proposed in medicare, food stamps, unemployment compensation, and the like. Finally, the continuing farm problem called for additional outlays of $45 billion, and all other outlays and offsets added another $45 billion to budgets.

Thus, just how much to blame Congress for budget deficits depends on how one views the budget changes and how they are calculated. If only the discretionary changes of $38 billion are counted, then Congress cannot be blamed for very much because these changes accounted for only 20% of the total changes of $186 billion. If one adds the entitlement cuts that were denied by Congress, the percentage rises to 43%. Of course, these cuts were preposterous, given the makeup of the Congress, and were never seriously considered acceptable. Republicans and Democrats alike backed away from severe cuts in the welfare state. David Stockman, for one, mourned the lack of support from traditional conservative Republicans: "The Republican quarrel with the American welfare state is over. The half-trillion-dollar budget which remains in 1986 after 5 years of sustained ideological challenge is there because the rank and file of GOP politicians want it for their constituents no less than the Democrats do."[1]

Yet even these numbers can be misleading because Congress did cut defense spending by over $61 billion from administration proposals. Congress balked

Table 5.2
Reasons for Differences in Budget Totals from Initial and Ending Amounts (in billions)

Reason	Fiscal Years 1982-89	Percent
Beginning Budget Totals	$ 7337.1	100.0
Policy Changes	109.7	1.5
Econ Conditions	10.6	0.1
Estimating Differences	49.2	0.7
Aid to Thrifts	16.9	0.2
Total Budget Changes	186.5	2.5
Final Budget Totals	$ 7523.5	102.5
Budget Deficits	$ 1412.7	
As % of Budgets	18.8	

Policy Changes:	Amount	As % of Policy Changes	As % of Deficits
Nat'l. Defense	$ -61.1	-55.7	-4.3
Nondefense	170.8	155.7	12.1
Discretionary changes	38.1	22.3	2.7
Entitlements	42.5	24.9	3.0
Farm	45.5	26.6	3.2
Other	44.7	26.2	3.2
Total Policy Changes	$ 109.7	100.0	7.8

Source: Office of Management and Budget, U. S. Budgets, Fiscal Years 1982-1989.

at some elements in the defense budget, and these reductions offset a large proportion of other congressional outlays. This modest resistance by Congress to the massive defense buildup completely offsets the discretionary spending of $38 billion, so it could be said that the additions to the budgets were paid for by cuts in defense spending. Even if the entitlements are added onto spending, the difference of some $19 billion net hardly justifies blaming Congress for the budget deficits. Because the budget deficits of the Reagan administration totaled a phenomenal $1412.7 billion, the share that could be attributed to Congress ranges from 2.7 to 5.7% of the deficits, not a terribly significant proportion given the fact that all changes to the original budgets account for only 13% of the budget deficits.

Thus, the charge that Congress was responsible for the budget deficits dissipates in the face of reality. In fact, it would appear that government spending cannot be blamed for much of the budget deficits that developed regardless of who was to blame. The lack of revenues was the real culprit.[2]

In addition to blaming Congress for the deficits and to deflect criticisms of these large budget deficits, Reagan also called for a line item veto power that would allow the president to strike any item from the budget without vetoing the entire budget. In addition, he called for a constitutional amendment to require the federal government to balance its budget annually. Neither of these possibilities was or is credible because the transfer of power to the president in the case of the line item veto would be enormous and contrary to the tenets of democracy; the annually balanced budget would result in perverse fiscal policy as indicated earlier and, although simple to understand, would be contrary to sound macroeconomic policy if followed.

So the Reagan administration took another tack, claiming that budget deficits did not matter that much. After years of maintaining all sorts of evils of deficits, from inflation to blocking economic growth, the conservatives took an about-face, reversed themselves, while proclaiming the need for a balanced budget amendment! Equally curious, the liberals who had downplayed the evils of budget deficits began now to worry about their effects. When we come to evaluating the legacy of the Reagan administration, these issues will be investigated further; for now, we are only interested in comparing the promise of the revolution with the results. As far as government spending and balancing the budget are concerned, the conclusion is obvious: The Reagan administration did not reduce federal government spending, and it did not balance the budget. In fact, it did the opposite.

Finally, in desperation, Congress passed the Gramm–Rudman Act that forced reduced spending by setting limits to the amount of the permissible deficit. The plan hoped to reach a balanced budget by gradually decreasing the allowable deficit until it disappeared. If in any one fiscal year, Congress failed to comply with the limits set, the Office of Budget and Management was empowered to cut spending across the board, with half coming from defense spending and half coming from other expenditures except for some poverty programs and Social Security.[3] This meat-ax approach to solving the deficit problem satisfied no one, neither those who feared cuts in national defense spending nor those who were protecting special interests. Economists found the Act to be nonsensical because it imposes restraints regardless of the state of the economy and makes cuts without regard to the efficacy of the programs—all would be cut without considering the merits of the individual items.

However, Congress was not about to vote against it because that would infer that it was not interested in reducing the deficit and that it had acted irresponsibly in the past, and without some constraints would do so again in the future. Everyone had the opportunity to engage in a great deal of political posturing, and the President and Congress could each blame the other for the deficit mess.

By the time this Act was passed, the budgetary process had already broken down, and each budget submitted by the president was regarded as DOA, dead on arrival. Now there was the potential for even greater confrontation. Despite all the furor caused by this silly Act, the deficit targets were never met in practice, causing even more public cynicism about the sincerity of all elected officials involved. After all, these people were sent to Washington to make these tough budgetary decisions, and if they could not do the job, why were they there? If they could do the job, why was this Act necessary?

THE COMPOSITION OF GOVERNMENT EXPENDITURES

If the Reagan administration did not succeed in reducing the size of government spending, it did manage to alter the composition of that spending. The Reagan administration mounted an assault on the welfare state, but it was only partially successful. Congress, although intimidated by the popularity of the president, balked at wholesale cuts or elimination of many social programs. Republicans, too, shied away from alienating their constituents who found many of the social programs to be desirable. Mr. Reagan simply did not have a mandate to dismantle the New Deal nor tamper with programs that had come to be part of the social contract made over the years. As many have observed, the American public wanted the programs; it simply did not always want to pay for them. Politicians can easily exploit this paradox and convince themselves that the programs themselves were being questioned.

Mr. Reagan needed little convincing because he brought to office the value judgments he had made years earlier about the efficacy of social programs in general and of the inability of government to solve social problems in any case. The Reagan administration also was convinced of the need for more spending on national defense; the United States apparently had become weakened over the past administrations and was now less well prepared for conflict than were the Russians. It was time, according to the Reaganites, to reverse the trend, and not only catch up to our adversaries but surpass them in military strength.

The attempt to eliminate the Department of Education and the EPA as part of the drive to reduce the government bureaucracy failed, and, in fact, Reagan ended up adding to it by creating the Department of Veteran's Affairs. Still, the administration was able to curtail the activities of various departments within the federal bureaucracy as it reduced their regulatory and administrative duties; in so doing, budget cuts in these departments were easy to justify. These general budgetary trends can clearly be seen in Table 5.3 which compares the changes in priorities from the Carter administration.

Just a glance at Table 5.3 reveals the shifts in federal spending that occurred in the Reagan years. National defense spending corrected for inflation rose to 26.5% of total outlays, up from 22.7% in 1980, an increase of over 68%! Most of the increase is accounted for by procurement expenditures and by increases in research and development, for example, star wars fantasies. The other major

Table 5.3
Composition of Government Spending, 1980 and 1989 (in billions of 1982 dollars)

Function	Percent of Outlays		Percent Change	Percent of GNP	
	1980	1989	1980–1989	1980	1989
National Defense	22.7	26.5	68.3	4.4	5.7
International Affairs	2.1	0.8	−43.5	0.4	0.2
Science, Space	1.0	1.1	64.9	0.2	0.2
Energy	1.7	0.3	−72.9	0.3	0.1
Natural Resources	2.4	1.4	−12.9	0.5	0.3
Agriculture	1.5	1.5	43.5	0.3	0.3
Commerce	1.6	2.6	132.1	0.3	0.6
Transportation	3.6	2.4	−2.8	0.7	0.5
Community & Region Development	19.0	0.5	−64.3	0.4	0.1
Educ., Training, Employ., & Soc. Service	5.4	3.2	−13.8	1.0	0.7
Health	3.9	4.2	55.9	0.8	0.9
Medicare	5.4	7.4	97.8	1.0	1.6
Income Security	14.6	11.9	17.5	2.8	2.6
Social Security	20.1	20.3	46.5	3.9	4.4
Veterans Benefits	3.6	2.6	6.1	0.7	0.6
Adm. of Justice	0.8	0.8	54.3	0.2	0.2
General Govt.	2.2	0.8	−48.3	0.4	0.2
Net Interest	8.9	14.8	140.8	1.7	3.2
Undist. offsetting Receipts	−3.4	−3.3	39.7	−0.7	−0.7
Total Outlays	100.0	100.0	44.6	19.3	21.6

Source: Office of Budget and Management, Historical Tables, 1991, and calculations by the author.

increase is evident in net interest paid; by 1989, it represented 14.8% of total outlays, an increase of 66% over 1980. The failure to raise the necessary revenue to pay for the increases in federal spending meant that the shortfall had to be borrowed; the result is inescapable—interest costs shot up, not just because the debt was large in dollar terms but also because interest rates were high as well, another result of deficit financing.

Looking at some of the areas *not* high on the Reagan list of priorities, one finds the minus signs indicating decreases in spending from the last Carter administration year. The list includes international affairs (−44%), energy (−73%), natural resources (−13%), community and regional development (−64%), education and training (−14%), and general government (−48%). Following the same list, some of the major cuts occurred in the conduct of foreign affairs (77%); in nearly all areas of energy, but particularly in supply (80%); in nearly all areas of natural resources, but particularly in pollution control (33%); in all areas of community development, in training and employment (62%); and, again, in most areas of general government.

Note where other increases occurred: in agriculture, health, medicine, income security, social security, and veterans benefits. Clearly these areas, including entitlement programs, were not as amenable to cuts because powerful special interest groups were involved. Moreover, many of these programs were too popular, as suggested earlier, and Congress could afford to resist severe attacks on them. Even conservatives were not willing to risk the wrath of the affected interest groups, leaving only the true believers on the right to continue the fight to reverse the trends in government spending.

Once again, another administration was unable to solve the problems in agriculture. The Reagan administration offered a new approach before retreating into the old methods. The Program in Kind (PIK) that offered farmers crops instead of money failed miserably, and, instead of saving funds, called for even greater expenditures when crops failed, and farmers sold their inventories. Government then had to buy crops at inflated prices to honor its pledges to farmers. In the end, the administration resorted to arguments that agriculture should be treated as just another industry and left to the marketplace. Of course, this view was not adopted.

Despite the shifts in the budget, it is clear that the administration fell well short of its goal of curtailing and redirecting federal expenditures. What it managed to achieve in this regard can be quickly reversed. The changes it made were not fundamental in nature and another administration could alter the spending priorities without major difficulty. The Reagan administration was unable to achieve its main goals because it lacked the authorization to do so by the electorate. It was only able to tinker with the budget instead of revamping it according to conservative principles. The welfare state remained intact, despite the most concerted attack on it for decades. The real success of the administration can be found in the military sector. Reagan was successful in convincing the nation that more defense spending was necessary, and in the process of reaching for the goal of number one in defense, militarized the economy.

CONCLUSION

The evidence suggests that the Reagan Revolution as far as it affected government spending never happened. Total government spending actually increased, the bureaucracy increased, and budget deficits rose dramatically. These developments were not what Reagan intended nor promised when he took office. True, there were some reallocations of government spending—more defense and less on other areas. Also true was the fact that government deficits prevented additional spending on old programs or precluded new programs from being proposed. What would have happened in the absence of the deficit constraints is speculative. Still, it must be counted as a sort of victory that new programs were not initiated and at least some spending might have been curtailed as a result of Reagan's known antipathy.

Yet in the areas where large expenditures are routine, in entitlement programs, the administration was unsuccessful in rolling back the clock and, in fact, found that these programs were popular with the public. The administration backed off quickly, and one major element in the Reagan revolution was sacrificed. It managed only to reduce some spending by its administration of existing programs, such as disability programs, only to find the courts reversing the administrative decisions. Other regulatory decisions may have been more successful but resulted in being considered mean-spirited because they hurt the disadvantaged disproportionally.

The point is that the much heralded revamping of federal spending was not very successful, and to the extent that it was, is easily reversible. The increases in defense spending were questioned long before the cold war disintegrated, and the threat from the USSR disappeared. In other areas, cuts that resulted from novel interpretations of regulations are easily reversed, and new programs can be quickly introduced. As a result, one of the main purposes for Reagan's participation in politics—to reduce government's involvement in the economy—was not really accomplished. No permanent revolution was ever likely or even possible as the conservative vision misread the public's attitude toward government spending; the public wanted the programs, it just did not want to pay for them.

REDUCING TAXES

The Reagan administration was much more successful in reducing tax rates than in reducing expenditures. The original plan called for a 30% across the board cut in tax rates, 10% in each of 3 years. After the tax rate reductions, the range of taxation would be from 10 to 50%, down from the existing range of 14 to 70%. The road to passage was not a smooth one, and it took all of Reagan's powers of persuasion to overcome Congress' reluctance to accept the possibility of large deficits that might result. Finally, an agreement was reached whereby the first year's tax reduction would be only 5%, and it was delayed at that, making the final tax reduction more like 23% than 30%. Still, it was a significant victory for the president and was perhaps his single most important economic triumph. Not many presidents could claim that they got most of what they wanted from Congress. Thus, the Economic Recovery Tax Act (ERTA) was signed into law in August 1981 with the appropriate fanfare.

The Act also gave the president most of the other provisions he asked for, including reductions in the gift and estate tax, the accelerated cost recovery system that allowed businesses to depreciate assets more rapidly, extensions and increases in IRA and Keogh benefits to more individuals, the indexing of the tax code, and the reduction of the top rate on investment income from 70 to 50%. These and other provisions gave the administration most of what it wanted and more than it hoped to receive. To argue, as some did then and some still do, that the full tax cut of 30% was not achieved or that cuts were delayed and as a consequence attribute these setbacks as the reasons why the tax program did not work out as planned is really not credible.

However, 1 year later, tax increases were enacted that may have limited the effectiveness of the tax cuts of 1981. The Tax Equity and Fiscal Responsibility Act of 1982 reduced some deductions of individuals and removed or scaled back some provisions for business such as the more generous depreciation allowances and safe harbor leasing agreements, increased the federal unemployment tax, and raised some excise taxes. Billed as the largest tax increase in history, the Act was expected to yield $99 billion in total over fiscal years 1983–85. In addition to these tax changes, gasoline taxes were raised by 5 cents a gallon in 1983, and Social Security taxes were increased in 1983, effective in 1984. Numerous further tax changes were made in 1985 that included increased excise taxes, reduced depreciation allowances, removal of the tax exemptions on some industrial development bonds, and the reduction of the holding period for capital gains from 1 year to 6 months.

These measures make an evaluation of the effects of ERTA more difficult to accomplish. Some of the stimulus that could be expected from cutting tax rates in 1981 could have been curtailed as a result of tax measures that either increased taxes directly or removed provisions from the original Act that were designed to provide incentives to economic agents. Without arguing the merits of these cases, there exists at least the possibility of offsets to the original tax designs.

With this brief historical background in mind, it is now time to look into the effectiveness of the taxation side of the Reagan agenda. Several early studies were conducted to try to estimate the impact on the economy of a Kemp–Roth-type tax cut. It is interesting to summarize these studies for later comparisons with actual results. The first study was undertaken by Data Resources, Inc. (DRI) in 1978.[4] It predicted ''solid gains'' in the short run (the period covered was 1979–83) in terms of increased output and employment, but over the longer run, inflation would dissipate most of the gains. That is, the real GNP would increase dramatically at first, but by 1982 would grow by 0.7 percentage points below what it would have grown without the tax cuts; similarly, the unemployment rate falls by 1 percentage point by 1981, but gradually climbs back up so that by 1983 it is only 0.5 percentage points below what it would have been in the absence of the tax cuts. High interest rates and inflation were blamed for the eventual reduction in the growth rates of the GNP and employment. Finally, the model predicted (without reductions in government spending) that the Laffer hypothesis is not correct. The increases in nominal GNP were not sufficient to recoup revenues lost in the tax cuts. In fact, the model predicted huge increases in the budget deficit, reaching $100 billion by 1983 and producing an increase in the public debt of $322 billion higher than without the tax reductions. Interest costs on the national debt of these deficits combined with rising interest rates are pushed up to over $16 billion by 1983.

The second study was done by the Congressional Budget Office (CBO). The

Table 5.4
Incremental Economic Impacts of the Kemp–Roth Tax Cuts for Fiscal Years 1979–83

	1979	1980	1981	1982	1983
Real GNP Growth Rates (percentage points)					
CBO	1.0	1.8	1.2	-0.2	-1.1
DRI	0.8	1.2	1.3	-0.7	-1.2
MPS	N/A				
Chase	N/A				
Inflation Rates (percentage points)					
CBO-CPI Basis	0.1	0.2	1.0	1.7	2.7
DRI-(GNP Index)	0.0	0.3	1.1	1.8	1.4
MPS	0.2	1.7	4.2	4.1	N/A
Chase	0.0	0.1	0.4	0.7	1.2
Unemployment Rate (percentage points)					
CBO	-0.1	-0.5	-1.2	-1.5	-1.3
DRI	-0.2	-0.6	-1.0	-0.9	-0.5
MPS	-0.4	-1.3	-2.0	-1.8	N/A
Chase	-0.2	-1.0	-2.1	-3.0	-3.4
Net Budget Cost (bill of dollars)					
CBO	16.0	38.4	64.4	74.8	79.1
DRI	22.4	46.4	72.4	80.4	99.1
MPS	N/A				
Chase	N/A				

Source: Congressional Budget Office, An Analysis of the Roth-Kemp Tax cut Proposal, (Washington, D. C.: U.S. Government Printing Office, 1978); and Allen R. Sanderson, DRI Readings in Macroeconomics, (New York: McGraw-Hill, 1981), 179.

same trends are evident in Table 5.4 from the CBO model as were predicted in the DRI model. Early gains were dissipated over time with the rate of growth of the GNP falling below by −0.2 percentage points what would have been the rate in 1982 and to −1.1 in 1983, and the inflation rate rising over time. The unemployment rate remains below what would have happened by −1.3 percentage points in 1983, more optimistic than the DRI model. Finally, the tax cut does not pay for itself as seen in the budget cost rising to $79 billion in 1983.

Two other studies are included in Table 5.4 for further comparisons. These results were included in the CBO study for that reason as well. Both studies show inflation accelerating over time with the MIT–Penn–SSRC model showing more dramatic increases. The Chase Econometric model, the most supply side of them all, shows a more dramatic reduction in the unemployment rate than the others.

These studies were conducted in 1978 when inflation was a more serious problem than it was in 1981, and some allowance must be made for using that starting point. Demand pressures caused by tax cuts without reductions in government spending would have added to the pressures already existing in 1978 to make inflation more likely; also, no allowances were made for Federal Reserve actions of the kind that actually occurred in the early 1980s. None of them could have foreseen the stringent monetary policy that accompanied the tax cuts, and their results reflect that omission.

These models are also different with respect to their construction of the U.S. economy so that it is instructive to compare the results of their simulations of the tax cut on the economy. It should be recalled that the Kemp–Roth tax cuts were unprecedented and, hence, not within the framework of these models. Thus, the results must be viewed with caution. They are included here to show that some evidence was available to suggest that the supply-side forecasts were likely to be overly optimistic, and perhaps disingenuous.

Despite these projections of the effects of the Kemp–Roth tax cut proposal, the administration rushed to put it into effect. Objections were disregarded as the supply-siders promised their reassuring results, if only the old outdated models were shelved. In the end, devotion to tax cuts became part, indeed the central ingredient, of the economic package and no amount of evidence to the contrary was or even could be entertained without jeopardizing the entire economic program. The economist's equivalent of the alchemist's search for the formula for making gold can be found in the supply-siders' search for a free lunch.

In turn, the supply-siders claimed that empirical studies performed with models of the past simply could not capture the reactions of people that their model was predicting. To that extent, they were correct because previous studies did not include the types and strengths of reactions that supply-siders were considering. More on this later, but the point here is that they could claim that the foregoing forecasts failed to provide for the proper responses of individuals and firms and are, thus, unreliable.

Thus, the question of the effectiveness of the tax cuts must be answered empirically. Although it is true that many would question the theoretical foundations of supply-side economics, the acceptance or rejection of it could not be satisfactorily determined or assessed without empirical results. Theoretical objections would not satisfy supply-siders nor opponents, and debates could always be labeled inconclusive.

Even so, the real question is "How does one measure the effects of the tax cut in isolation from other economic (and noneconomic) events that were taking place at the same time? This is an old and familiar problem in economics, but in cases like this, the problem takes on an extra dimension. These tax cuts were unprecedented in U.S. history and, hence, affected many decisions in ways that may not have been observed when past models were constructed.

For example, with large tax cuts there are likely to be large changes in aggregate demand in addition to the postulated changes in aggregate supply. When after-tax incomes rise, every model would predict that individuals would spend a portion (major?) of the added income, and, hence, increases in personal consumption would account for a substantial part of the tax reduction. However, if the supply-siders were correct, a large increase in saving would result, leading to a substantial increase in aggregate supply. Funds for investment would now be more readily available at a reduced cost, and firms would be more willing to invest. Also, as the after-tax wage rate rose due to the tax cut, workers were supposed to substitute work for leisure now that the price of leisure had risen. Again as the after-tax rate of return on investment rose, firms should have been willing to purchase additional capital stock. Both of these tendencies would have increased the supply of goods, increased productivity, encouraged economic growth, and forestalled inflation because the added goods production would offset and demand pressures on capacity. Finally, everyone would begin to shift resources out of unproductive uses that were induced by high taxes into more productive uses that did not depend on how the tax code treated the investment. The tax code would play a less important role in the allocation of investment opportunities.

The trouble is that all the empirical evidence available from attempts to measure past reactions to changes in taxes were drawn from experiences of many years ago when a much different economy was in existence. Some effects were studied when the economy was at full employment, or when inflation was markedly lower than the early 1980s, or in response to changes in taxes that were much more modest, and so on. Extrapolation of these studies to the experience of 1981 was either unwarranted at worst or questionable at best.

Nevertheless, extrapolation is just what must be done when no other course is possible, as long as the limitations are acknowledged. Therefore, a very brief description of the evidence gathered from past studies may be appropriate. Regarding the effects of tax cuts on the supply of labor, it was found that males did not respond to tax changes. They were either unable or unwilling to adjust their hours of work in response to changes in after-tax wage rates. For a 1% change in wage rates, they altered their supply of labor from a range of 0% to 0.9% for low income workers. (This is the substitution effect which measures the responsiveness of the quantity supplied of labor to a *small* change in the after-tax wage rate with income held constant. Note the word "small" in the definition of the substitution elasticity.)

Females, on the other hand, did show some response to after-tax increases in the wage rate as they appeared more flexible. Women's response to the same 1% change in wage rates varied over the range of 0.1 to 2.5%. The studies that reached these conclusions were published in the early 1970s using data that reflected the work habits of women in the 1950s and 1960s. Clearly, the experience of women in the labor force in the 1980s is far different from that of women in earlier decades. As such, these estimates are clearly suspect when applied to periods when the behavior of women in the labor force had undergone a dramatic change.[5]

On the basis of these data, the CBO concluded that the overall response to an increase in the after-tax wage rate was nowhere near that required for the tax to be neutral in regard to revenue loss. The tax cut was approximately 10% for the average worker, meaning that the labor supplied would have to increase by more than 10% if the tax cut was to pay for itself. According to the past estimates, the labor supply would increase by only 1–3%, clearly not sufficient to make up for the revenue loss.

As for saving, the evidence is unambiguous: Most economists do not regard the saving rate as being affected by changes in taxes. Supply-siders maintained that saving would increase following the tax cut as the after-tax return would increase. Further, the additional saving should encourage investment spending which would foster economic growth, increase labor productivity, increase employment, and so on. There is little evidence for this view, and besides the short-run effects of additional investment on either the growth in the capital stock of the nation, or on revenues received from taxing the additional income from capital would be very small. If there is anything to the claim that tax cuts would alter the return to capital and, hence, foster greater capital formation, it would have to be a long-run proposition and, hence, one not easily traced back to the original tax reduction.[6]

On the demand side, the stimulus to the economy caused by tax reductions should result in an increase in national income by some multiple of the increase in spending. The increase in incomes cause taxes to rise and revenues to increase. In other words, there are feedback effects that offset the revenue loss of any tax cut.

RESULTS OF THE TAX CUTS

Did the tax cuts positively affect the supply of labor? The answer is yes but the effect was small and much less than postulated by supply-siders. One study by Gary Burtless found that the two main avenues that were supposed to increase employment, the tax cuts and the reductions in or limitations of social programs, had little affect. After allowing for cyclical affects, he found that "among men in their prime working years, . . . average annual hours rose 2.3% to 4.1%. Among women between 25 and 54, . . . average annual hours rose about 3.5%."[7] These numbers are modest enough, but Burtless went on to conclude "if the high unemployment rate of the 1980s is attributed to Reagan administration policy, higher unemployment has just about offset the supply-enhancing effects of its tax and transfer policies."[8]

With labor responses of these magnitudes, it is clear that tax revenues are going to fall; the tax cuts will result in greater revenue losses and will certainly not pay for themselves. An early study by Jerry Hausman concluded that a

30% tax cut would increase female labor supply by 9.4% and reduce tax revenues by 16%. For males, labor supply would increase by 2.7% while tax revenues would fall by 23%.[9] Because more recent estimates of labor supply responses indicate a smaller response for females and larger responses for males, a 20% reduction in tax revenues would be a useful approximation using Hausman's analysis. Using the methodology developed by Hausman, Robert H. Haveman found that, at best, the percentage change in the labor force due to the tax reductions would be about 3.8%, and that includes an estimate for the effects of reductions in social programs that would push people to work; at the lower end of the estimates, Haveman found only a 1.3% change in the labor force. Warning us that the estimates should be interpreted with care because they are rough, he concluded that these estimates are not even close to the responses needed for the tax cuts to be self-financing.[10]

Benjamin M. Friedman estimated the decline in tax revenues as approximately $154 billion in 1986 even allowing for demand-side effects. Because tax revenues for that year were $349 billion, the decline would amount to 44% of revenues for just that year.[11] Lawrence Lindsay, using an entirely different procedure to estimate the revenue loss, found that in 1985 the loss would be about $33 billion or about 10% of the tax revenues of that year.[12] Lindsay's approach is much more favorable to supply-side arguments and uses some assumptions that others might find questionable.

Estimates from the Department of Commerce of the *direct cost* (same incomes using 1980 tax rates) of the tax reductions are available. For instance, the loss of revenue from ERTA would have been $181.2 billion in 1985 and $225.6 billion in 1986. Offsetting these loses are gains from the Tax Equity and Fiscal Responsibility Act of 1982 that increased revenue by $42.6 billion and $57.3 billion in the same periods.[13] The indirect effects of demand-side changes and incentive effects on the supply side are what cause the problems in estimating the total revenue effects in the period.

Unfortunately, a definitive estimate of the revenue loss from the tax cuts is not available now nor may ever be. Without pausing to critically evaluate these studies, it is evident that the actual revenue loss may be too difficult to estimate precisely. Too many events, both economic and noneconomic, complicate the analysis of tax reductions of this magnitude where incentive effects cannot always be measured and value judgments creep in to prevent unbiased results.

One final estimate can be made using the CBO's study of feedback effects of changes in fiscal policy; in this case, cuts in the personal income tax.[14] The CBO estimated the feedback effect of a 3% reduction in individual income tax rates assuming an "accommodating" monetary policy. Revenue gains from increased economic activity were estimated, and these offset the revenue loss from the tax cuts; however, there are additional outlays that might be necessary after the tax cuts that, in turn, offset the revenue gains. The main outlay increase is interest costs on the national debt caused by the added borrowing to finance the tax cuts.

Table 5.5
Estimated Feedback Effects and Revenue Loss of Tax Cuts

	1982	1983	1984	1985	1986
Feedback Effects:					
Total	11	13	12	10	5
Revenues	19	37	45	50	57
Interest Costs	-12	-29	-38	-43	-49
Direct Loss:(in bill)a					
ERTA	-52	-108	-145	-181	-226
Feedback:	6	14	17	18	11
Net Revenue Loss	-46	-94	-128	-163	-215
Deficit (on NIA Basis)	-146	-176	-170	-197	-207

a. Revenue loss on national income accounts basis; feedback
effects calculated on a unified budget basis.
Source: For feedback effects, Congressional Budget Office, How
Changes in Fiscal Policy Affect the Budget: The Feedback Issue,
1982, Table 3, 22; For Direct Loss, Richard C. Ziemer, "Impact of
Recent Tax Law Changes," Department of Commerce, Survey of
Current Business, April, 1985, 28.

Table 5.5 shows the estimates of feedback effects and the loss of revenue
associated with the tax cuts of 1981. The numbers in the table indicate the
percentage of direct revenue loss that is offset by feedback effects which reduce
the budget loss. A negative sign indicates that the feedback effect reinforces
the direct loss rather than offsetting it.

The estimates in Table 5.5 must be viewed with extreme caution. They are
not presented for their accuracy, but only to provide rough guidelines to measure the results against the other studies. The feedback estimates were made
for a 3% reduction in personal income tax rates, not the 23% reductions of the
Kemp–Roth tax cuts, and the effects of the corporate tax rate reduction are not
included. What violence that does to the estimates is unknown, but surely some
adjustments are necessary for the unprecedented tax reductions of ERTA. Furthermore, the estimates were derived from several econometric models that use
different assumptions about the structure of the economy, use different budgets
(national income accounts versus unified budgets), and so on.

If the numbers in Table 5.5 were accurate, the net revenue loss of the tax cuts would account for a major portion of the budget deficits that actually occurred in the years noted. They would account for 32% of the deficit in 1982 to over 100% in 1986. Even if they are only half correct, the tax cuts would still account for a major portion of the deficit, and that is the point of this exercise. The supply-side estimates of the revenue effects of the tax cuts were simply overly optimistic, and it is likely that the tax cuts added significantly to the budget deficits that followed. The exact amounts may be debatable, but this much seems evident: The tax cuts were not self-financing.

TAX REFORM

The lack of concern given to the accuracy of the estimates of the effects of the ERTA tax cuts is probably due to the diversion of attention to new tax proposals that quickly followed its passage. The tax cuts, whatever the exact magnitude of the revenue loss, soon revealed the unequal impact of their provisions. Higher income groups benefited at the expense of low income groups. The distribution of the tax burden shifted and made the tax structure unfair. In an unpublished study of the effects on the distribution of income and taxes paid, the CBO concluded that between 1981 and 1983, the progressivity of the tax system declined. Except for the top 1% of income recipients, who paid a higher tax rate because they received a disproportionate share of pretax income gains, the tax payments for the lower income groups increased at a greater rate than did the rates for higher income groups.[15] Again, as with the revenue loss, the exact numbers are not the issue; the perception was that the tax cuts were unfair. (Later, the actual changes in the distribution of income will reinforce this perception.)

The perception of unfairness turned attention away from tax cuts to tax reform. Dozens of plans were proposed to make the tax system fairer, simpler, and easier to comply with. The administration did not escape the movement because during the campaign of 1984, Mr. Reagan was asked repeatedly about further tax changes, including those needed to combat the now obvious budget deficits and to address the unfairness issue. Reagan cleverly deflected all questions and criticisms by referring to a tax study underway by the Treasury Department. A good campaign ploy perhaps, but what the economists at the treasury eventually provided was not greeted with great joy and enthusiasm by the rest of the administration.[16]

Once unveiled, the treasury tax proposal was quickly branded as antibusiness and too radical for serious consideration. It would have eliminated the investment tax credit, required that depreciable assets be corrected for inflation and that depreciation allowances approximate economic concepts, taxed capital gains (adjusted for inflation) as ordinary income, eliminated some subsidies for some industries, curtailed the use of tax-free state and local bonds, and closed some tax shelters. Despite the reduction of corporate income tax rates (to 33% for all corporations), the proposal was attacked by the business community. For individuals, the rate schedule would be reduced from 14 marginal rates to three— 15, 25, and 35%. However, it would also make some fringe benefits taxable and reduce or eliminate the tax deductibility of items that aroused much opposition, for instance, all state and local taxes would no longer be deductible.

The treasury was sent back to work to come up with a better proposal, presumably more acceptable to business leaders and Reagan constituents. Treasury II, as it was called, restored the special treatment of capital gains with a maximum rate of 17.5%, liberalized depreciation allowances, and some industry subsidies were reinstated. Changes for individuals were not as dramatic. Meanwhile, the House and the Senate were busy with tax bills of their own, more liberal than Reagan's, and the president threatened to veto the more liberal House version. All appeared lost as special interests attacked both versions, winning enough to destroy all notions of simplicity and fairness. Two men, Daniel Rostenkowski, chair of the House Ways and Means Committee, and particularly Robert Packwood, chair of the Senate Finance Committee, managed to discard much of the baggage that had become attached to their bills, and steered the conference committee to a resolution of the seemingly impossible task of producing a compromise that was to become the Tax Reform Act of 1986.

The Tax Reform Act of 1986, summoned into existence by the cry from all quarters and echoed by Reagan for a tax system that was "clear, simple and fair for all," unfortunately fulfilled none of these desires. It was no clearer than earlier tax codes, no simpler in its arcane provisions, and no fairer than other plans mentioned would have been. Most people were expected to end up paying the same amount of taxes, with some 15% paying higher taxes and some paying less. About 6 million people would be removed from the tax rolls by higher exemptions and standard deductions, but the tax rates were reduced to two, 15 and 28% from 14 marginal rates starting from 11 to 50%. The special treatment of capital gains was eliminated, and interest charges, sales taxes, two-earner deductions, and other deductions were disallowed or diminished. Unemployment compensation and scholarships and fellowships would be taxed, and IRA contributions would be limited. Some tax shelters were closed and the minimum tax was strengthened. For business, the top corporate tax rate was reduced to 34%, the investment tax credit was repealed, and depreciation was made less favorable for real estate and more favorable for fixed investment.

It is not the purpose here to criticize this tax action, nor to continue to detail the other tax actions that preceded or followed it in the Reagan administrations. The interest here is to ascertain the end results of all these tax changes, and the provisions of them are included only to the extent that they help us understand the distribution of the tax burden. The 1986 tax law did restore some progressivity to the tax code, but it did not take us back to the pre-1981 tax distribution. This can be seen in Table 5.6, but before addressing the issue of

Table 5.6
Comparison of Effective Federal Tax Rates by Population Decile, 1977, 1984, 1988

	Year			Percent Change		
	1977	1984	1988	1977-84	1984-88	1977-88
Decile						
First	8.0	10.5	9.6	31.3	-8.6	20.0
Sec	8.7	8.5	8.3	-2.3	-2.4	-4.6
Third	12.0	13.2	13.3	10.0	0.8	10.8
Fourth	16.2	16.3	16.8	0.6	3.1	3.7
Fifth	19.1	18.5	19.2	-3.1	3.8	0.5
Sixth	21.1	20.1	20.9	-4.7	4.0	-0.9
Seventh	23.0	21.5	22.3	-6.5	3.7	-3.0
Eighth	23.6	23.0	23.6	-2.5	2.6	0.0
Ninth	24.5	23.8	24.7	-2.9	3.8	0.8
Tenth	26.7	23.6	25.0	-11.6	5.9	-6.4
Top 5%	27.5	23.3	24.9	-15.3	6.9	-9.5
Top 1%	30.9	23.1	24.9	-25.2	7.8	-19.4
All Deciles	22.8	21.7	22.7	-4.8	4.6	-0.4

Source: Congressional Budget Office, <u>The Changing Distribution of Federal Taxes: 1975-1990</u>, October 1987, 48.

fairness, it is necessary to note one of the major reasons why the tax burden in the United States has become less equitable: the tax on earnings that is used to support the many programs that can be labeled simply Social Security.

After running into a firestorm, Reagan dropped his proposals for the curtailment or elimination of the Social Security program and opted instead to appoint a commission to examine the issue, particularly the financing of benefits because the fund was in danger of depletion. Backing away from the conservative dream of eliminating the program entirely, Reagan was able to deflect the criticisms and salvage some political capital by shifting the burden to an independent commission. The commission, headed by Alan Greenspan, labored long and hard, and finally emerged with recommendations that essentially avoided all the difficult questions and recommended essentially only a tax increase to rescue the fund for another 40 years.

Payroll taxes are regressive, but the issue of fairness did not hinder the commission. Reagan and Congress eagerly accepted the advice of the commission and everyone was happy to be rid of this thorny issue. Besides, the increased Social Security taxes would help reduce the budget deficit. Although not meant for that purpose, this fortuitous help was more than welcome, particularly when the public would not be conscious of this deficit offset and would not care when they became aware.

The Congressional Budget Office examined the changing distribution of the *federal* tax burden for the years 1975-90. The results of their analysis are shown in Table 5.6. Just a glance at the table reveals that the tax burden became more inequitable from 1977 to 1984. Generally, the tax burden rose for the bottom half of the income distribution and fell for the top half. Indeed, the top three deciles saw their tax burdens fall, and the top 5% and 1% saw their burdens fall dramatically, by 15% and 25%, respectively. In fact, progressivity disappears for the top three deciles with the top 1% of income recipients paying the same rate as those in the eighth decile.

From 1984 to 1988, a period that included the reform act of 1986, the effective tax rates increased for nearly all income groups, and some progressivity was restored to the tax structure. The top income groups saw their rates increased by greater amounts than lower income groups. For the entire period in question, 1977–88, the tax structure clearly was tilted toward less progressivity as the lowest income group saw its effective tax rate rise by 20% while the top tenth saw its rate fall by 9.5%. The effective rate of the top 1% of the income distribution actually fell by 19.4%.

One could always quarrel with the methodology, or the precision, of the CBO in arriving at these estimates, but it would be difficult to escape the conclusion that the tax structure was made less progressive in the period.[17] The inequitable tax changes in the period were clearly recognized at the time and were to cause much unrest among the critics of the Reagan administration. It will be necessary to return to the issue of fairness later in the discussion of the distribution of income and wealth.

CONCLUSION

Fiscal policy in the Reagan administration exhibited all the signs of schizophrenia that characterized most of its policies. An expansionary fiscal policy, led by the militarization of the economy, was not the aim of the administration when it drafted its plan. The increases in national defense spending was supposed to be offset by reductions in the civilian sphere. Congress did not go along with the complete dismantling of the New Deal and the welfare state. Its resistance was bound to lead to trouble, for the administration did not have a mandate to eliminate all the social programs enacted in the past 50 years. Reagan's victory led the conservatives to labor under the miscomprehension that the public was voting for a complete change in philosophy; what the public voted for was hope—hope that somehow there were easy answers to the economic woes that were besetting the nation. Reagan promised them that, and the voters responded.

Yet the public wanted those social programs but were unwilling or unable to pay for them. Reagan completely misread the mood of the country in this regard and was annoyed that Congress reflected the wishes of the public by resisting the wholesale dismantling of some very popular programs. What Reagan was able to accomplish was to forestall the introduction of any new programs or the enlargement of existing ones. Not satisfied with this achievement, he continued to blast Congress for failing to follow the lead of his administration in reducing government spending in areas that he felt were wasteful and unnecessary.

The tax cuts did not work as promised, and revenues fell short of predictions. Together with the failure of government expenditures to fall, deficits were inevitable. Once again blaming Congress for the deficits, the administration never did propose a balanced budget, and Congress did not add significantly to the spending plans in the budget. Even if Congress had added no additional spending, the Reagan budgets would still have resulted in large budget deficits. Pointing fingers at others simply cannot conceal the basic flaws in supply-side economics and conservative budget dreams.

Cutting social programs for the disadvantaged members of the society is harsh enough, but when the lower income groups are asked to bear a larger share of the tax burden as well, the entire fiscal policy is seen to be unfair and inequitable.[18]

NOTES

1. David Stockman, *The Triumph of Politics* (New York: Harper and Row, 1986), 401.

2. A similar conclusion was reached by Benjamin Friedman, *Day of Reckoning* (New York: Brown Brothers Harriman, 1988), 131–132.

3. The original Act called for the Comptroller of the Currency to determine when the deficit exceeded the limits set and to determine how to cut the budget to reach the predetermined deficit goal. The Supreme Court declared this unconstitutional because the Controller of the Currency is part of the legislative branch and the budget is the responsibility of the executive branch.

4. Stephen Brooks and Otto Eckstein, "Economic Analysis of the Kemp–Roth Proposal," in *DRI Readings in Macroeconomics,* ed. Allen R. Sanderson (New York: McGraw-Hill, 1981), 176–180.

5. Most of the estimates on the response of the supply of labor are taken from Glen G. Cain and Harold W. Watts, eds., *Income Maintenance and Labor Supply* (New York: Academic Press, 1973). See the following articles: Orley Ashenfelter and James Hickman, "Estimating Labor-Supply Functions," 265–278; Michael J. Boskin, "The Economics of Labor Supply," 163–180; Glen Cain and Harold W. Watts, "Toward a Synthesis of the Evidence," 328–367; Robert Hall, "Wages, Income, and Hours of the U.S. Labor Supply," 102–162. See also Jerry Hausman, "Labor Supply," in *How Taxes Affect Economic Behavior,* eds. Henry Aaron and Joseph Pechman (Washington, DC: The Brookings Institution, 1981), 27–83 and Maravin Kosters, "Effects of an Income Tax on Labor Supply, in *The Taxation of Income from Capital,* eds. Arnold C. Harberger and Martin J. Bailey (Washington, DC: The Brookings Institution, 1969), 301–324. For additional sources and summary of the evidence, see Congressional Budget Office, *An Analysis of the Roth–Kemp Tax Cut Proposal,* 1978, 15–17.

6. For a more thorough examination of personal saving, see George M. von Furstenberg, "Saving," in *How Taxes Affect Economic Behavior,* 327–402.

7. Gary Burtless, "The Supply-Side Legacy of the Reagan Years: Effects on Labor

Supply," in *The Economic Legacy of the Reagan Years,* eds. Anandi P. Sahu and Ronald L. Tracy (New York: Praeger, 1991), 61.

8. Ibid. 62.

9. Jerry Hausman, "Stochastic Problems in the Simulation of Labor Supply," in *Behavioral Simulation Methods in Tax Policy Analysis,* ed. Martin Feldstein (Chicago: University of Chicago Press, 1983), 68–69.

10. Robert H. Haveman, "How Much Have the Reagan Administration's Tax and Spending Policies Increased Work Effort," in *The Legacy of Reaganomics,* eds. Charles R. Hulten and Isabel V. Sawhill (Washington, DC: Urban Institute Press, 1984), 119.

11. Friedman, *Day of Reckoning,* 247.

12. Lawrence Lindsay, *The Growth Experiment* (New York: Basic Books, 1990), 76.

13. Department of Commerce, *Survey of Current Business,* April 1985, 28–31.

14. Congressional Budget Office, *How Changes in Fiscal Policy Affect the Budget: The Feedback Issue,* 1982.

15. Congressional Budget Office, *Effects of the 1981 Tax Act on the Distribution of Income and Taxes Paid,* Staff working paper, August 1986, II.1

16. For a quick understanding of the major plans that were being considered, see Joseph A. Pechman, ed., *A Citizen's Guide to the New Tax Reforms* (Totowa, NJ: Rowman & Allanheld, 1985).

17. Whenever the question of tax equity is raised, the problem of tax incidence (who bears the burden of various taxes in the tax structure) surely follows. The CBO made some assumptions about how taxes are borne as follows: The individual income tax is assumed to be borne by the families that pay the tax; the social insurance payroll tax is assumed to be borne by workers and is allocated to employee compensation; the corporate income tax is calculated in two ways, reflecting the controversy over the incidence of this tax. In one calculation, the burden is assumed to be on capital, and in the other, on employees (used in Table 5.6). Excise taxes are assumed to be shifted to the consumer and allocated in proportion to expenditures on taxed goods and services. See Congressional Budget Office *The Changing Distribution of Federal Taxes: 1975–1990,* October 1987, 19–25.

18. For a passionate discussion of these issues and more, see Robert Lekachman, *Visions and Nightmares* (New York: Macmillan, 1987). Consider the following passage on page 116:

Social Policy is too important to be left to economists: "Free" health, education, and housing markets threaten to dissolve historically fragile ties of community. Segmentation of services; conversion of medical care, decent housing, and adequate education into so many additional commodities available in quantities and qualities determined by income and wealth; and denial of a public interest in minimum levels of the essentials of existence for all define more than an uncaring society. They threaten the social stability upon which corporations and other income maximizers depend.

Chapter 6

Monetary Policy and Inflation in the Reagan Years

In its *Program for Economic Recovery,* the administration indicated that it wanted a monetary policy that would be consistent with its overall program: "One that would be consistent with noninflationary expansion of the economy." More specifically, it wanted the growth rates of money and credit to be reduced by 1986 to one-half of those that existed in 1980.[1] By 1986, the administration predicted that the inflation rate would have fallen to 4.2% as measured by the CPI. In this chapter, we will see if the monetary authorities gave the administration what it wanted.

Paul Volcker, Chairman of the Board of the Federal Reserve System, was appointed by President Carter at a time when inflation was a serious problem in the United States. Well trained for the job, Volcker relished the task of combating inflation, the number one enemy of orderly financial markets. On October 6, 1979, the Fed announced that its targets for monetary control would switch from controlling interest rates to controlling monetary aggregates.[2] The monetarists who had been advocating this route for years finally had their day. Recall that interest rates rose dramatically as a result, for example, the prime rate which was near 11% a year earlier, now rose to near 15%, and the federal funds rate rose from about 9% to 14%. These significant increases in interest rates, and those that followed, helped defeat Jimmy Carter in his bid for re-election. By election time in 1980, the prime rate was around 17%, and the federal funds rate around 16%, high enough to frighten everyone.

Still, once control over monetary aggregates becomes the object of monetary policy, interest rates are free to fluctuate to whatever levels are necessary to achieve the targeted growth rates of the money supply. The Fed can concentrate on either controlling the money supply or interest rates; it cannot control both because the demand for money is beyond its control.

EARLY MONETARY POLICY

As far as monetary policy is concerned, the Reagan administration started off on the wrong foot. It forecast a GNP growth of 11.1% for 1981 (12.5%, 12.4%, and 10.8% for the rest of the first term), but its monetary plans were inconsistent with these growth rates. Monetary growth was set at about 5% and velocity (how quickly the money supply turns over), if it followed its trend growth, would grow at about 3%. This growth of money and velocity would not be sufficient to finance the growth of over 11% in GNP. Either the GNP growth rate was overestimated, or the money supply growth rate was too low. If neither of these growth rates were incorrectly forecast, then the velocity growth rate would have to increase to about 6% per year, or about twice its normal growth rate. Because falling interest rates were forecast by the administration, this abnormal growth of velocity would be inconceivable. (Interest rates and velocity vary directly: Falling interest rates would mean *falling* velocity because less is sacrificed in holding money rather than other assets at lower interest rates.)

The administration was informed of this inconsistency in its economic plans but chose to ignore it, choosing instead to stick with its rosy scenario.[3] To acknowledge the incompatibility of parts of its economic program would be to upset the favorable expectations it hoped to generate. Once admissions of error were permitted to creep in, the entire economic program might come under closer scrutiny. It is no wonder, then, that the administration was eager to push its program through before more thoughtful analysis was allowed to question the details, and lead to possible rejection.

MONETARY POLICY IN THE FIRST TERM

In the latter half of the Carter administration, the growth of the money supply, M1—demand deposits and currency, was high relative to past trends. In the last half of 1980, for instance, M1 was growing at a rate of 16.9 and 10.9% (quarterly compounded annual rates) for the third and fourth quarters. (See Table 6.1.) As indicated above, interest rates were also high by historical standards, and prices, as measured by the implicit GNP price index, were growing at rates of 8.8 and 11.3% (quarterly compounded annual rates) for the final quarters of 1980.

These growth rates furnished Ronald Reagan with sufficient campaign fodder to enjoy and declare that the economy was out of control and had to be subdued; interest rates must come down, he said, and inflation must be brought under control. Accordingly, a tighter monetary policy was necessary. Table 6.1 shows the reduction in the growth rate of the money supply, M1, in the period 1981I–1982II. The Federal Reserve, under the guidance of Paul Volcker, was only too eager to comply with the wishes of the Reagan administration. Volcker, too, was anxious to halt inflation and restore orderly financial markets.

After the Reagan administration took office, the Federal Reserve began to restrict the growth of the money supply in earnest, and in the process helped drive the economy into the severe recession (depression?) of 1981–82. Prices fell more rapidly than anyone had expected, from 12.4% in the CPI in 1980, to 8.9% in 1981, and 3.9% in 1982. The GNP implicit price index fell also from 9.7% in 1981 to 6.4% in 1982, and to 3.9% in 1983.

Interest rates fell also, but not as rapidly as prices, and, thus, *real* interest rates remained high. The real prime rate (nominal prime rate minus inflation in

Table 6.1
Growth Rates of GNP, M1, and Velocity (compounded quarterly data at annual rates)

Year and Quarter	GNP	M1	Velocity
1979I	9.8	5.2	1.9
II	7.5	10.3	0.7
III	13.6	9.6	1.4
IV	8.1	4.6	1.8
1980I	11.7	6.9	1.7
II	0.9	-4.3	-0.2
III	9.7	16.9	0.6
IV	15.5	10.9	1.4
1981I	22.1	4.7	4.7
II	6.0	8.2	0.7
III	13.1	3.1	4.2
IV	2.5	4.6	0.5
1982I	-0.3	10.7	0.0
II	4.7	2.2	2.1
III	2.5	6.3	0.4
IV	3.9	16.2	0.2
1983I	8.5	13.4	0.6
II	12.3	12.2	1.0
III	10.1	9.8	1.0
IV	10.6	7.1	1.5
1984I	15.4	6.4	2.4
II	8.9	6.7	1.3
III	5.8	4.7	1.2
IV	4.7	3.8	1.2
1985I	7.9	10.8	0.7
II	5.6	10.5	0.5
III	7.0	15.2	0.5
IV	6.2	11.7	0.5
1986I	7.2	9.0	0.8
II	2.6	16.6	0.2
III	5.9	18.1	0.3
IV	3.4	19.1	0.2
1987I	8.4	13.7	0.6
II	8.7	6.6	1.3
III	7.7	0.6	12.8
IV	8.6	5.1	1.7
1988I	5.4	3.3	1.6
II	8.7	6.5	1.3
III	7.3	5.3	1.4
IV	7.6	2.3	3.3

Source: St. Louis Federal Reserve Bank, <u>Monetary Trends</u>, and <u>National Economic Trends</u>, various issues.

Table 6.2
Inflation and Real Interest Rates

Year	Prime rate	Federal Funds rate	CPI	Real Prime rate	Real Federal Funds rate
1980	15.3	13.4	12.4	2.9	1.0
1981	18.9	16.4	8.9	10.0	7.5
1982	14.9	12.3	3.9	11.0	8.4
1983	10.8	9.1	3.8	7.0	5.3
1984	12.0	10.2	4.0	8.0	6.2
1985	9.9	8.1	3.8	6.1	4.3
1986	8.3	6.8	1.1	7.2	5.7
1987	8.2	6.7	4.4	3.8	2.9
1988	9.3	7.6	4.4	4.9	3.2

Source: Council of Economic Advisors, *Economic Report of the President,* various years.

CPI) rose from 2.9% in 1980 to 10% in 1981, and 11% in 1982 before falling back to still rather high rates of 7 and 8% in 1983 and 1984. The real federal funds rate rose from 1% in 1980 to 7.5% in 1981, and to 8.4% in 1982 before falling to 5.3 and 6.2% in 1983 and 1984, respectively. (See Table 6.2.) The same tendency for real interest rates to remain high by historical standards continued in the second Reagan administration. Although the real rates did fall somewhat, they remained above the levels that prevailed before the 1980s. The failure of real interest rates to fall along with the fall in inflation probably reflects the banks need to recover profits lost in the 1970s when real interest rates were sometimes negative. Banks were reluctant to give up this opportunity to profit at the expense of debtors who had benefited earlier.

So in the first term, the administration was getting the monetary (and fiscal!) policy it wanted, but it had not foreseen the cost of such a policy. Inflation was reduced as well as *nominal* interest rates. Not only was the Federal Reserve cooperating with the administration but it was also being given credit for bringing down inflation and interest rates (real interest rates were not given the same attention by the general public). Much to the consternation of the Reagan administration, Paul Volcker was seen as the second most powerful person in Washington, if not the country. The administration wanted credit for the main achievements of the first term, the reductions in inflation and interest rates, but the public was honoring Paul Volcker and the Fed while muting its criticisms of the Fed for its role in causing the recession.

The economy began its steep decline in the last part of 1981 when the unemployment rate climbed to over 8.6%, and continued its rise in the first half of 1982 as the unemployment rate reached 9.5% in June. Real GNP was falling at a rate of over 5% in the last and first quarters of 1981 and 1982. In the past when monetary policy began to hurt the economy to this extent, the Fed usually relented from its tight monetary policy and retreated into moderation. The Federal Reserve was forced by public outcry to be sensitive to the pain being caused by its actions.

This time the Fed persisted well into the recession and did not reverse its policies until the summer of 1982 by which time the unemployment rate had risen to about 10%. It then permitted the money supply to grow more rapidly (see Table 6.1) as the growth of M1 rose from 2.2% at annual rates in the second quarter of 1982 to 6.3% in the third quarter and to 16.2% in the fourth quarter. It also abandoned its experiment with monetarism and began to broaden its targets for monetary policy away from strictly controlling the money aggregates.

What made the Fed give up on monetarism? Just a glance at Table 6.1 reveals one of the reasons: the velocity of M1, GNP/M1, began to misbehave. Departing from past trends, the growth rate of money velocity rather strangely fell despite the high *real* interest rates. If the velocity of M1 was becoming unstable and unpredictable, then the proper change in the money supply could not be determined either. Hence, to concentrate on the control of the money supply, as monetarists advocated, would not be possible. If velocity varies, a given change in the money supply would not have predictable changes in money and credit to finance the national output. In short, the money multiplier, which determines the growth of money and credit for a given change in the money supply, would not be stable or predictable either, and a given change in M1 might result in too little or too much money for the circumstances. Eventually, in October 1982, the Fed was forced to abandon M1 entirely and focus on M2, a broader monetary aggregate.

Without pursuing the matter that requires much more esoteric detail, it is sufficient to indicate that the evidence was enough to convince many to declare monetarism dead, at least for the time being.[4] Of course, there were attempts to explain the decline in velocity, but they were not convincing to the critics. For example, falling prices and falling nominal interests rates usually are associated with falling velocity as the cost of holding money falls. In addition, the banking deregulation of 1980 that created or expanded new types of accounts (NOW, super NOW, money market, etc.) played havoc with the definitions of money and with money multipliers because shifts among accounts upset the predictability of money multipliers.

Monetarism and the simplicity of controlling monetary aggregates, fell from the prominence it once enjoyed whereby the stock market waited breathlessly for the weekly data on the money supply to be released on Friday afternoon. Now, instead of the accolades, it was blamed for the recession by many people, but especially by the supply-siders who saw their theory wrecked by what they considered an inappropriate monetary policy that maintained high interest rates and discouraged real investment.

COSTS OF RECESSION

It is clear that in the battle against inflation, not everyone is called to duty. In general, the lower income groups are asked to sacrifice for the benefit of the nation. The upper income groups must rearrange their portfolios, and the lower income groups must rearrange their lives. It is one thing to protect one's assets in a period of inflation; it is quite another to maintain a household in the face of unemployment. The price of goods becomes immaterial if one has no income to buy. As demonstrated again and again, the poor do not benefit from efforts to reduce inflation because inflation affects all income groups about the same. However, to combat the alleged evils of inflation, recessions are often called upon to fight the battle. It is here, when unemployment develops, that the poor are asked to pay a disproportionate share of the burden.[5]

The shifting of the burden to the poor will be seen again in the discussion of the changes in the distribution of income over this period. Here the question is more direct: What did it cost us to reduce inflation? One estimate made by Sawhill and Stone found that a milder recession with unemployment of about 6% instead of the actual 10+% cost households $1557 in the period 1981–83 and $3425 for the period 1980–86. These are considerable sums to pay for inflation that was in the process of declining anyway. Sawhill and Stone estimate that over half of the observed decline in inflation, 8.6% from 1980 to 1983, was due to a revision of the treatment of home ownership in the measurement of inflation (19% of total decline), and the remainder was accounted for by the fall in energy and food prices (34%). Thus, about 48% of the decline in consumer prices was due to the recession and unemployment.[6] The point is that the severe recession was not necessary to achieve the goals of the administration; a more gradual approach to the problems of inflation and high interest rates would have been far less costly and more humane.

Of course, the administration was not interested in delving into the costs of their actions. They either believed that its actions were costless—the free lunch syndrome—or they were callous to the suffering necessary to reach their goals so quickly. Speed was important to them, again testifying to their anxiety and possibly fear that their economic program would be discovered as being untenable. They had to, and did, "hit the ground running."

MONETARY POLICY IN THE SECOND TERM

The recovery began in 1983 and lasted throughout the remainder of the Reagan administration. The unemployment rate gradually fell to 7.4% in 1984, and eventually to 5.4% in 1988. Real GNP increased at an average annual rate of about 4% from 1982 to 1988. Inflation, as measured by the CPI, stabilized at about 3.8% until it climbed to 4.4% in 1987 and 1988. These are the essential economic data to preface the discussion of monetary policy in this period.

As seen, the growth rates of monetary aggregates were no longer the only

Table 6.3
Monetary Trends in the 1980s

Period	Growth rate Of M1	Growth rate M2	Target Ranges		CPI
1982IV-1983IV	10.0	12.2	none 7-10%	M1 M2	3.8
1983IV-1984IV	5.4	8.0	4-8% 6-9%	M1 M2	3.9
1984IV-1985IV	12.1	8.9	4-7% 6-8.5%	M1 M2	3.8
1985IV-1986IV	15.3	9.3	4-7% 6-9%	M1 M2	1.1
1986IV-1987IV	6.2	4.2	none 5.5-8.5%	M1 M2	4.4
1987IV-1988IV	4.3	5.2	none 4-8%	M1 M2	4.4

Source: St. Louis Federal Reserve Bank, Monetary Trends, various issues; Federal Reserve Bulletin, various years.

guide to monetary policy after 1982. Still, they were important considerations in an era when monetarism was still popular and still influential. Looking at the data on monetary aggregates reveals some interesting and potentially damaging evidence concerning the ability of the monetary authorities to control the money supply (now defined many ways) and the importance of controlling it anyway. Not only was the definition of the money supply giving the monetary authorities headaches but the demand for money was shifting and causing some disconcerting problems for the Fed. The monetarist assumption that the Fed could control the money supply by simply controlling monetary aggregates in the face of shifting demand for money became questionable. In technical terms, the money supply was being determined endogenously (determined by factors within the working of the economic system) not exogenously (determined by the monetary authorities). If the latter is denied, another blow to monetarism would result.[7]

The growth of monetary aggregates can be seen in Table 6.3. Both the growth of M1 and M2 fluctuated about their target ranges for most of this period, often exceeding them by substantial margins. Yet prices were falling or had stabilized. If, as monetarists claimed, the growth of the money supply was the main determinant of the price level, then again their theory received a severe challenge in the 1980s. Particularly in the middle years of the 1980s, the rate of monetary growth was far in excess of targeted ranges, and still prices were not rising. Clearly, other factors were at work in the period, including the prevention of price increases due to the severe competition from abroad and fluctuating exchange rates, with an overvalued dollar up to 1985 when the United States became a debtor nation. Whatever the cause, monetarism was badly damaged, perhaps fatally.

THE STOCK MARKET CRASH

Some of the uneven distribution of rewards from the Reagan tax cuts and spending decisions flowed into speculation in the stock market. In place of the increase in real investment that the administration hoped for, financial investment soared instead. Instead of the increase in real capital spending, luxury consumption spending on private planes and vacation homes was the order of the day.

Even in the midst of the severe recession of 1981–82, the stock market boomed. There was no apparent reason for the boom, for there were no signs of high profits by business nor any sign of any industrial boom that might account for the favorable expectations. There was, however, a great deal of speculation; there seemed to be no tomorrow in these years. Perhaps Mr. Reagan's optimism was infectious, or, better, his hands-off approach to the economy signaled the financial community to shrug off any restraints, end its caution, and follow the path of greed. The Reagan administration's indifferent attitude toward antitrust administration, its obvious pro business, antilabor bias, and its fanatical belief in free markets, and so on all contributed to the general accommodation of the reckless pursuit of money while the favorable climate lasted.

Fueled by the phenomenal explosion of corporate takeovers, mergers and acquisitions, financial futures and options markets, computerized trading strategies (program trading), and corporate restructuring, the entire financial community went wild making millionaires out of fresh MBAs and crooks out of the old master speculators and takeover artists. Financial innovations were cheered by free-market advocates as promoting efficiency without recognizing the potential for instability as well.

All this stock market activity was taking place against a backdrop of a banking industry in deep trouble. Banks were failing in numbers not seen since the great depression. In 1980, the FDIC closed or assisted 10 banks; in 1987 the number rose to 203, and the number of "problem" banks rose from 223 in 1981 to 1575 in 1987. Some 650 banks had been closed or assisted from 1980 to 1987, and the number was still growing when the Reagan years came to an end. One other piece of evidence to demonstrate the disregard for caution in the financial community was the overall financial condition of the commercial banks: in 1980, 3.7% of them were losing money; in 1987, nearly 18% were. Thus, while the banking system was in trouble, the rest of the financial world seemed unconcerned—a rather remarkable situation.

Greed was in, risk was out. Governments refused to raise taxes or reduce spending; consumers were enticed to buy now and not postpone gratification. Future consequences for such behavior were dismissed, and anyone who warned of them was regarded as a doomsayer. Consumers borrowed, governments borrowed, everyone spent as if accountability was absent, and debt accumulation was nothing to worry about.

This orgy of paper swapping had to end sometime because it was built on nothing but paper and rosy expectations. The bull market began on August 13, 1987 when the Dow Jones average was 776.92; it reached a high of 2722.42 on August 25. The end came with the dramatic stock market crash of October 19, 1987 when the Dow Jones average fell from 2246.74 to 1738.42, a 508.32-point drop or 22.6% in one day! This was a far greater fall than the 12.8% decline that occurred in the stock market crash of 1929. In one day, $500 billion in wealth had been erased, and $1 trillion lost from the high in August!

Of course, panic ensued in both the financial and political communities. The predictions for another depression like the one in 1929 were widespread, and alarmists of all kinds were eager to forecast one calamity or another. Ignoring the speculative orgy of the past 5 years, the blame for the collapse was laid to James Baker, secretary of the treasury, for his threat to let the dollar fall against the German mark, and to the Federal Reserve for declaring the economy healthy and inflation under control while nudging interest rates upward. Perhaps these events helped precipitate the collapse, but a better explanation can be found in the unwarranted boom in the first place; there was no reason for the boom, so why the surprise when the bubble burst?

Forecasts of another depression helped restore some rationality to political circles as the shaky condition of the economy became apparent. The budget deficits along with the trade deficits revealed the cause of the upswing in the economy since 1983. The federal government had used its credit card to promote prosperity, just as the consumers had used theirs. Once the veil had been lifted to reveal the true source of the nation's prosperity, some of the sheen over the growing economy was removed. The go-go years began to fade as the headlines were filled with recriminations, and junk bond dealers and takeover specialists were depicted as mere criminals. Congress blamed the administration, and the president blamed Congress for the deficits, the state of the economy, and anything else in the attempt to shift the blame for which both were responsible.

The forecasted depression did not materialize. In the first place, the reduction in wealth would not affect consumption as much as might be expected. For each additional dollar of wealth, only 3 to 6 cents affects consumption. Although this seemingly small amount could be significant in the huge reduction of wealth, the concentration of wealth restricts the decline in consumption. In addition, there are now programs in place that cushion the decline in income: federal deposit insurance, Social Security, unemployment compensation, welfare programs, and so on. These programs, not in place in 1929, provide safeguards against the unchecked loss of income. Moreover, the federal government has assumed responsibility for the functioning of the economy and would be expected to intervene with fiscal and monetary measures to restore economic stability.

In this section, monetary policy is the central issue. What did the Federal Reserve do in the face of the stock market crash? Chairman Greenspan immediately calmed financial markets by vowing to provide whatever reserves to the banking system that were necessary to prevent any panic. This move was absent in 1929, and its absence helped to contribute to the financial panic that ensued. The Federal Reserve honored its pledge as it poured reserves into the banking system; even interest rates declined slightly as a result.

Thus, the Federal Reserve took the proper action under the circumstances. Its first duty was to reassure financial markets. Yet, it also validated all the excesses that occurred in the previous 5 years. Like it or not, it sanctioned the uninhibited financial actions, speculation, and financial institutional innovations. By stepping in, it protected the market from chaos but forgave it from its excesses and abuses. The Fed also was acting on behalf of the Reagan administration. Again it gave the administration exactly what it wanted.

CONCLUSION ON MONETARY POLICY

This brief review of monetary policy in the Reagan years was not meant to be a complete accounting of all the monetary actions taken in the period nor a critique of them from whatever perspective. What can be stated is that the Reagan administration got substantially the monetary policy it was seeking. Although the growth of monetary aggregates was not reduced by as much as the administration wanted in the beginning, that is, to half those that prevailed at the time the economic plan was made by 1986, too many other events in the interval made such a target unrealistic.

In the early years, the fight against inflation required a tight monetary policy. The Fed cooperated and, despite the resulting recession, continued the tight policy until its aims were achieved. The administration could hardly ask for more, whatever its convenient criticisms of the Fed's actions. Although it became an easy target for the administration, the Federal Reserve cannot be blamed for the failure of the economic plan.

In the later years, so many other events were intruding on the economy that the Federal Reserve's actions must be seen in broader terms than simply satisfying the needs of the executive branch. Exchange rate problems, deregulation of the banking sector, shifts in the demand for money and velocity puzzles, the continuing pursuit of price stability, the stock market crash and speculation, the decade of mergers and acquisitions, the accumulation of public and private debt, and the expanding economy after 1983 left the conduct of monetary policy more complicated than it was in the early years when the goals were clearer. Still, it can be said that the actions of the Fed were at least consistent with the administration's general desires.

NOTES

1. *A Program for Economic Recovery,* a message to Congress dated February 18, 1981, 22–23.

2. The Federal Reserve announced on that day that it would be taking actions to "assure better control over the expansion of money and bank credit, help curb speculative excesses in financial, foreign exchange, and commodity markets, and thereby serve to dampen inflationary forces." It planned to change its daily operating procedures in the conduct of monetary policy that "involves placing greater emphasis in day-to-day operations on the supply of bank reserves and less emphasis on confining short-term fluctuations in the federal funds rate." "Announcements: Monetary Policy Actions," *Federal Reserve Bulletin* (October 1979), 830.

3. According to Niskanen, David Stockman was told of the inconsistency by Beryl Sprinkel of the Treasury Department, but "decided to maintain the GNP forecasts. . . ." For more details of the development of monetary policy, see William A. Niskanen, *Reaganomics* (New York: Oxford University Press, 1988), 155–189.

4. The St. Louis Fed, one of the most vociferous defenders of monetarism was not ready to give up on monetarism so easily. In several articles, it attempted to explain away the puzzles of declining velocity and reversals of money multipliers. See, for instance, the articles that appeared in its *Review:* John A. Tatom, "Recent Financial Innovations: Have They Distorted the Meaning of M1?" (April 1982), 23–35; John A. Tatom, "Was the 1982 Velocity Decline Unusual?" (August/September 1983), 5–15; and Courtenay C. Stone and Daniel L. Thorton, "Solving the 1980s' Velocity Puzzle: A Progress Report" (August/ September 1987), 5–23. *Business Week* was less guarded in its "The Failure of Monetarism," 4 April 1983, 64–67. The Council of Economic Advisors in its *Economic Report of the President of 1983* simply declared the problem of the decline in velocity as "not fully understood" (21). For a more detailed study, see Stephan Goldfeld, "The Demand for Money Revisited," *Brookings Papers on Economic Activity,* 1973:3.

5. See the discussion in Douglas A. Hibbs, Jr., *The American Political Economy* (Cambridge, MA: Harvard University Press, 1987), 77–89.

6. Isabel V. Sawhill and Charles F. Stone, *Economic Policy in the Reagan Years* (Washington, DC: The Urban Institute Press, 1984); or see their contribution, "The Economy," in *The Reagan Record,* eds. John L. Palmer and Isabel V. Sawhill (Cambridge, MA: Ballanger Publishing Co., 1984), 69–105.

7. For a succinct summary of monetary policy in this period, see Stephen H. Axilrod, "U.S. Monetary Policy in Recent Years," in *Federal Reserve Bulletin* (January 1985), 14–24.

Chapter 7

Regulation in the Conservative Administrations

The Reagan administration made regulatory relief one of the cornerstones of its economic plan. In its *Program for Economic Recovery,* it stated its commitment to reverse the trend toward regulation as it included: "The third element of our economic program is an ambitious reform of regulations that will reduce the government-imposed barriers to investment, production, and employment."[1]

Mr. Reagan had been preaching that government was the problem in many areas and, in particular, in its intrusive behavior in the regulatory area. "Get government off the backs of industry" or some similar phrase was meant to convey the perception that burdensome regulations were hampering U.S. business, hurting the competitiveness of U.S. firms versus foreign firms, raising costs, and shunting investment into nonproductive areas to comply with regulations of all kinds. Armed with the shocking estimate of the cost of regulation put at over $100 billion a year (in 1979) by Murray Weidenbaum, the administration was convinced of the need to reverse the tide and relieve the overburdened and harassed business firm.[2]

Critics were quick to attack the study that estimated the cost of regulation of $100 billion as being seriously flawed because it included the budgets of some regulatory agencies as costs, paperwork costs of business such as filling out IRS forms and the like, import quota costs, productivity losses caused by employees complying with regulations, and so on. In addition, no benefits of regulation were considered. Through repetition, however, the number of $100 billion as the cost of regulation endured.

It was also pointed out that the foreign firms which were outcompeting U.S. firms were subject to additional and more stringent regulations than their U.S. counterparts. Still, the perception persisted in an administration not overly concerned with empirical evidence. The administration was able to garner sympathy for its views by citing numerous cases of regulatory horrors, bureaucratic ineptness, complicated and contradictory rules, and aimless enforcement. Many who were subject to one regulatory abuse were easily convinced of the general extrapolation to all regulations.

Indeed, regulations had increased in the 1970s. In fact, the Nixon administration enacted more regulations than any other, and the trend was not diminished in subsequent administrations. In addition to regulations for specific industries, there were the general social ones for the attainment of clean air, clean water, safe food and drugs, workplace safety, consumer protection, and so on. Business began to compute the costs of these regulations and, of course, complained. Regulations were increasingly blamed for more and more of the ills that beset the U.S. firm. Rising prices, falling profits, declining productivity, undermining competitiveness, wasting resources and manpower, and requiring investment to comply with regulations were all identified with overregulation that held back the firm and robbed it of resources to invest in R&D and more productive capital goods.

Much of this had the ring of plausibility, and anecdotal examples of misguided regulatory behavior reinforced the surface credibility. Not many were anxious to identify the decline of U.S. industry with mismanagement; not many were pointing fingers at irrational union behavior. Who would take the blame for inferior products, resistance to changes in technology, and for seeking greater profits abroad and abandoning production in the United States? It was easier to blame the "faceless bureaucrat" who administered those burdensome regulations that hindered the growth and profitability of the firm or industry. This is not to deny that there are costs involved in regulation, sometimes burdensome ones. Moreover, bureaucratic bumbling is legion in the regulatory field. Thus, many complaints were justified, and regulatory reform was a valid concern of everyone involved.

It is against this background that the Reagan administration announced with great fanfare its antiregulatory stance. The fact that there were too many economic burdens placed on business only served to buttress the administration's free-market philosophy. Too much interference into private decision making was not only costly but ran counter to the minimal role for government that was the basic ideology of the administration. The lesson was clear: Keep regulation to a minimum where regulation serves a useful role, but eliminate it whenever possible, particularly at the federal level, when the apparent benefits are small.[3]

EARLY APPROACHES

The administration acted quickly, and during its first month in office took steps to indicate its determination to end the burden of regulation. The Task Force on Regulatory Relief was established to review and assess existing regulations and scrutinize new proposals with a view toward avoiding overlapping and duplication and, of course, reducing the role of regulation in general. It was headed by Vice-President George Bush and included major officials of the administration, including the secretaries of treasury, commerce, labor, the director of OMB, and the chair of the CEA. Clearly, these appointments were designed to foster the belief that the administration was indeed serious about regulatory impediments.

The Council on Wage and Price Stability (CWPS), established by President Nixon and extended by Carter, was abolished as being ineffective and market distorting. As the remnant of Nixon's wage and price control system, its job under Carter was to establish wage and price standards to control inflation, the scourge of the 1970s. In an administration committed to the free market as an article of faith, there would be no room for such an agency that interfered with private decisions. That the market is the best vehicle for establishing wages and prices is the hallmark of capitalism, and any attempt to intervene must be resisted by free-market devotees.

In the same vein, efforts were made to decontrol the price of domestic oil. It was hoped that the removal of this "cumbersome and inefficient" system of regulations would spur domestic output of oil, lessen the dependence on foreign oil, and encourage conservation. The demise of another federal bureaucracy was an added bonus.

Reagan also sent a memorandum to agency heads asking them to postpone the effective dates of pending regulations and requesting them to delay the implementation of new regulations for 60 days. The delay was felt necessary to permit new appointees to become familiar with the regulations and to permit the new Task Force on Regulatory Relief to become operational.

Finally, and most important, the president issued an executive order in February, 1981 designed to improve the regulatory process but clearly directing more power to the executive branch in regulatory matters. The order required all executive agencies to use cost–benefit analysis in all regulatory affairs. In the examination of past regulations or in the consideration of new ones, the costs of the regulations and the benefits of them were to be included in the analysis. The agencies were required to "determine the most cost-effective approach for meeting any given regulatory objective, taking into account such factors as the economic condition of industry, the national economy, and other prospective regulations." [4]

To carry out this procedure, the Reagan administration borrowed, despite the lack of acknowledgement, the formal structure from the Carter administration. Carter also wanted to control the regulatory process by giving the executive branch more power to oversee changes in regulations to prevent undue costs and inflationary pressures. The Regulatory Analysis Review Group (RARG), established by executive order, became the focus for regulatory review. The Regulatory Council was established to bring regulators and cabinet officials together to review and discuss regulatory matters and to issue a semiannual calendar of forthcoming regulation changes.

In the Reagan plan, the OMB was given the major responsibility for overseeing regulatory changes. Each agency was directed to prepare a Regulatory Impact Analysis that was to be reviewed by the OMB Office of Information and Regulatory Affairs (OIRA) before they were published in the Federal Register. OMB was thus given enormous power to oversee any change in regulations before they were made public. In addition, the agencies were directed to prepare a semiannual agenda of new regulations that were being considered or changes in old ones. As a result of these requirements, the administration would be kept informed of any activity in the regulatory field. Again, the administration signaled its serious concern for the regulatory issue by its appointments to key positions: James Miller was appointed head of OIRA and Murray Weidenbaum was made chair of the Council of Economic Advisors. Both economists were identified with the antiregulation, free-market camp.

These actions, and particularly the routing of regulatory changes through OMB, were the subjects of much controversy. Defenders, such as Niskanen, found them to be quite a good start in the deregulation process but, according to him, did not go far enough to make a serious reversal of past trends. He generally approved of executive control over the regulatory process and found that "the able people who led OIRA probably pushed the White House regulatory review process as much as possible, ... Their aggressive actions to review, modify, or delay regulatory proposals initiated by the executive agencies, however, were ultimately checked by both Congress and the courts."[5]

Critics, however, were less enamored with the OMB and its tactics.

Granting OMB superagency status over regulations and mandating economic analysis . . . created a new regulatory landscape . . . with the presidential agencies fearful of issuing new regulations, or introducing too many new initiatives. . . . With its power to monitor the regulatory performance of the executive agencies, OMB kept the agencies so busy with requests for additional information that it held *de facto* control of their agencies as well as their output.[6]

Of course, after repeated badgering by OMB, the agencies learned to curtail their regulatory changes, sending a chilling effect throughout the administration as far as regulatory matters were concerned.

Thus did the administration erect the institutional framework to control, limit, and forestall regulatory actions. The mechanisms apparently were not sufficient, and to ensure that Congress and the courts could not circumvent or overcome the bureaucracy, the administration was particularly anxious to appoint people as agency heads who were not likely to propose new regulations anyway. If antiregulators were put in charge of federal agencies, they would not be proposing new initiatives nor using their positions to press for innovative responses to problems that involve regulations. For example, Anne Gorsuch (now Burford) was appointed head of EPA with no knowledge of environmental affairs; Thorne Auchter was appointed head of Occupational Health and Safety Administration (OHSA) with a record of safety violations in his construction company; and James Watt was appointed secretary of the interior with a known penchant for economic development of public resources. In these (and many other) cases, the appointees were overtly hostile to the causes of agencies they were to head.

There are many other equally glaring examples, and, in fact, all through the administration, appointees to federal posts were unsympathetic to the purpose or rationale of the agencies they headed or served. When it came time to appoint people to office, conservative ideology took precedence over knowledge and experience. The lack of qualifications for the job did not prohibit the Reagan administration as it had previous ones. In fact, one study found that Reagan appointees had much less experience than appointees of other presidents.[7]

Of course, appointing people through a test of ideological purity is one way to ensure allegiance to the conservative crusade and to promote the aims of the administration. Another way is to "remove, transfer, or demote old-time civil servants deemed uncooperative or ideologically suspect."[8]

RESULTS

According to one of the principle proponents of deregulation, Murray Weidenbaum: "The Reagan administration virtually stopped the growth in the issuance of new rules, [but] it did not make any significant cutbacks in the structure of regulation. For the most part, it left laws unchanged . . . [and] although regulatory reform was one of the four original pillars of 'Reaganomics' . . . , it never received as high a priority as the other three."[9] Niskanen, too, regrets the lost opportunity to deregulate on a more widespread scale, but admits that "the Reagan administration was only moderately successful in reducing or reforming the several types of economic regulation, . . . [but] The Reagan attempt to reform these [social regulations] . . . was a near-complete failure."[10]

The assessment of these influential men in the Reagan administration is based on their comparisons of the promise of the commitment to deregulation with the record of actual achievements. Without reviewing the entire record of proposals in each agency with the degree of success with them, some summary remarks can be made, leaving the details to others. The major successes in deregulation came in the form of several Acts that managed to win the support of Congress. The Bus Regulatory Reform Act of 1982 deregulated bus fares, allowed firms to make changes in routes and permitted freer entry and exit into the industry. The Shipping Act of 1984 permitted shipping firms to adjust rates and types of service. The Garn–St. Germain Act of 1982 authorized banks to offer new types of accounts, permitted savings and loans (thrifts) to make more commercial and consumer loans, liberalized the ownership of S&Ls, allowed deposit insurance funds to be used to bail out failing banks, reduced the interest rate differentials between banking institutions, and, in general, revolutionized the banking industry. (This Act, designed to rescue the S&Ls and modernize the banking system, actually exacerbated the problems that later led to massive bank failures. More on the effects of this example of deregulation is found in Chapter 10.)

Despite the hue and cry over the evils of regulation and the condemnation of government's interference in the marketplace, there was little evidence of the commitment to deregulation to match the rhetoric. The administration was not able or willing to attack the regulation of the agricultural sector. Its own program, payment-in-kind (PIK), was a dismal failure, leaving the farm sector in shambles. The administration finally abandoned attempts to seriously reform agricultural regulation, and toward the end was simply making noises about returning the sector to free-market forces, knowing that option was hopelessly unrealistic.

Much can be said of the other agencies in which regulation was presumably onerous. The FCC did manage to stir quite a controversy between producers and TV networks by changing a few rules in the regulation of TV syndication rights but did not confront any other major issues. AT&T was allowed to divest itself of portions of its market to other companies in return for the right to enter into other areas of telecommunications. This ended one of the major, long-running antitrust suits that solved nothing. In energy matters, no major changes were made after the initial deregulation of gas prices in 1981. Reagan's vow to eliminate the Department of Energy (as well as the Department of Education) failed to materialize, and little was done in this area.

The same scenario can be repeated in the case of the other federal agencies; there is little point in reviewing the case studies of each agency.[11] With much fanfare, bold statements were made condemning regulation and blaming it for many of the ills that were besetting the U.S. economy. The administration found that many of the regulations were popular and were regarded as required to protect economic agents of one kind or another from the vagaries of the marketplace. When business firms sought protection from the marketplace, regulations were supported; they were opposed only when accountability was demanded.

The administration found resistance from those who regarded regulation as necessary in an advanced industrial society.

It is our major protection against the excesses of technology, whose rapid advances threaten man's genes, privacy, air, water, bloodstream, lifestyle, and virtual existence. It is a guard against the callous entrepreneur, who would have his workers breathe coal dust, and cotton dust, who would send children into the mines and factories, who would offer jobs in exchange for health and safety, and leave the victims as public charges in hospitals and on welfare lines.[12]

WHAT WENT WRONG?

Without question, regulatory reform was high on the president's agenda from the very beginning. He attributed many of the ills of the U.S. economy to the unnecessary burdens placed on business. U.S. firms were put at a competitive disadvantage versus the rest of the world. The rhetoric was simple, strong, and clear. Furthermore, he could take advantage of the path already cleared for him by Carter's deregulation successes. Why, therefore, was not more accomplished?

Critics could easily point out that the benefits of deregulation were oversold and that the costs were overstated. Still, a strong push might have overcome these reservations if the public was convinced of the president's arguments. He had prevailed in other areas where many doubts were manifest.

So the first explanation of failure in this area must be laid at the administration's feet. It simply put a higher priority on other parts of the economic agenda. The tax cuts and the defense buildup were more important and claimed much more attention. Tax cuts were crucial to getting the economy moving again, and national defense spending was necessary to restore the United States to military prominence. The administration worked diligently in these areas, relegating other parts of the economic plan to secondary importance.

A second explanation can be found in the administration's lack of a specific plan for deregulation. It seemed content to assert the evils of *all* regulations, and it did so in generalizations that appeal to devotees of simple solutions but found opposition from those directly involved in them. Thus, it did not appreciate that many regulations were popular with the public, and not everyone shared the belief that regulations could do only harm. Lacking a plan for phased deregulation, it could only attack verbally at first, and then retreated at the first sign of opposition. Clean air and clean water regulations, for instance, were very popular with the public, Congress, and the states that often had more stringent regulations than required by federal regulations.

So the administration backed away from frontal attacks on these regulations and on regulatory reform generally, fearing that they would "clutter the legislative agenda with controversial issues and dilute administrative resources on Capital Hill."[13] Niskanen maintains that James Baker, Chief of Staff, backed away from legislative changes to regulations unless the chances of winning were a certainty and that he refrained from some regulatory reforms out of political considerations.[14] According to Goodman and Wrightson, the administration chose not to pursue a gradual course of deregulation but to opt for a confrontational stance that left little room for compromise. So it adopted what they called a management strategy that avoided dealing with Congress or negotiating with special interest groups or the public. The management strategy called for executive domination of regulatory administration by centralizing oversight in the OMB. Actions of the rulings of the agencies and the OMB would presumably not be as noticeable as direct assaults on the regulations themselves. Opposition would, thus, be limited or thwarted.[15]

Successes were temporary, however, and soon the opponents realized what was happening. Congress balked at the power given to OMB and challenged the administrative bureaucracy established to change regulations. Moreover, the defiant administration, insisting on absolute loyalty, appointed agency heads who were not only antagonistic to the regulations of the agencies they represented but often were inexperienced and ill-informed as well. Their public remarks that denigrated regulations in one way or another simply demonstrated their insensitivity and were self-defeating as they alienated everyone. The administration abandoned true regulatory reform, then, and settled for reducing regulations by administrative actions. Some would call the attempt successful, but whatever the degree of success of this strategy, it was a long way from the original intent found in the rhetoric of the economic plan. Gradually, the rhetoric about deregulation diminished as well. Once the management strategy was challenged, once the public rallied behind regulations it favored, and once special interest groups recovered from the administration's end run, the administration retreated from its lofty goals. Even the agency heads, so combative and arrogant, were relieved of their posts, some by way of scandal and others by way of public intolerance of them.

It is difficult to quarrel with the conclusion of Goodman and Wrightson

That the Reagan strategy has undermined public confidence in regulatory institutions. It has politicized regulatory administration; undercut the relationship between Congress, agencies, and the executive office in regulatory policy making and implementation; debilitated regulatory agency management capacities and research capabilities; increased tension in the intergovernmental system; and produced a legislative backlash that has foreclosed prospects for reforming a number of important regulatory statutes in the future. . . .[16]

Here is the verdict of one administration member, William Niskanen, sympathetic to the goals of deregulation: "The Reagan program of regulatory relief promised more than it delivered. The failure to achieve a substantial reduction in or reform of federal regulations, building on the considerable momentum established during the Carter administration, was the major missed opportunity of the initial Reagan program.[17]

In reviewing the progress made by the Reagan administration in regulatory matters, some supporters of reform assigned a great deal of importance to the people who are involved in overseeing them.

We believe that the explanation for success and failure [of the Reagan regulatory program] is more straightforward. Where heads of agencies understood the institutional incentives with which they were dealing, embraced solid analytical procedures, and displayed a real commitment to achieving market-oriented reforms, progress was made. Where such an approach was lacking, politics reigned supreme and little was accomplished.[18]

The same theme is echoed with regard to antitrust policy during the Reagan administration. "Because the character of antitrust policy during the Reagan years has been shaped by the personalities of its administrators rather than by fundamental changes in law or institutions, it leaves little or no legacy. . . ."[19] As was the case with regulatory reform, the record of antitrust receives only modest approval by basic supporters of the thrust of the Reagan plans. Successes are few—the settlement of long-standing cases against IBM, AT&T, Exxon, and the cereal industry—but failure to adopt merger guidelines for the future and failure to revise the antitrust laws to reflect current economic theory represent lost opportunities, perhaps for some time. Critics of the administration might well quarrel with the claimed "successes" of these important cases, but that is not the issue here.

CONCLUSION

No doubt the administration was successful in forestalling new regulations and in reducing the burdens of some of the existing ones, but there seems to be little question that it failed to accomplish what it so grandly intended when it took office. Its view of regulations was either simply not shared by the rest of society or it failed to make the effort to convince others through the more difficult route of negotiation, compromise, and persuasion. Ideology was not sufficient justification for expecting the public trust; the case had to be established. Whatever opportunities it had, it squandered many of them by the often uncompromising and arrogant posture of agency heads who in the end turned out to be the worst enemies of deregulation. As indicated earlier, apparently more successes occurred when regulators knew what they were doing. The blame must then rest with the appointment process for the failure to achieve more in this area. Perhaps the Reagan administration was not as serious about deregulation as it claimed to be; perhaps campaign rhetoric was stronger than the will to struggle for change.

The record here is, of course, incomplete, and there has been no attempt to investigate the many decisions made by regulatory agencies to support conclusions of success or failure. Others have examined the agencies in detail, and the interested reader can consult the many references supplied but not detailed in this chapter. But is difficult to avoid the assessment that in deregulation, as elsewhere, the promises and rhetoric of the administration exceeded what was achievable and ideological intransigence prevented genuine accomplishments.

NOTES

1. *A Program for Economic Recovery,* a message to Congress dated February 18, 1981, 2.

2. See Robert DeFina and Murray L. Weidenbaum, *The Taxpayer and Government Regulation* (St. Louis, MO: Center for the Study of American Business, Washington University, 1978).

3. Another reason to oppose regulation, and one that is consistent with conservative philosophy, is that the wrong level of government is involved. The federal government is too far removed from the problems to deal with them effectively. The states and localities should be the agencies to regulate. Of course, the administration was willing to ignore this argument when it came to social program regulations. More on this and other aspects of regulation will be discussed later. This latter point was observed by many; see for instance, George C. Eads and Michael Fix, "Regulatory Policy," in *The Reagan Experiment,* eds. John L. Palmer and Isabel V. Sawhill (Washington, DC: The Urban Institute Press, 1982), 132.

4. *A Program for Economic Recovery,* a message to Congress dated February 18, 1981, 20.

5. William A. Niskanen, *Reaganomics* (New York: Oxford University Press, 1988), 132.

6. Susan J. Tolchin and Martin Tolchin, *Dismantling America: The Rush to Deregulate* (New York: Oxford University Press, 1983), 41–42. They quote one unnamed official as follows:

OMB pretends it isn't there. We can recommend but we can't do anything. Technically, OMB has no authority, but uses bribery and blackmail instead. The executive order says we can consult, but the agency can't do anything while we consult. We can drop it into a black hole while the politicians decide what to do with it. It is just window-dressing to a power grab. We're not doing heavy analysis. The economic analysis is just window-dressing for the executive order. (74)

7. Chester Newland, "A Mid-Term Appraisal—The Reagan Presidency: Limited Government and Political Administration," *Public Administration Review* (January/February, 1983), 1–21.

8. Marshall R. Goodman and Margaret T. Wrightson, *Managing Regulatory Reform: The Reagan Strategy and Its Impact* (New York: Praeger, 1987), 39.

9. Murray Weidenbaum, *Rendezvous with Reality* (New York: Basic Books, 1988), 237.

10. Niskanen, *Reaganomics,* 124, 125.

11. See Niskanen, *Reaganomics,* 118–130 for a brief summary of the regulatory agenda. Also see Tolchin and Tolchin, *Dismantling America,* for numerous examples of regulatory problems and solutions, or lack of them.

12. Tolchin and Tolchin, *Dismantling America,* 22.

13. Goodman and Wrightson, *Managing Regulatory Reform,* 201.

14. Niskanen, *Reaganomics,* 131.

15. Goodman and Wrightson, *Managing Regulatory Reform,* 201–202.

16. Ibid. 210.

17. Niskanen, *Reaganomics,* 115.

18. Thomas F. Walton and James Langenfeld, "Regulatory Reform under Reagan—the Right Way and the Wrong Way," in *Regulation and the Reagan Era,* eds. Roger E. Meiners and Bruce Yandle (New York: Holmes and Meier, 1989), 42.

19. William F. Shugart II, "Antitrust Policy in the Reagan Administration: Pyrrhic victories?" in *Regulation and the Reagan Era,* 100.

Chapter 8

Some Results of Reaganomics

Chapters 5 and 6 outlined the economic plans of the administration, or what it hoped to accomplish. Along the way, some results of its policies were indicated, although not in detail. These chapters were designed to suggest what was planned and, to some extent, how the plans would be carried out. Where it was deemed important, some results were mentioned immediately. In this chapter, some of the more significant outcomes are summarized to gauge the success or failure of the administration's economic plans and to prepare the groundwork for subsequent chapters that deal more significantly with its legacy.

The economic plan was directed toward the achievement of some specific and measurable goals; for example, reducing the rate of inflation, increasing saving and investment, stimulating the growth of labor productivity, and thereby the number of jobs, all of which should have encouraged economic growth. It is time to examine what happened to these important magnitudes, for it is on these outcomes that the administration's plans must ultimately be judged.

ECONOMIC GROWTH

In its original economic plan, the administration forecasted a real GNP growth of 1.1% in 1981, rising to 4.2% in 1982, 5.0% in 1983, 4.5% in 1984, and then falling to 4.2% in 1985 and 1986. In subsequent years, the Council of Economic Advisors revised its forecasts downward, to 1.4% for 1983, but rising to about 4% for the 1984–88 period.[1] In later years, the CEA kept insisting that 4% real growth was realistic but that the rate may fall to 3.9% in 1989 due to the fact that "the economy's long-run growth potential most likely is below 4 percent."[2] These projections continued until 1987 when the CEA revised them downward to 2.7% in 1987 and 3.6% in 1988, all the while claiming that the "stronger real growth reflects the long-term benefits of tax reform, as well as factors that will improve growth in the current year and carry forward in later years."[3]

Putting aside this contradiction, the record shows that real GNP growth averaged 3.0% over the Reagan years, not very different from the record of the previous decade (1971–78) of 3.2% and about equal to the record of the Carter years of 3.0%. However, the post-World War II real GNP growth, from 1949

Table 8.1
Accounting for Real GNP Growth

ITEM	CEA Projections for 1984–1990	Actual 1981–88
Population growth	.9	1.2
Participation rate growth	.6	.5
Labor Force Growth	1.5	1.7
Employment growth rate	.3	.3
Civilian employment	1.8	2.0
Adj. to estimate nonfarm business sector:[a]		
employment share	.6	.3
avg. weekly hours	-.2	-.1
Total hours	2.2	2.2
Productivity growth	2.0	1.4
Output of nonfarm bus. sector	4.2	3.7
Less: nonfarm output as share of real GNP	.3	.7
Real GNP growth	3.9	3.0

[a]Nonfarm business sector data are used instead of data for the entire economy because accurate data on hours worked are not available for the entire economy.

Source: Council of Economic Advisors, *Economic Report of the President, 1985*, 43; Council of Economic Advisors, *Economic Report of the President, 1989*, 286.

to 1980, averaged 3.4%, so growth in the Reagan years was below this long-run average and cannot be called extraordinary in any way.

What went wrong? Using the administration's projections for the 4% rate of growth in real GNP might reveal the source of the overoptimism. Table 8.1 supplies the necessary data.

Using the data of Table 8.1, it is clear that the major difficulty in the administration's forecast of real GNP growth can be found in two factors: slower productivity growth and slower growth in the nonfarm business sector. Once again the overoptimism of supply-side economics is apparent. Instead of the incentive effects that were to spur productivity growth and increase the supply of labor, we find the results do not substantiate the claims. Even the administration was forced to recognize the obvious and in its later *Economic Reports,* it lowered the growth rates for the 1990s to 3.2%, all the while continuing to claim that "reductions in marginal tax rates on labor income initiated during this administration are expected to encourage labor force participation in the years ahead."[4]

Taking a closer look at the determinants of real GNP growth, it appears as if the administration underestimated the growth of the civilian labor force. The predicted growth rate of 0.9% for the 1980s turned out to be less than the actual rate of 1.2%. The CEA did not explain its estimate except to state that the adult population had been declining for some time now that the baby boom was over. This may be correct, but for the time period under consideration, the decline simply was not that rapid.

The population growth rate, together with the growth in the labor force participation rate, determine the growth rate of the labor force. The labor force participation rate grew at a rate of 0.4% in the 1980s, somewhat less than the administration had predicted using the incentive effects of supply-side economics. In fact, the civilian labor force participation growth rate for males actually declined by 0.2% in the decade, whereas the rate for females increased by 1.2%. It will be argued later that the increase in the labor force participation rate for females was not due to incentive effects of taxation but to the decline in family incomes, forcing a secondary earner into the labor force to maintain living standards. (Interestingly, the rate for teens remained constant over the decade.)

The unemployment rate remained above the targeted rate of 5%, and the nonfarm sector did not grow as rapidly as predicted. However, the lingering problem of the decline in the growth rate of labor productivity is evident. The growth rate of about 1.4% over the period is far below the 2% rate that the administration kept forecasting. The measurement of productivity may be controversial, but the importance of the measure cannot be overstated. The administration based its optimistic forecasts on several developments: the older, more experienced labor force; the decline in energy prices; the increase in research and development expenditures that should contribute to technological change; and some beneficial effects of tax reform. At the same time, it complained about the negative effects of subsidies and burdensome regulations.

Labor productivity is influenced by many factors, and economists disagree about their importance. However, everyone agrees that the quality of the labor force is an important ingredient. Both the education of the labor force and its health are crucial parts of the qualitative dimension. Yet, the administration did little about these elements. It threatened to eliminate the Department of Education and ignored the health problems of the nation. In fact, it maintained that the nation's schools were improving at a time when others were warning of the crisis in education.[5] The critics were right; the nation was falling behind other nations in education, and repeated evidence was and is still being presented to substantiate the claim. A similar crisis was and is evident in health care.

Of course, labor productivity is influenced by the physical capital with which labor has to work. Both the quality and quantity of capital are important determinants of labor productivity. More capital per worker (capital deepening) increases labor productivity, but perhaps even more important is capital improvements through technical change. Ironically, such improvements are likely to require a more skilled labor force but that has not been forthcoming. More sophisticated capital may even require less labor input over time, but this feature has received scant attention.

The quality of physical capital can be influenced by public policies that encourage research and development (R&D). Unfortunately, the administration decided to promote R&D in the military field, and the spillover benefits to the private sector of military technology are not substantial. Public policy can also influence the quantity of capital through taxation practices. The administration claimed that its tax initiatives would foster saving and, hence, investment. In addition, its more generous depreciation provisions would stimulate capital formation and, in general, create a climate wherein entrepreneurs would once again respond to higher after-tax returns to undertake the inevitable risk associated with real investment. As we will see in the next section, the administration's fiscal policies were not very successful in achieving the response necessary for capital formation.

In summary, the Reagan administration did not fulfill its promise to increase the rate of economic growth. Its policies did not stimulate labor participation and productivity growth rates nor did it create the conditions necessary for long-term improvements in the critical areas needed for future increases. Its health and education policies were lacking, and its capital formation policies did not work as planned.

SAVING AND INVESTMENT

The promise of increased economic growth was derailed by the failure of saving and investment to attain the levels needed. It was claimed by the administration, supply-siders, and many others not identified with either group that Americans do not save enough and, hence, private investment is less than it would be, and a slower growth rate is the result. No one questioned the need for greater economic growth because it had long been held to be crucial to increasing living standards, providing jobs and opportunities to succeeding generations, and creating the conditions whereby increasing wealth would more willingly be shared by the winners with the losers. Moreover, intergenerational transfers would be easier in a world of an aging population, and conflicts among groups would be ameliorated if everyone had more. These and other benefits made, and still make, economic growth a major goal of most economies.

To achieve economic growth, more investment in plants, equipment, and buildings is necessary. Investment in physical capital is required to provide additional output, jobs, opportunities and to take advantage of new technology that would increase efficiency. Of course, increases in human capital in the form of education, job training, and, in general, the upgrading of the skills of workers and managers is required as well if the maximum benefit from fixed investment is to be achieved.

Again, no one questioned the need for additional, higher rates of investment in the U.S. economy; the question was how to accomplish it. Governmental efforts to stimulate investment must necessarily be roundabout and come largely through the tax code that grants tax incentives, investment tax credits, and accelerated depreciation allowances.

The Reagan administration, turning Keynesian theory on its head, decided that additional saving would stimulate investment. Accordingly, it proposed schemes to increase saving through tax cuts on both incomes and estates, IRA enlargement, all-savers accounts, generous depreciation rules, a capital gains tax reduction from 70 to 50%, tax credits on incremental R&D spending, and reductions in tax rates on small corporations. Not all of these measures were designed to increase saving, but the general thrust of ERTA of 1981 was clearly to encourage more saving. The 1986 tax reform measure reversed some of these provisions, eliminating the capital gains reduction and the investment tax credit, reducing the R&D and depreciation allowances, while decreasing corporate income tax rates. The trade-off was essentially the reduction in marginal tax rates to three (or four) rates and presumably a simpler and fairer tax code.

Regardless of its sometimes contradictory tax and spending proposals, the administration continued to call for additional saving as the means to increase investment. Yet, the offsetting tax policies over the course of the Reagan years rendered the administration's investment efforts inconsequential.[6] Its record in this regard is provided in Table 8.2, where the total of gross private domestic investment is shown along with how it was financed. In our national income accounting, the sum of household saving, business saving, and governmental saving must equal gross private domestic investment. If total saving is insufficient to finance investment, foreign capital inflows must make up the difference.

In Table 8.2, it is clear that total saving was able to finance domestic investment right up to the Carter administration, when it became necessary to rely on foreign investment. In the Reagan years, however, much more reliance was necessary on foreign sources to finance domestic investment—amounting to 1.9% of GNP from 0.1%—a phenomenal increase. Instead of increasing saving to finance investment, the United States was saving less!

Looking further at Table 8.2, gross private investment as a percent of GNP did not increase in the Reagan years and, in fact, was less than in the Carter and Nixon/Ford administrations. Gross investment was about 8% lower than in

Table 8.2
Saving and Investment (percent of GNP)

	1950s	Kennedy/ Johnson	Nixon/ Ford	Carter	Reagan
Gross Private Domestic Invest	16.2	15.5	15.8	17.1	15.7
Fixed	9.6	9.8	10.4	11.3	10.8
Residential	5.6	4.6	4.6	5.2	4.5
Inventory	1.0	1.1	.7	.6	.4
Financed By: National Saving	16.0	16.3	16.3	17.1	13.8
Private	16.1	16.8	17.3	17.5	16.6
Household	4.7	4.7	5.8	4.7	3.7
Business	11.4	12.1	11.5	12.8	12.9
Government	-.1	-.5	-1.0	-.4	-2.8
Federal	.1	-.5	-1.5	-1.6	-4.1
State & Local	-.2	-	.5	1.2	1.3
Financed by; Net Foreign Capital Inflows/ Outflows (-)	-.1	-.7	-.4	.1	1.9

Note: Totals may not add due to rounding.
Source: Computations made from data supplied in the Economic
Report of the President, 1991.

the Carter years, and, moreover, both fixed and residential investment were less.

National saving fell in the Reagan years to an average of just 13.8% of GNP down some 20% from the Carter administration and down 15% from long-term averages. Households reduced their saving by 1 percentage point while business remained fairly constant. The trouble, of course, must come from the public sector; here, federal government saving plummeted to −4.1% of the GNP, down some 150% over the Carter and Nixon/Ford experience. The large government deficits of the Reagan administration reduced the total saving available for private investment, and foreign sources had to make up the difference.

We will examine the consequences of these developments later, but one observation is necessary to insert here. Just a glance at Table 8.2 is enough to dispel the notion that private saving finances investment. Over the period since 1950, household saving barely manages to finance *residential* investment—investment in private housing. Business has been the main contributor to fixed investment. Thus, although it is true that American households save less than other nations, first, they always did, and, second, what they did save financed only residential investment. This fact, although obvious from the data, is often lost in the discussion of household saving and investment.

Finally, foreign investment in the United States grew rapidly in the Reagan years, the consequences of which we also postpone. However, it should be noted here that foreign investment takes two general forms: direct and financial. Direct investment is defined as investment in a new venture in the United States of at least a 10% interest in an American firm; financial investment is defined as stocks and bonds of U.S. firms or government securities. Foreign direct investment in the United States grew rapidly in the 1980s constituting about 27% of foreign investment in 1988 and causing much public alarm. Portfolio investment accounted for the remainder, furnishing the saving that the private sector and government agencies failed to provide.

WHAT WENT WRONG WITH SAVING AND INVESTMENTS PLANS

In view of the fact, noted above, that personal saving has been low since the 1950s, the explanations for the low saving rate in the 1980s appears to be ex post justifications for a failed policy or simply rationalizations. The decline in personal saving has not been fully explained; however, here are a few of the more plausible explanations.[7] First, there is the wealth effect of a booming stock market. As stock values rose, the increase in wealth did not require personal saving, and consumption increased. The consumption of luxury goods could be expected to rise because the stock market gains would be concentrated among the few. No doubt some of the gains were plowed back into the stock market, further fueling the boom. Of course, the purchase of durable goods would rise as well, and adherents of the permanent income theory of consumption regard this as a form of saving.[8] This wealth effect might have been at work in the booming 1980s prior to 1987, but would it have been strong enough to account for much of the decline in saving? Probably not, although the issue raises new concerns for equity among households.

Another explanation can be found in the age distribution of the population. The population group that does most of the saving, 45–64, grew slowly during the period while the groups who dissave, the young and the elderly, grew more rapidly. But by itself, the slow demographic changes would not account for the dramatic decline in the saving rate because the population has been exhibiting such shifts for some time. Besides, the saving behavior of the population is not always consistent.[9]

Finally, Friedman mentions tne decline in pension fund contributions by corporations because interest rates rose by enough to fulfill promises made to honor retirees without putting in as much to the funds. Contributions to pension funds are counted as personal saving by the national income accountants so that the data would show a decline in saving even if households saved the normal amount.

But Friedman shows that personal saving had begun to decline even when pension contributions were rising.[10] So, again, some of the source of the decline in personal saving can be identified but not enough to account for the observed shortfall.

It follows that households did not respond to the saving incentives to the extent predicted by the administration. Summers and Carroll conclude that the low national saving rate "is traceable to combination of federal deficits and a continuation of a long-term downward trend in private and personal saving. . . . the most reliable way for the federal government to increase national saving is to reduce its own borrowing."[11] Consumption, not saving, was stimulated by the administration's policies.

INVESTMENT

Apparently, investment in the Reagan years did not depart significantly from historical averages. Despite all attempts to encourage investment, either through tax cuts or through the reversal of past expectations, the administration was not successful in increasing the proportion of national output that is devoted to investment spending. Recall that one of the aims of the economic plan was to create a climate in which businessmen would be encouraged to invest because of the new economic regime; expectations would be changed to match the favorable economic forecasts for the future. Obviously, whatever favorable expectations were developed did not result in comparable investment motivations because the response was unimpressive.

It would be possible to end the discussion about investment spending here with the observation that the administration's efforts failed to influence this important variable. However, total investment spending conceals a much more significant trend: the disturbing composition of investment. Table 8.3 gives a quick summary of the composition of investment spending in the latter part of the Reagan years. The early recession years of 1981–82 are omitted because they could distort the analysis, and only the recovery years from 1984 are considered, allowing for a possible lag in the response of investment in a consumption-led recovery. Only some general trends are wanted here anyway, and no great harm is likely if we concentrate on the years when the administration's economic program would have taken hold.

In Table 8.3, total private fixed (nonresidential) investment is first separated into structures and equipment. As is readily seen, the structures component declined steadily, reaching only 25% of fixed investment in 1988 while producers durable equipment rose steadily to 75% of the total. Industrial structures remained fairly even, but investment in farm and mining structures fell dramatically. In the case of mining, the decline is about 47% in just 4 years, with most of the decline accounted for by the fall in petroleum investment of about 56%. No doubt the decline in the profitability of oil production and refining can explain this observation.

Table 8.3
Composition of Private Real Investment (percent)

Item	1984	1985	1986	1987	1988
Total Fixed					
Nonres Investment	100.0	100.0	100.0	100.0	100.0
Nonresidential					
Structures	33.8	33.0	29.7	27.3	25.1
Bldgs. ex farms	51.8	57.3	61.2	63.2	64.5
Industrial	8.8	10.0	9.8	9.9	10.5
Other	43.0	47.3	51.4	53.3	54.0
Utilities	17.0	16.8	19.8	18.2	17.8
Farm	2.0	1.3	1.4	1.5	1.3
Mining	27.7	23.5	15.9	15.0	14.7
Other	1.3	1.9	1.8	2.2	1.7
Producers Durable					
Equipment	66.2	67.0	70.3	72.7	74.9
Information	35.7	39.2	41.7	43.9	44.5
Industrial	22.2	21.3	20.2	19.1	19.1
Transport	21.1	20.2	19.4	18.7	18.8
Other	21.4	19.8	19.1	18.9	18.1

Source: Department of Commerce, Survey of Current Business,
various years.   Data compiled from national income accounts.

Before turning to the equipment component of fixed investment, it may be useful to compare the experience in the Carter years. Averages over the period 1977–80 reveal that no such trends are observable in the composition of structures. Structures accounted for about 29% and equipment 71% of fixed investment. Aside from the steady decline in farm structures (about 30% over the period), there are no real discernible trends to be found.

Returning to Table 8.3 for a look at producers durable equipment, it is clear that the proportion of fixed investment devoted to equipment rose over the period, by 13%. It is equally evident that the major increase—25% of equipment investment—occurred in the area of information processing and related equipment, mainly computers and office equipment. The remaining elements of producers durable equipment expenditures declined over the period. As a proportion of total equipment, industrial equipment fell 14%, transportation equipment fell 11%, and all others fell by 15%. Without examining the data in detail, it is striking that the information processing component increased so dramatically as to swamp in importance the increases in other areas so that its proportion of total equipment actually rose over the period.

Comparing the Carter years reveals that information processing and related equipment and communication equipment spending rose dramatically in those years as well—by over 67% for information processing and over 55% for communication equipment. The trend toward an information society began in the 1970s, and continued in the 1980s. Transportation equipment spending fell by

25%, mainly in autos and trucks. Energy problems could easily account for this decline. Other elements of equipment spending did not show any noticeable trends in the Carter years.

This same interesting development about information processing was observed by Barry Bosworth in an early study in which he concluded: "There is room for doubt about the role of the 1981–82 tax reduction in the recovery of business investment in 1983–84. Total investment has increased substantially . . . [but] more than 90 percent of the growth in business investment since 1979 is due to the rise in outlays for office equipment, business automobiles, and commercial structures." [12] In the latter years of the Reagan administration, the situation was essentially the same. Investment in shopping malls and office buildings creates temporary jobs but not the more desirable wealth-producing ones. As we will see, the expansion in these investment areas was excessive, leading to further problems of excess capacity and defaulting bank loans that seriously damaged the nation's banking system.

The increase in investment spending would be even more worrisome if the investment in computers and some furniture and related items for home use (counted as business use) were to be subtracted from the total. The point is that this type of investment is not the job-creating kind. Processing information more efficiently is laudable, but the productive capacity of the nation is hardly enhanced if only information is processed better. Jobs in the production of wealth-creating goods was the goal of the administration; it was to restore the good, productive jobs that the administration sought. Clearly, if the composition of investment is any guide, it did not succeed. It is imperative, then, to examine the source of the job creation in the period. The administration boasted of having created 17 million jobs in its two terms. Where and what were they?

EMPLOYMENT GAINS

The case for the employment gains made in the 1980s was made by the Council of Economic Advisors in its *Economic Report of the President, 1988.* It claimed that 15 million jobs were created since the upswing in the economy starting in 1982. Furthermore, the unemployment rate fell by 4.9 percentage points over the period. [13] Both of these claims are true, although measuring the decline in the unemployment rate from the end of the recession of 1981–82 is somewhat misleading. Still, the unemployment rate did decrease in the 1980s from 7.1% in 1980 to 5.5% in 1988.

Moreover, the number of jobs created in the period is significant, particularly when compared with the record of western Europe where little job growth took place. The economy was clearly responding and exhibiting flexibility during this long period of economic expansion. The adaptability of the U.S. economy to changing economic conditions is remarkable in many respects and should be acknowledged as one of its more commendable features. Similar flexibility has been observed in the past when, for example, women entered the labor force in increasing numbers without causing unsurmountable problems.

The administration was not content to relate these gains but felt compelled to answer its critics by making more extravagant claims. It claimed that all groups shared in the employment gains—minorities, Hispanics, youth—and all regions as well. "These gains demonstrate the principle that economic growth benefits all groups who participate in the economic system," it declared. The report continued: "Employment gains during the current expansion have been largest in higher paying occupations. Nearly two-thirds of the new employment growth has been in managerial, professional, technical, sales, or precision production occupations. . . . It has been less vigorous in lower paying, low skilled occupations and in part-time work." [14]

Reading these quotes, one would get the impression that the recovery was extremely beneficial because it created mainly the better paying jobs and apparently narrowed the inequality among workers. Both of these claims are misleading. First, the growth in the high paying jobs occurred from a low base and will not employ a very large number of people. The growth in lower paying jobs will appear much smaller because the base was large to begin with, and more important, more people will be employed in these jobs.

Ryscavage and Henle found just the opposite as they concluded "during the 1980s earnings inequality had accelerated among male and female full-time, year-round workers and had increased among whites, black men, Hispanics, and workers in various occupations and industries." [15] Because the inequality among workers increased in the decade, the gains from the reduction in unemployment and from job creation cannot be as widespread or as evenly distributed as the administration claimed. Inequalities in labor income are affected by both supply- and demand-side factors and, surprisingly, are not as readily explainable as might be imagined. In a period of plentiful labor while firms were downsizing and streamlining, many responses affect the labor market: wage concessions, two-tier wage structures, givebacks of escalator clauses, increases in part-time work, greater subcontracting to smaller firms, and so on. Added to these developments, the size of the labor force grew by some 21.5 million in the decade and, equally important, the participation of women in the labor force grew from 51 to 57%.

Clearly, much study remains to be done concerning the labor market trends in this period and the growing inequalities among workers. One thing is likely, the administration's boasting of the improved conditions of all components of the labor force was premature and inappropriate. [16]

One of the major reasons given for the observed inequalities in the wage and salary structure is the shift from manufacturing (or other high-paying) jobs into service occupations (or low-paying jobs). Without entering into the debate about the deindustrialization of the U.S. economy, it is still instructive to examine the changing structure of U.S. jobs. Table 8.4 shows the employment changes in selected industries in the period 1979 to 1989.

Table 8.4

Employment Change in Selected Industries from 1979 to 1989

Industry	Employment Change (in Thous)	Industry Employ (%)[a]	Avg. Hourly Earnings[b]
Total Private	16,978.0	83.7	9.66
Goods Producing	-827.0	23.6	
Mining	-236.0	0.7	13.25
Bituminous Coal	-116.3		
Construction	837.0	4.9	13.52
Heavy Construct	-128.9		13.42
Special Trade Contract	847.3		14.30
Manufacturing	-1428.0	18.1	10.39
Durable Goods	-1224.0		11.19
Primary Metals	-471.4		12.59
Fab Metals	-272.4		10.72
Machinery, ex. elect	-339.3		11.62
Nondurables	-204.0		9.96
Textile mfg	-159.0		7.85
Apparel	-212.8		6.45
Printing and publ.	371.8		11.09
Service Producing	19,584.0	76.4	
Transportation	569.0	5.3	12.61
Railroad	-261.5		16.28
Trucking and Warehouse	320.5		11.70
Air transportation	253.6		
Wholesale Trade	1,030.0	5.7	10.39
Retail Trade	4,586.0	18.0	6.53
Food Stores	972.7		7.24
Auto dealers & service	344.8		8.69
Eating and Drinking Places	1,856.8		4.88
Misc Retail	636.0		6.86
Finance, Insur. & Real Estate	1,839.0	6.3	9.54
Services	9,780.0	24.8	9.39
Hotels & lodging	543.6		6.86
Business Services	2,882.8		9.28
Health Services	2,642.5		10.13
Educ services	539.1		
Social services	655.6		

a. Employment in government, 16.3%, is not included in total.
b. As of December, 1989.
Source: Employment data from U.S. Department of Labor, BLS,
Monthly Labor Review, September, 1990, Tables 1 and 2; Earnings
data from Employment and Earnings, January 1991, Table C-1.

It is one thing to claim, as did the Reagan administration, that it created some 17 million jobs; it is quite another to omit any mention of the type of jobs created. Barry Bluestone and Bennett Harrison maintain that the jobs created are low-paying ones and that the high-paying ones have either disappeared or have been exported abroad.[17] The data in Table 8.4 appear to offer prima facie confirmation of their conclusions.

The economy did indeed create 17 million jobs, but just a glance at the data reveals that the goods-producing sectors lost 827,000 jobs and that these jobs were relatively high-paying ones, paying roughly $13 per hour. The service-producing sector gained 19.6 million jobs, and these jobs paid roughly $9 per hour. In fact, the service sector now accounts for over 76% of all employment in 1989 (up from 70% in 1979) and the goods-producing sector accounts for 24% (down from 30% in 1979).

Looking more closely at the data, the manufacturing sector lost nearly 1-1/2 million jobs, mainly in the durable goods sector where wages averaged between $11 and $12 per hour. The wholesale and retail trade industries gained nearly 5.5 million jobs that paid $5–6 per hour less. Another 5.5 million jobs were created in the business and health services industries where the pay was higher as the job classifications were much broader in these areas. So the jobs created were not the high-paying professional ones that the administration called our attention to in its assertions. Furthermore, of the fastest growing industries between 1979 and 1989 identified by the Department of Labor, all of them are in the service sector; of those industries most rapidly declining, most of them are in the goods-producing industries. Moreover, of the 30 industries adding the most jobs in the period, the overwhelming majority are in the service-producing areas.

Clearly, there is enough evidence here and elsewhere to justify the concern that the U.S. economy is creating the wrong type of jobs. The high-paying, wealth-creating jobs are disappearing and being replaced by lower-paying service type jobs. Although it may be true that as an economy advances, more service type jobs will be demanded, it is also true that an economy cannot prosper on just the service sector. The standard of living of the nation must decline, especially when the productivity of labor is declining as well. The growing inequalities in the wage structure also is exacerbated, posing possible social problems but, more important, problems with effective demand: *Who will buy the output if wages are declining?*

We will address this question, as well as others hinted at, later in the book. For now, we may conclude that the Reagan administration was too sanguine and too boastful in its clamor about the number of jobs created during its tenure. A closer look reveals some troubling trends for the U.S. economy and some problems for future generations.

NOTES

1. *Economic Report of the President, 1983,* 144.

2. *Economic Report of the President, 1984,* 198.

3. *Economic Report of the President, 1987,* 60.

4. *Economic Report of the President, 1989,* 286.

5. *Economic Report of the President, 1987,* 49.

6. Charles W. Bischoff, Edward C. Kokkelenberg, and Ralph A. Terregrossa, "Tax Policy and Business Fixed Investment during the Reagan Era," in *The Economic Legacy of the Reagan Years,* eds. Anandi P. Sahu and Ronald L. Tracy (New York: Praeger, 1991), 21–39. The authors provide tests of several leading investment theories, but even at best the responsiveness of investment to tax policies is still weak. As Kevin J. Murphy, who commented on this article, put it, "Reagan was not really a supply-sider with respect to capital" (41).

7. Why households save has been the subject of intensive research in recent years. Much remains to be done, however, before a full understanding is possible. Even the definition of saving is not as straightforward as one might think. The national income accounting definition used here, for instance, ignores capital gains and treats all consumption goods as final goods, a procedure that fails to consider that households may save in the form of durable goods, and so on. By all accounts and most definitions, however, the saving rate has declined, and so for the purposes of this chapter, simplicity was selected over technicalities. For those interested in the complex issue of saving in the United States, two books cover the main issues and should be consulted: Laurence J. Kotlikoff, *What Determines Savings?,* (Cambridge, MA: The MIT Press, 1989); and F. Gerald Adams and Susan M. Wachter, eds., *Saving and Capital Formation* (Lexington, MA: Lexington Books, 1986).

8. For instance, see William A. Niskanen, *Reaganomics* (New York: Oxford University Press, 1988), 254.

9. See Lawrence Summers and Chris Carroll, "Why is the U.S. National Saving Rate So Low," *Brookings Papers on Economic Activity* 2 (1987): 607–635. Benjamin M. Friedman, after citing this article, concluded that "at best, age-based differences in saving behavior are too small to have reduced saving by much." *Day of Reckoning* (New York: Brown Brothers Harriman, 1988), 259.

10. Benjamin Friedman, *Day of Reckoning,* 258–259.

11. Lawrence Summers and Chris Carroll, "Why is the U.S. National Saving Rate So Low," 608.

12. Barry P. Bosworth, "Taxes and the Investment Recovery," *Brookings Papers on Economic Activity,* 1 (1985): 1–38.

13. *Economic Report of the President, 1988,* 58.

14. Ibid. 60–61.

15. Paul Ryscavage and Peter Henle, "Earnings Inequality Accelerates in the 1980s," in U. S. Department of Commerce, BLS, *Monthly Labor Review* 113(December 1990): 3–16. The quote is from pages 13–14. For a longer historical view of inequality in wages and salaries, see W. Norton Grubb and Robert H. Wilson, "Sources of Increasing Inequality in Wages and Salaries, 1960–1980," U.S. Department of Commerce, BLS, *Monthly Labor Review* 112(April 1989): 3–11. Although outside the time period of this book, some of their conclusions are worth reporting. They found that inequality

in wages and salaries had increased in the period 1960–80. Although this trend is true for men, it is not true for women; moreover, regional shifts within the United States do not explain very much of the observed inequalities. However, sectoral shifts from manufacturing to service industries did affect overall inequality among workers. This trend, as we will see, continued in the Reagan years, and higher-paying jobs were lost to lower-paying ones, despite the administration's claim to the contrary. One interesting finding, not explained by the authors, was that inequality increased *within* sectors as well as between them.

16. Interested readers in some of the preliminary results and the problems involved in these issues might well consult, Gary Burtless, ed., *A Future of Lousy Jobs?: the Changing Structure of U.S. Wages* (Washington, DC: The Brookings Institution, 1990).

17. See their testimony before the Joint Economic Committee, *The Great American Job Machine: the Proliferation of Low-Wage Employment in the U.S. Economy*, a study prepared for the Joint Economic Committee, December 1986.

Part III

The Legacy

Chapter 9

The Legacy of Reaganomics

In this book, it may be too soon to speak of legacies; more hindsight is needed before making summary judgments about the lasting effects of the Reagan administrations. Still, some preliminary assessments are irresistible, particularly in regard to the short-run effects, some of which are readily observable. Final judgments will have to await the verdicts of history, of course, with the benefits conferred by hindsight. Yet, future historians may well benefit from the early assessments of contemporary ones so that failure to venture into the difficult area of appraisal could be considered unnecessarily evasive. Whatever the pitfalls, Part III is devoted to early judgments and to whatever insights they may provide. Wherever possible the analysis will be divided into short-run and long-run legacies.

ON GOVERNMENT IN THE ECONOMY

It is ironic that the Reagan administrations that disavowed the government as a solver of problems, as a sector capable of leading the nation in its development, and as a partner in the restoration of the belief in progress should accomplish just the opposite. Reagan restored faith in government while proclaiming constantly that government was the problem. The strong, decisive, and perennially optimistic president was able to resurrect the confidence in the presidency from the levels of disrespect and distrust that had been growing since President Johnson.

Make no mistake, the Reagan administrations attempted to reduce the role of government when they thought it feasible, and continually paid lip service to the conservative principles of limited government. Cited as the most ideological administrations, they did not live up to the advance billings. These were conservatives who talked of a laissez-faire government but who continually intervened into the economy for the benefit of their clients; these were conservatives who talked of free trade but who concocted intervention schemes that made free trade a mockery. It became quite clear that the administrations were willing, even anxious, to intervene and use government's power to aid their special constituents whenever they needed help. However, as we will see, when nonclients' interests were involved, they reverted to their ideological principles of limited government, which included self-reliance as a key feature.

So the special quotas for steel and autos, the relationships with the defense contractors, the overlooking of the emerging problems in the banking sector, the attempts to commercialize public lands, the awarding of special deals with real estate friends, and so on through the dreary list of the subversion of government for the benefit of the few. Free markets and open competition were slogans for the fourth of July, not principles to be followed in practice.

Of course, the people attracted to government service in conservative administrations are not likely to have great faith in or devotion to the tasks to which they were assigned. Hence, they used government for their own purposes or helped their friends do so. The number of officials indicted or convicted of illegal activities (over 140) in these administrations is startling, far surpassing anything of its kind in the nation's history.

Republicans were known to represent business interests in the past, but Reagan was able to build a coalition of groups that went beyond this caricature. By appealing to family values, latent bigotry, anticommunism hysteria, religious principles, and by speaking the language of the common person, he was able to garner support from groups previously alienated or ignored by the mainstream parties. Consequently, he was able to win the elections but was unable to govern without reverting to the former biases of the Republican party—favoring business and financial interests. The family and social values that Reagan espoused in public, but was not particularly attached to in private, helped keep the disenchanted in line, but after he was gone from office, and his personal magnetism with it, this coalition would begin to disintegrate.

Thus, in the short run, a new coalition was forged but, lacking a dynamic leader, is not likely to last far into the future. Mr. Reagan was unwilling, and perhaps unable, to take the time necessary to make the coalition a permanent one. Building a lasting organization of the groups brought into the political process would have taken enormous energy and a genuine commitment, neither of which Reagan possessed. This matter, however, is best left to the political scientists for analysis. It is time we returned to the economic aspects of government in the economy.

FISCAL POLICY—GOVERNMENT SPENDING

Fiscal policy has been downgraded since the initial failure to employ it properly during the Vietnam war experience.[1] The failure to increase taxes then and the inability to reduce expenditures since has gradually eroded the confidence in fiscal policy as a useful instrument of government intervention. The Reagan administrations have exacerbated the problems of fiscal policy to the point where it is nearly obsolete. Perhaps because it has been identified with liberalism, perhaps because it was convenient to identify the opposition with the "tax and spend" label, or perhaps to conform to the conservative ideology, the Reagan administrations downplayed the role of fiscal policy in its rhetoric (except to condemn it) and nearly destroyed it as a result of its actual policies. (The

Clinton administration, just assuming office as this is written, may well reverse the trend.)

Looking first at the expenditure side, it is easy to compare the promises made with the results. Reagan took office promising to reduce the government's role in the economy. It was part of "government is the problem" perception that was an integral component of his philosophical base. By any measure, the result was the opposite. For example, real federal government spending as a percentage of GNP was 7.7% in 1980 and was 8.2% in 1988. Earlier data in Chapter 5 confirm this result; government spending did not fall, it rose.

All this is quite familiar by now; however, as discussed earlier, the composition of government spending changed. The economy was militarized in the 1980s, as spending on national defense rose from 5.4% of GNP in 1980 to 6.5% in 1988. In the Reagan years, $1.9 trillion was spent on national defense. In the short run, such huge expenditures helped produce record budget deficits and, no doubt, helped stimulate the economies of many states that rely on defense dollars. Moreover, the national economy was likely a beneficiary of defense spending. Without it, the economy would not have experienced even the growth that it did in this period.

Our concern here is with the effects of such data, not the recitation of them. One effect that can only be mentioned here is the role played by the increase in the U.S. national defense spending in the collapse of the USSR. The Soviet Union's economy simply could not match the increase in defense spending and was forced to withdraw from the arms race. The Soviet economy, already functioning poorly, was in no condition to spend more on defense or maintain an empire without seriously risking internal strife that would threaten the government and the existence of the type of economy it invented. Was the Reagan military buildup responsible for the collapse or was the economy already tottering? Or was the existence of a pragmatic leader, such as Gorbachev, a necessary condition for the relaxation of hostility and the cold war?

Others will have to answer these questions, as well as the charge that the weapons created by the United States did not even have to work—all that was necessary was to outspend the Soviets or indicate a willingness to do so. Actual defense capability was a secondary consideration.

The longer-run effect of militarization on the economy is what happens to the economy that becomes so dependent on defense spending? If the defense spending works as planned and the enemy is vanquished, additional spending becomes difficult to justify. What happens when an empire, built up at a heavy cost of resources, is no longer needed and becomes superfluous? This is the long-run legacy of the militarization of the economy, and the problems created by it may prove intractable in the short-run and formidable in the long-run. An economy that has transferred resources to the demands of national defense will have difficulty reversing the flow; there is no shortage of consumer goods to satisfy nor are investors stymied for lack of materials for producer goods. Rebuilding the infrastructure, improving education, investing in housing, creating an industrial policy, and so on are possibilities for using some of the funds released from defense spending, but the philosophy of recent administrations conflicts with such endeavors, leaving little hope that such avenues will be pursued.

Yet, if defense spending is reduced drastically in the face of obsolescence and defense establishments are closed, millions will lose employment, and many states will experience economic hardships for which they are unprepared. A faltering national economy will be in no position to help. Many military people and defense contractors and workers will find their services redundant, and they will be forced to return to the civilian sector. Atomic physicists may have options, but what of minorities who sought a military career for want of opportunity who now find themselves competing for scarce jobs in an economy not particularly anxious for their return.

Indeed, an economy so heavily dependent on defense spending will face many such problems. The tragedy is that such economies never prepare for the day when such expenditures will be unnecessary. Everyone enjoys the benefits of defense-aided booms, but no one is prepared for the pain of retrenchment. But to continue defense spending without a conceivable enemy will be seen as wasteful, particularly when so many domestic problems remain unsolved; to reduce spending will invite economic decline, but transfers of funds to those domestic programs will be resisted due to ideological and bureaucratic concerns. In the end, the failure to prepare for such an eventuality will condemn the nation to a long period of painful readjustment that can only be curtailed by a leader of foresight and courage willing to shed past concepts of national defense and reestablish a different system of priorities.

To see what a difficult task that is, let us consider the other elements of government spending in the 1980s. When campaigning for office, Reagan vowed to reduce waste in government, meaning the reduction in the bureaucracy as a first approximation; after taking office, waste took on a broader meaning, that is, reducing unneeded social programs. His aim was to provide for the "truly needy" by providing a "safety net" that included some core social programs while eliminating the unnecessary ones. The safety net included those programs that were not means tested such as the basic retirement program of Social Security, unemployment compensation, veterans' programs, aid (cash) to dependent families, and some payments to the elderly poor. All other social programs were vulnerable to elimination.

In September 1981, Stockman began to propose deep cuts in the Great Society programs such as subsidized housing, urban development, education grants, student aid, Head Start, Jobs Corp, health, job training, and social service grants. He declared quite simply: "Given where we are on taxes, defense, and Social Security, these programs are going to be eliminated in next year's budget." [2] I think he spoke for the majority of Reagan supporters, in and out of government, when he declared, "The existing welfare programs are family-destroyers. They subsidize a culture of poverty, dependency, and social irresponsibility." [3] This conservative thought is a far cry from the liberal responses in the 1960s and even far removed from the previous Nixon–Ford Republican administrations that expanded social programs, a fact that Stockman bemoaned.

Of course, such sentiments ran counter to the prevailing public sentiment on social programs, and the administration did not receive a mandate to dismantle them. In fact, the Great Society programs enjoyed wide public and congressional support as poll after poll revealed; the public simply did not enjoy paying for them, and Congress was less than anxious to disclose the costs.

Scholars have been engaged in lengthy debates over the efficacy of government-sponsored social programs, and there is no room to address the issues here for it would take us far afield from the purpose of this chapter. [4] However, only Reagan conservatives would endorse the foregoing statement of David Stockman; others would be more cautious in their assessments.

As might be expected, Congress was among the latter, and it did not go along with the Reagan cuts in social programs as it tried to preserve as many as possible from the budget cutters. Still, the administration was able to secure reductions in many social programs as Congress was put on the defensive in view of the massive budget deficits. Table 9.1 presents the evidence.

Looking first at the means tested programs (based on income), it is clear that the administration was able to slow the growth of these programs. These are the programs that affect the lower strata of the population, the ones loosely identified with "welfare" payments. Obviously, these programs are the ones that reach out to the poor in the nation; these are also the ones that are most controversial. Still, the cuts seem unnecessarily cruel, especially when combined with the increase in taxes on the lower income groups. Most of the program's recipients do not vote, however, and remain relatively voiceless. Who will defend programs that are costly and debatable in their effects? Surely not the Reagan administrations that were willing to eliminate them without performing the necessary cost–benefit analyses. (Stockman claimed to have done so before Congress, but that was impossible in the time allotted for the task.)

The data in Table 9.1 reveal that the growth of means tested programs were slowed in nearly all programs. Comparing the growth rates with the Carter years, one finds that Medicare spending fell from an annual rate of 5.4% to 3.5%, food stamps from 5.3% to −3.1%, child nutrition from 3.9% to −2.0%, student loans from 52.9% to −2.6% and eventually to zero, and so on. Note the decline in real AFDC ("welfare"), veteran's pensions, and SSI (Supplemental Security Insurance) even before the Reagan cuts; such programs increased in nominal terms, but when corrected for inflation, the benefits were declining. Indeed, all of these programs were failing to keep up with inflation, and, thus, the recipients were falling behind. These trends continued into the Reagan administrations, exacerbating the problem.

Especially noteworthy is the SSI program designed to aid those particularly in need—the aged, blind, and disabled. The Reagan administration reviewed

Table 9.1

Average Annual Growth Rates for Major Entitlement and Mandatory Spending Programs (adjusted for inflation and population growth)

	1975–1988	1975–1981	1981–1987	1981–1987[a]
Means tested programs:				
Medicaid	4.6	5.4	3.5	4.6
Food stamps	1.0	5.3	-3.1	-2.4
SSI	0.2	-3.0	2.3	4.5
AFDC and CSE	-1.3	-1.9	-0.6	-1.5
Veteran's pensions	-4.1	-4.0	-4.6	-2.5
Child nutrition	1.0	3.9	-2.0	-1.1
Guar student loans	20.4	52.9	-2.6	0.0
Other	17.3	29.5	0.4	0.4
Total Means tested programs	1.8	2.8	0.3	1.1
Nonmeans tested programs:				
Social Security	2.5	3.3	1.9	0.8
Medicare	7.1	8.4	6.5	5.3
Other retirement/disability:				
Federal civilian	4.2	5.7	1.6	0.5
Military	1.6	3.5	0.0	-1.2
Other	-3.6	-1.5	-4.6	-5.7
Unemployment compensation	-6.4	-3.8	-5.6	-3.0
Other programs:				
Veterans' benefits	-4.1	-6.6	-3.4	-4.6
Farm price supports	16.3	21.7	26.9	26.9
Gen revenue sharing	-100.0	-12.0	-100.0	-100.0
Social services	-4.1	-4.7	-3.8	-3.8
Other	5.0	0.6	-0.3	-0.3
Total nonmeans tested	2.0	2.2	2.1	2.1

a. Adjusted for population growth specific to each program.
Source: Adapted from Committee on Ways and Means, U.S. House of Representatives, Background Material and Data on Programs within the Jurisdiction of the Committee on Ways and Means, March 15, 1989, 1227.

the records (not the people involved) and determined that many recipients were unqualified for the program. It arbitrarily proceeded to strip many of them of benefits. The courts overturned most of these cases in favor of the recipient. Many of these reversals, however, were ignored by the Social Security Administration. In 1992, federal officials agreed to reopen thousands of such cases, and large awards are expected. Perhaps a quote from one court decision will suffice to indicate the seriousness of the administration's conduct: ''Claimants who lose or are denied benefits face foreclosure proceedings on their homes, suffer utility cutoffs and find it difficult to purchase food. They go without medication and doctors' care; they lose their medical insurance. They even die from the very disabilities the agency denies they have."[5] Note that in Table 9.1 the ironic result is that growth rates for SSI, adjusted for population changes, appear to increase in the Reagan years. Of course, if the population served by the program is slashed by arbitrary agency decisions, then the growth rate for the remainder will grow!

Guaranteed student loans were reduced by the administration and did not grow at all if the program is adjusted for population changes in this category. The tightening up of requirements for a guaranteed loan, together with the reduction in outright grants, forced many students to go heavily into debt for those able to continue and forced many to forego an education for those who could not manage the burden, the poor and minorities. Together with Reagan's desire to eliminate the Department of Education, such restrictions on higher education seekers surely runs counter to the need for a highly skilled labor force to meet the requirements of the technical revolution and to meet the challenge of global competition.

Among some of the other social programs, unemployment compensation fell during the Reagan years from past experience, as did other social services. In addition, general revenue sharing was eliminated in Reagan's ill-fated attempt to form a "new federalism." The first administration managed to consolidate a large number of categorical grants (for specific purposes such as community development) into 10 block grants in which the states and localities were free to determine how to spend the funds. Later, the administration sought to continue the restructuring of grants to the states by agreeing to assume the burden of the Medicaid program in return for the states' assumption of the AFDC and food stamp programs as well as some 40 other programs; the federal government would provide a fund of $28 billion over 4 years that the states could claim until the funds ran out. Needless to say, the states rejected this "opportunity" to assume these responsibilities, preferring block grants and recognizing that these programs would call for tax increases eventually.

The administration failed to solve the farm problem as shown by the continued growth of farm price supports. Its policy of payment in kind (PIK) (from crops in storage) instead of cash payments failed miserably, and there was no real alternative to past practices. Thus, although Reagan economists preferred the free-market approach to the farm problem, the amounts spent on price supports rose instead of being phased out.

Looking over the entire set of programs, it is clear that the growth of means tested programs fell, whereas the growth of nonmeans tested programs remained constant. Because the means tested programs affect mainly the poor and disabled, the conclusion that any savings made in social program costs came at the expense of the most disadvantaged members of the society is inescapable. To attempt to reduce the size of government at the expense of those who look to it for support does not square with many people's perception of social justice. Other, more powerful constituencies were able to protect themselves from arbitrary budget-based decisions. These are generalizations, of course, but others have documented the consequences of these policy actions.[6]

The implications of these spending patterns will become evident when we review some of the societal divisions created by them. For now, it is possible to suggest that such reductions in government expenditures hurt those at the bottom of the income distribution and were bound to have repercussions on the society as a whole. Not only were the distributions of income and wealth adversely affected, but the net result was a further polarization of the society into white versus black, cities versus suburbs, male versus female, and, in general, the haves versus the have-nots. In 1992, such divisions would erupt in Los Angeles, leaving many to ask Why? Part of the answer can be found in the polarization caused by government indifference in the 1980s.

FISCAL POLICY—TAXATION

The results of the Reagan administrations' tax policies have already been reviewed in Chapter 5. Most of the studies of their effects have concluded that most of the tax cuts benefited upper income groups while those at the bottom received little in the way of tax relief. This is true of the 1981 tax cuts, but in the 1986 tax legislation, many at the bottom were excluded from taxation; however at the same time, some of the progressivity of the tax code was lost in the reduction in the number of tax rates. The end result was some tax reform, some simplification of the tax code, and some tax reductions.

Yet, the Reagan tax policies are perceived as unfair, and there is much evidence to support that contention. Despite efforts to refute that claim, and despite the fact that much discussion has been evoked over the issue, the consensus is growing that the tax changes in the 1980s favored the upper income groups at the expense of those in the middle and bottom.

Putting aside the esoteric studies of the issue, the perception of unfairness will not disappear any time soon. If people think they have been treated unfairly, they are likely to react in ways to redress their grievances. Those in the middle of the income classes have already clamored for relief, and politicians are likely to respond, once more cluttering up the tax code with hasty provisions. Those at the bottom will conclude, once again, that government services the upper classes and ignores or mistreats them. The loss of faith in government as a solver of problems, as a source to look to for support when market based results appear too overwhelming, will surely erode their hopes of advancement and dash their belief in progress.

One seeks in vain to find such data among the myriad of economic statistics collected, charted, and analyzed. A society, it is said, is ultimately judged by how it treats its most disadvantaged members. By such a standard, the Reagan administrations would receive a failing grade. Why the disregard of the most disadvantaged? In the words of one of Reagan's harshest critics, "Rich Americans rent politicians. Middle Americans vote. Poor Americans remain home on election day. The political payoffs shovel whipped cream to the wealthy, pastry to families of moderate income, and crumbs to the poor.'' [7]

However intriguing such important questions are, they are not the main issue in this chapter. We are more concerned here with taxation as a tool of fiscal policy, more with stabilization than redistribution. Here too, the Reagan administrations nearly destroyed the use of taxation for purposes other than merely tax relief.

Reagan did not invent tax reductions as a form of relief, but he institutionalized it and made it sound respectable. It is noteworthy that over the past several decades, tax cuts have been made repeatedly, whereas tax increases were seldom utilized. It all started with the Kennedy/Johnson tax cuts in 1964 when the government opted for tax reductions instead of increases in public spending to stimulate a stagnating economy. Galbraith warned with astonishing prescience that once conservatives grew accustomed to tax reductions, they would forever favor them over government expenditures whenever the choice was possible. He clearly saw one of the basic shortcomings of Keynesian countercyclical policies that others had ignored or denied.

Subsequent tax reductions in the 1970s were used as indirect means of indexing the tax code for inflation. Inflation in the 1970s pushed people into higher tax brackets which precipitated higher tax bills. Tax reductions were used to relieve the social pressures brought to bear on several administrations to adjust the tax burden.

In brief, Galbraith was right and the nation grew accustomed to tax cuts. The Reagan administrations capitalized on this attitude that was reinforced by states and localities placing limits on property taxes—the so-called tax revolt. The growing distrust of government that began with Johnson merely reinforced the belief that government would misuse the funds and that the funds were better off in private hands; fiscal conservatism gained in popularity.

All that was needed by the Reagan administrations was the notion that tax cuts were also self-financing via supply-side predictions, and the nation was easily persuaded to continue along the same route traveled by previous administrations. Simple explanations and convoluted rationalizations may well account for the ready acquiescence where caution might have prevailed, but the fact is that supply-side predictions were appealing, probably because everyone wanted to believe in them. Still, when economic conditions call for a tax increase, such deep-seated biases against taxation will prevent a proper policy from being considered or enacted, and lead to inaction.

Consider the lack of support for tax increases to finance the Vietnam War, the surrender to inflation in the 1970s, and, of course, the failure to address the huge budget deficits in the 1980s. When George Bush ran for the presidency in 1988, he capitalized on the asymmetrical views of taxation with the pledge of ''no new taxes,'' and the nation responded in predictable ways. How many politicians are willing to propose a platform that calls for increases in taxes—how many votes can he or she count on? One does not win votes by working in the national interest, no matter how appropriate.

Of course, tax increases have occasionally been enacted, one, in fact, in 1982. But this tax measure was designed to correct the excesses in the 1981 tax act, particularly in the reversal of tax provisions for business that were simply outrageous. Tax revenues increased but that was not the aim; the administration responded to heavy criticism and was forced to retreat. Tax increases in 1986 on businesses were designed to make the measure revenue neutral. But the reduction in taxes for individuals was paid for by increasing taxes on business that would discourage investment by decreasing depreciation deductions and eliminating the investment tax credit. Clearly, tax measures were being driven by their affects on revenues not on economic merits or repercussions.

Thus, we find that despite being one of the least taxed nations among advanced economies, Americans still consider themselves overtaxed. In fact, among the 20 most advanced countries in the world, the United States ranked 11th in terms of total tax revenues as a percent of GDP (Gross Domestic Product) in 1955, 14th in 1980, 17th in 1984, and 16th in 1988 (using GNP data). Of the 18 countries for which data are available, only Japan and Switzerland collected less revenue. Of course, these numbers should not be taken as conclusive in regard to relative tax burdens, but they do indicate in a crude way that U.S. residents are not terribly overburdened to the extent often stated.

However, thanks to the Reagan administrations and other politicians who promoted tax cuts, such convictions are now part of the conventional wisdom; thanks to these same politicians, many of whom stressed the waste in government operations, asking for tax increases is likely to be strongly resisted precisely because people feel overtaxed already. U.S. residents simply do not connect taxes paid with what they receive from government; they see only the necessity for self-denial and sacrifice. It is curious that a society that demands so much from the public sector should not recognize its reliance on government and be so unwilling to pay for the services for which it constantly expresses the need.

What this means is that one element of fiscal policy has been seriously undermined. Cutting taxes will continue to be popular, as always, whereas raising them will be strongly resisted and nearly impossible to obtain. No doubt future tax increases will occur, but they will be subject to so much debate that timely actions will be even more improbable than they are now. A sense of crisis will be crucial to secure prompt action and meaningful changes to the tax structure.

BUDGET DEFICITS

It used to be that conservative Republicans decried budget deficits as the cause of inflation, high interest rates, crowding out of private investment, burdening future generations, damaging to international trade, and so on. Liberal Democrats, on the other hand, were accustomed to downgrading the significance of budget deficits as they denied the importance of the foregoing list of evils. All that changed in the 1980s, as both sides hurried to switch sides and select the opposite posture.

Ronald Reagan had always been a staunch antideficit politician. Promising a balanced budget after assuming office, he launched into one of his favorite themes in his inaugural address: "For decades we have piled deficit upon deficit, mortgaging our future and our children's future for the temporary convenience of the present. To continue this long trend is to guarantee tremendous social, cultural, political, and economic upheavals." To repeat such rhetoric now seems almost satirical given that his administrations produced greater budget deficits than all previous administrations combined.

But the upheavals predicted by Reagan have not occurred yet, nor are they likely to. The huge deficits did teach us some lessons: Deficits do not cause inflation as previously thought by conservatives; they do not necessarily cause high interest rates; monetary policy caused them in this period; if eventually deficits do cause higher interest rates, as Martin Feldstein concluded and was fired as chair of the CEA for so thinking, then capital will be attracted to this country, driving up the value of the dollar and hurting U.S. exports; they do not cause crowding out, particularly in a period of slack; the deficits were actually the cause of the expansion that occurred following the deep recession[8]; the burdening of future generations may be worse than previously thought now that much of the debt is held by foreigners.

The problem with the debate over the economic effects of the budget deficit is not that all the statements in the previous paragraph are undisputed, indeed some are still controversial, but that the deficits came to be viewed as relatively harmless. Because many of the predicted results of the deficit had not been realized, some came to the conclusion that there was no need to worry. Having put aside their prior fears, Republicans found solace in such reasoning. So they could ignore the high real interest rates and their relations with the overvalued dollar, and the foreign trade deficit. They could ignore the interest costs of the national debt; in 1981, interest costs were $69 billion or 10.1% of federal outlays, in 1988, they were over $151 billion or 14.3%, more than was spent on all social programs combined! What was saved by cutting social programs was now being used to cover interest costs—transfers of income to higher income groups at the expense of the lower income groups.

Meanwhile, the Democrats began to voice increasing concerns that the huge deficits were hurting the recovery and redistributing income. Furthermore, the deficits were preventing the introduction of new programs or getting in the way of funding the old ones. What they did not wish to entertain was the notion that Reagan, following the advice of Milton Friedman, was quite aware of their frustration; cut taxes first, and reductions in government spending will follow. (The old conservative Republican view was the opposite—cut spending first, then cut taxes). Here is Reagan in his first speech to the nation: "There were always those who told us that taxes couldn't be cut until spending was reduced. Well, you know, we can lecture our children about extravagance until we run out of voice and breath. Or we can cure their extravagance by simply reducing their allowance."

So the concern about deficits and the drive for a balanced budget nearly vanished from administration concerns. Of course, there was support for a balanced budget amendment to the constitution, and the line item veto power appeared in speeches from time to time, but real concern about budget deficits and how to remedy them disappeared from top priority matters. If deficits appeared to be harmless, why worry about them?

It was the Democrats who began to worry. Senator Moynihan (D., NY) probably spoke for many when he said

The Reagan administration came to office with, at most, a marginal interest in balancing the budget—contrary to rhetoric, there was no great budget problem at the time—but with a real interest in dismantling a fair amount of social legislation of the preceding fifty years. The strategy was to induce a deficit and use that as grounds for the dismantling.[9]

There is certainly enough suspicion to make Moynihan's statement acceptable, and evidence is available and consistent with the claim. David Stockman's description of the budget process in the early years lends credence to the claim that one of the major aims was to reverse years of social legislation as quickly as possible. This aim would hardly be alien to a conservative administration. The problem with Moynihan's thesis is that the administration did not act in concert on the budget issue. True, the administration did attract budget-balancers to Washington, but it also invited monetarists and supply-siders. These groups were not committed to balancing the budget; they had their own agendas to follow. In fact, these groups often acted at cross purposes, as previously pointed out, and their agendas were contradictory, for example, monetarists produced high interest rates, supply-siders wanted more fixed investment that is encouraged by low interest rates.

Still, it is possible to retain Moynihan's assertion as an ultimate aim of the administration, without abandoning their ideological desire to achieve a balanced budget. The administrations often paid lip service to many conservative beliefs, so it is possible that a balanced budget was just one more item to be included to placate Reagan.

Economists were not helpful either. Many of them shared the belief in a balanced budget and were anxious to press for one, even if a constitutional amendment was necessary. On the other hand, economists like Robert Eisner and Robert Heilbroner were demonstrating that concern over budget deficits was misplaced. They claimed that if the deficits were measured correctly, for example, in real terms for Eisner and eliminating capital items for Heilbroner, the real deficit would be reduced and appear to be in manageable proportions.[10]

Such conclusions served to complicate arguments over deficits and permit politicians to choose whichever side they needed to support whatever actions they were advocating. Combined with the Gramm–Rudman fanaticism, the pronouncements that deficits were basically harmless, and the measurement fallacies, all public discussions about the deficit degenerated into confusion and, of course, inaction.

Our main concern is not with the sociology of group dynamics but with the effects such perceptions had on fiscal policy. Obviously, with large budget deficits, new programs or new approaches will be resisted, and old ones must be perennially justified. But what happens to stabilization policies? Conservatives might respond that stabilization policies are unnecessary or ineffective because the economy is self-regulating and is better left alone. Particularly in the long run, maintain conservative economists, the economy is basically stable and will return to some sort of equilibrium. Without disputing the veracity of that claim, politicians cannot be left alone, and social pressures to "do something" become overwhelming and they do not have time to wait for the long run to arrive.

Under such circumstances, what fiscal response can be made when it might add to the already large budget deficit? It would always be possible for politicians to say that they would like to respond to the economic situation but are prevented from doing so because of the deficit. The result is paralysis. Spending cuts are contentious, and special interest groups are vigilant. Tax changes are asymmetrical with only tax decreases receiving consideration while increases are shunned.

Clearly, huge budget deficits have destroyed rational fiscal policy actions. Politicians will hesitate to use the available fiscal tools and justify inactions because of adverse affects on deficits. Conservative economists can always be quoted who maintain that fiscal policy is ineffective or unnecessary anyway; their theoretical models of rational expectations demonstrate that economic agents anticipate such policy actions and take actions that in the end subvert the public policy. The general public may not appreciate such abstractions, but they are just one more means for politicians to avoid taking action. Of course, events may well force their hands, but by this time the economic situation could have grown worse, requiring much stronger policies than the ones that could have been used earlier.

In brief, fiscal policy has been denigrated by budget deficits, economic theory, and political ideology. The latter two causes are subject to reversals by future administrations and economists; budget deficits, however, will be around for some time and could continue to thwart proper fiscal policies. Along with Moynihan's conclusions, that is some legacy.

NOTES

1. For an enlightening discussion of fiscal policy in this period see, Arthur Okun, *The Political Economy of Prosperity* (New York: W. W. Norton, 1970). See also, An-

thony S. Campagna, *The Economic Consequences of the Vietnam War* (New York: Praeger, 1991).

2. David Stockman, *The Triumph of Politics* (New York: Harper & Row, 1986), 323.

3. Ibid. 406.

4. For example, see the one that inspired the Reagan people, George Gilder, *Wealth and Poverty* (New York: Basic Books, 1981) and another conservative author Charles Murray, *Losing Ground* (New York: Basic Books, 1984). For different views, see Sar A. Levitan's many works, such as *Programs in Aid of the Poor* (Baltimore, MD: Johns Hopkins University Press, 1985); and the very influential book by David T. Ellwood, *Poor Support* (New York: Basic Books, 1988). These are but a few of the many studies on the topic in question.

5. Quoted in Robert Pear, "U.S. to Reconsider Denial of Benefits to Many Disabled," *New York Times,* 19 April 1992, 1. Pear claims that the awards could range from $3000 to $6000 a year for missed benefits for up to four and a half years.

6. Among the many evaluations, see the liberal views of Robert Lekachman, *Visions and Nightmares* (New York: Macmillan, 1987); also see the conservative view from Kevin Phillips, *The Politics of Rich and Poor* (New York: Random House, 1986).

7. Lekachman, *Visions and Nightmares,* 13.

8. See William A. Niskanen, *Reaganomics* (New York: Oxford University Press, 1988), 108–113, for an insider's view of changing positions within the administration. Niskanen suggests that the budget deficit is seen as wrong from a moral point of view; it is wrong to borrow to finance current operations and let future generations pay the bill.

9. Daniel Patrick Moynihan, "Reagan's Inflate-the-Deficit Game," *New York Times,* 21 July 1985, E21.

10. See Robert Eisner, *How Real is The Federal Deficit* (New York: Free Press, 1986); and Robert Heilbroner and Peter Bernstein, *The Debt and the Deficit* (New York: W. W. Norton, 1989).

Chapter 10

Monetary Policy and the Banking Industry

When Mr. Reagan took office in 1981, Paul Volcker was chairman of the Federal Reserve System. Volcker and his colleagues at the Fed were committed to fighting inflation, and so on October 6, 1979 they decided to redirect monetary policy away from controlling interest rates to controlling monetary aggregates. Heavily influenced by monetarists who believe that controlling the money supply is crucial for controlling inflation, the Fed began to adopt their prescriptions for monetary policy. Simply put, monetarists were using a variant of the quantity theory of money; the crude equation for it is $MV = PY$, where M is the stock of money (M1 then), V is velocity or the number of times a dollar is turned over in a period, P is the price level, and Y is real output. If V is presumed to be constant, then changes in M will result in changes in PY, national income. However, the closer the economy is to full employment and Y becomes fixed, changes in M will be met with equal proportional changes in the price level, P.

Even without full employment, it is clear that changes in the money supply will affect the price level. The lesson is clear as well: Control the money supply if you wish to control prices. However, if the Fed controls the money supply, then interest rates are free to adjust to whatever levels are necessary to bring the supply of money equal to the demand for it; interest rates are free to find whatever rates are consistent with demand and supply.

Hence, reductions in the rate of growth of the money supply in 1979 and 1980 to control inflation resulted in unprecedented increases in the rate of interest. For example, 3-month treasury bills rose from just over 7% in 1978 to 10% in 1979 to 14% in 1981; the prime rate rose from 9% in 1978 to over 12% in 1979 and to over 20% in 1981. All interest rates rose in similar proportions, and only returned to lower levels in the summer of 1982 when the Fed abandoned its monetarist experiment. Real interest rates, however, remained higher than past experience would have justified.

Ironically, candidate Reagan berated the Carter administration for the high interest rates and then President Reagan retained the same monetary policy until the restrictive monetary policy caused the depression of 1981–82 and proved too severe to continue. Still, it was Volcker's monetary policy that was later given credit for reducing inflation much to the chagrin of the Reagan administration that wanted to claim that victory for itself.

Thus, Reagan took office with a monetary policy begun in the Carter administration but one with which he would not have been displeased. Bringing down inflation was one of his major goals, and in his economic plan, the necessary monetary policy was left to the Federal Reserve.

MONETARY POLICY AND DEREGULATION

As we have seen, the Federal Reserve wrestled with controlling monetary aggregates with the assumption that the velocity of money would remain predictable. Unfortunately for the monetarists, velocity did not behave properly and began to decline in the 1980s. The less reliable the past relationships between income, money, and velocity became, the more the Federal Reserve retreated from its commitment to pursue the monetarist's path.[1] While not abandoning control over monetary aggregates, it began to shift its emphasis to interest rates, particularly the federal funds rate.

In 1987 it was forced to abandon control over M1 entirely, which formerly captured the demand for transaction balances. The Federal Reserve's job of controlling financial conditions for the economy was becoming more difficult, and it began the search for more reliable indicators. True, there were explanations for the decline in velocity—the rapid decline in inflation and interest rates were major factors—as people began to hold more money balances now that the cost of doing so was reduced.

But a large part of its difficulties can be traced to deregulation of financial markets and to the creation of new financial instruments. For example, people formerly used checking deposits for transaction balances, but these balances did not pay interest. Now with deregulation, people sought accounts that paid interest on deposits; they could keep more money idle in these NOW accounts without sacrificing income—the opportunity cost was low. Clearly, the velocity of M1 began to fluctuate and became unreliable for policy purposes. After 1986, interest rates were free to vary with market conditions, and even more switching could occur. Now money market funds were available, ATMs made switching convenient, and the public was becoming accustomed to moving funds as needed to take advantage of changing market conditions.

The point of all this is that the Federal Reserve was left without a clear indicator of monetary conditions. It was no longer able to focus on some summary variables to gauge its actions or measure its success. This by-product of deregulation has hampered the Fed in doing its main job (as it sees it) of maintaining orderly markets and preventing inflation.

The longer-term question is how will the Fed conduct its future monetary policy. If we assume that the past relations among income, money, and velocity are no longer reliable, on what will the Fed base its monetary policy? In the short run, it may choose to become more eclectic and include a variety of variables to consider. This may well confuse the Fed watchers and make individual responses to economic conditions more uncertain. Ironically, it would make it possible for the Fed to surprise the market by its policies and thereby thwart the market's ability to anticipate its actions. For rational expectations believers, this would make monetary policy more effective! Economic agents would not be able to outguess the Fed quite so readily and thus take actions that would anticipate the results of such actions and make policies ineffectual. Thus, with unexpected signals and multiple policy determining variables, the Fed's actions would be effective in the short run.

The Federal Reserve could, however, choose to ignore or minimize its involvement in the short run thus acknowledging its inability to respond to conditions quickly. In this scenario, the Fed might choose to lengthen its horizons and pursue longer-term goals while letting the short-term problems relatively free to self-correct. For example, it could choose an inflation target for a given period and stick to policies it thinks would facilitate reaching this goal. Over the longer run, the relations among income, money, and velocity might conform to a more predictable pattern and enable the Fed to use this longer-term stability to justify an adherence to a course of action that might otherwise be questioned. A lower target rate of inflation, say, could conflict with short-term economic conditions that might require more stimulation and thereby risk inflation above the long-term inflation target. Something like this scenario could be inferred from the Fed's early reaction to the recession of 1990; it was slow to react and timid in response. Again, inflation fears seemed to have been responsible.

A less active monetary authority would comfort monetarists and other economic and political conservatives who object to overmanagement anyway. On the other hand, those who advocate continued Fed intervention would find such a policy philosophically objectionable. In the long run, the setting of targets would again please conservatives, particularly if the main target was the price level. Adherence to the goal might prove difficult, to be sure, but the commitment to the idea would be welcomed as a needed change from the overreaction to temporary disruptions in the economy. Of course, a more progressive philosophy would emphasize that short-run economic conditions cannot be abandoned and must be addressed. Long-term goals may be desirable, but they cannot be pursued without regard for the present.[2]

Thus, the Fed could be put in the strange position of being swayed by political and economic philosophy more than presently. Ideology, always present anyway, would play an even more important role in the Fed's responses. The choice between the short-run actions and long-run goals need not be an either/or situation, of course, but the lack of clear policy instruments to follow could result in a kind of short-term paralysis that would lead to longer-term horizons by default.

Deregulation and the rapid pace of financial innovations have led to unforseen problems for the conduct of monetary policy. Free marketers, anxious to free the hands of bankers, have inadvertently tied those of the Federal Reserve System. Although they may welcome such restraints, they still must spell out the role of the Federal Reserve under the new and unfamiliar conditions caused by financial market changes. Those who advocate the same or more market intervention by the Fed will also have to find new or revised instrumental variables to guide the Fed and devise policies more appropriate to markets where participants respond in different ways from the past.

In any case, the Federal Reserve will have to reestablish its credibility with the public now that its operating rules are no longer discernible and its policies no longer obvious. Because the public will no longer be certain about either what its stated goals are or what the Fed is basing its policies on, a new kind of trust must be developed if monetary policy is to be effective. No one believes that will be easy.[3]

THE SAVINGS AND LOAN DEBACLE

The origin of the problems of the savings and loan associations (S&Ls) is found in the inflation following the buildup for the Vietnam War. The additional spending in 1966 for the undeclared war in Vietnam started a round of inflation that was to last for some time, eventually causing Nixon to impose wage and price controls, and OPEC to impose an oil embargo. The source of the inflation, the role of inflationary expectations, the rapid rise in energy prices, and the problems caused by stagflation are not the concern here.[4] The effect of inflation on the banking system is the issue here.

Up to this time, interest rate ceilings on time deposits were adjusted periodically to remain above market rates. After 1966, market interest rates soared, but interest rate ceilings were kept constant to protect the thrift institutions from self-destructive competition and mortgage markets from competition from commercial banks, now subject to interest rate ceilings as well. Attracted by higher returns, funds flowed out of these accounts in a process called disintermediation until the very solvency of the banks was threatened. For example, in 1976 the inflow of new savings into the S&Ls was $34.4 billion, by 1980 it was $10.7 billion, and by 1981 it was −$25.4 billion. Some banks did fail in 1981 but were insured by the FDIC that arranged for mergers with stronger banks or sales to new owners. As might be expected, the search began for new types of deposits and/or gimmicks to avoid the regulated interest rate ceilings. The banking structure would never be the same after this episode, as it learned how to avoid regulations and thwart the regulators. No bailout was necessary, but the problems of the thrifts were growing more and more severe. Many thought that there was a need for thrifts to diversify and expand their loan opportunities beyond the mortgage markets to which they had been tied if they were to compete with commercial banks.

The first attempt at rescue was the Depository Institutions Deregulation and Monetary Control Act of 1980 that phased out the interest rate ceilings by 1986. In phasing out the interest rate ceilings, the Act freed the banks to compete for funds in the market. Although the S&Ls were able to compete for funds, they were also stuck with mortgages that were issued at much lower interest rates in the past. They were paying high interest rates to attract short-term funds and receiving low interest returns on long-term loans—a sure prescription for disaster. Their collective net incomes turned negative in 1981 and 1982, and removal of the rate ceilings did not provide the promised relief from insolvency. Something more was necessary.

The deregulation act of 1980 also provided for an increase in insured deposits by the FSLIC from $40,000 per account to $100,000. This last-minute insertion into the bill received little or no attention at the time nor was there any previous pressure to increase the insured amount, but the change in insurance coverage was to prove unwise to the industry in a very short time because they could now compete for large, and unregulated, deposits up to $100,000. Moreover, the S&Ls were permitted to offer NOW accounts, invest in consumer loans, and experiment with other types of mortgage loans. Finally, the Act removed state usury ceilings, giving the banks the authority to charge interest rates more in line with market rates.

Because removal of interest rate ceilings was not the panacea, the S&Ls remained in deep trouble. By mid-1981, 75% of the S&Ls were losing money and 50 were insolvent and many others could not meet the minimum capital requirements.[5] Still, the movement toward deregulation was inexorable and finally was formalized in the Garn–St. Germain Depository Institutions Act of 1982. Its provisions along with new regulations, in the words of one regulator, "didn't deregulate the industry, they unregulated it." The Act allowed the S&Ls to:

1. Offer money market funds free of interest rate restrictions
2. Invest up to 40% (up from 20%) of their assets in real estate and commercial loans
3. Make consumer loans up to 30% of assets (up from 20%)
4. Make home and apartment loans without regard to meeting any fixed percentage of the loan to appraisal value (loan to value tests)
5. Convert from mutual banks to stock ownership to attract more capital
6. Issue adjustable interest rate mortgages

At or around the time of the passage of the Garn–St. Germain bill, states such an California were attempting to rescue the S&Ls with new regulations, among them:

1. Permitting a single entrepreneur (down from 400) to own a thrift institution without any clear community need as was previously required.
2. Permitting the use of noncash assets (a boon to landholders) in the capitalization of a thrift.
3. Permitting loans without any down payment—the bank financed 100% of the loan.

4. Permitting thrifts to make real estate loans without regard to location. Previously loans were limited to local markets where knowledge of the market would be valuable.

5. Permitting troubled banks to use some creative accounting practices to meet capital requirements. "Goodwill" was allowed to be capitalized and other "voodoo" accounting practices sanctioned in order for the thrifts to appear in better financial shape. These funny monies accounted for over 40% of net worth of the thrifts in 1986.[6]

Looking over these changes, it is obvious that there was an open invitation for abuse. In many cases, that is exactly what happened. Using government-backed deposits, speculators and freeloaders could gamble with risky ventures because they could not lose. If the risky loans proved worthwhile, the bank won; if the loans proved worthless, the deposits were guaranteed anyway—so what if the bank failed! In the meantime, many avenues were open to bank officials to conceal the actual financial state of the bank, including government-sanctioned creative accounting.

Bank regulators were no match for the creative financing schemes of the banks, often dealing in huge sums devoted to massive real estate projects and shopping centers. The Reagan administration cut back on the number of regulators in the belief that the market would take care of errant behavior, and those who remained were low paid and ill-prepared to follow the machinations of these clever financial manipulators.

So the door was open to swindlers, high rollers, speculators, money launderers, and ambitious entrepreneurs. Taking advantage of the government-insured deposits and the desire of the government to preserve the banking system, seemingly at all costs, they loaned out funds in areas in which they were unfamiliar, favored friends and relatives, refinanced poor and nonfunctioning loans, and generally ran the banks as private preserves.[7]

Not all of the bank failures were the result of fraud and malfeasance; many were due to changing economic conditions. Loans to energy producers, mainly in oil, made when energy prices were booming quickly became worthless once the price of oil collapsed. The dramatic decline in inflation in the 1980s also hit all loans based on the expectation of continued high prices. Shopping centers, office complexes, and housing developments were created in the boom period, and when the recession of the early 1980s hit and jobs were lost in the energy fields, these investments proved superfluous and their values declined. Many banks that invested in such ventures or financed them themselves, now found their balance sheets were works of fiction.

Nor does it necessarily follow that the deregulation legislation was to blame for the woes of the S&Ls. Regulatory agencies and the federal insurers, the Federal Home Loan Bank Board (FHLBB), and the FSLIC must bear a good part of the burden. For this story, it is necessary to turn to public policy toward the banking industry in this period.

PUBLIC POLICY AND THE BANKING CRISIS

When the Reagan administration took office, the S&L industry was already in serious trouble. With interest rates at record highs since 1979, the S&Ls could not continue to pay these high rates while receiving low rates on their loans. The experiment with monetarism was wreaking havoc on the solvency of the thrift industry. The drive to reduce the rate of inflation, largely through monetary means, might have been popular in many circles, but not with the managers of the S&Ls. Moreover, Fed Chairman Volcker made it quite clear that the Fed would not relent in its efforts to eliminate the problem of inflation. The deregulation act of 1980 did not help the thrifts and probably made things worse.

The early bank failures in 1981 were resolved by the FDIC without much public notice or concern, although there were newspaper accounts of banks getting into trouble. However, it was obvious then to the FHLBB, and to all of us at least in retrospect, that it was only a matter of time until most of the S&Ls would be insolvent. What was the administration's response?

The administration was fully committed to deregulation, to the unwavering belief in competition, and to the reliance on markets rather than government to solve problems. In addition, Reagan was absolutely opposed to bailouts of any kind. Accordingly, the administration, represented by Donald Regan, held the belief that the problems of the S&Ls were temporary and would be solved by the marketplace in time. The high interest rates would fall as the policies to reduce inflation became effective; the inability to attract funds would be solved as soon as interest rates were deregulated, and they could compete for funds like everyone else; and deregulation would make the S&Ls comparable to commercial banks and, therefore, their temporary problems would disappear. Both the Treasury and the Office of Budget and Management (OMB) were firm in their declarations that no funds existed for bailouts of any kind.[8]

It was left to the insuring institutions to remedy the situation. Realizing that there would be no financial help from the administration and aware that the number of precarious banks would bankrupt the FHLBB reserves, Richard Pratt, the new appointee to head the FHLBB, found ways to preserve the banking system without bailouts. He began the merger or sale of failing institutions, some 400 in 2 years, and began the process of bending rules and creating accounting gimmicks to preserve confidence in the banking system. Counting "goodwill" as capital, reducing capital requirements, writing up fixed assets to market values, permitting sales of S&Ls to bank holding companies, and allowing interstate acquisitions of S&Ls were some of the means employed to bolster the balance sheets of failing thrifts and conceal the actual conditions of the thrifts from the public and Congress.[9] So successful was the attempt to preserve the banking system that when Pratt left in 1983, there were hundreds of banks that were operating that would have been declared insolvent under the old regulatory rules.

Ironically, had the administration (and Congress) been willing to confront the problem and not been blinded by its ideological dogma, the problem could have been solved with a minimum of difficulty. Had the failing thrifts been closed, merged, or sold, the cost would have been something like $10–15 billion. Senator Moynihan's plan to purchase mortgage loans issued at low interest rates from the S&Ls by the government until market interest rates declined and the thrifts could have recovered would have cost an estimated $10 billion. A large sum to be sure, especially for an administration keeping an eye on the deficit, but minuscule when compared to the ultimate cost of bailing out the industry after letting insolvent banks continue in operation.

Now begins a period of one of the most irresponsible and incomprehensible policy pursuits in the history of the United States. Given the ease with which an S&L could be established, the minimal amount of capital necessary, the relaxation of rules governing the areas where loans could be made, and permission for interstate banking and bank holding companies, of course money flowed into the thrift industry. They were becoming attractive investments for speculative types, adventurous entrepreneurs, high rollers, swindlers, money launderers, and similar groups who saw a means to high rewards with little risk. For a time, it appeared that the problem was indeed self-correcting, and attention moved away from any banking crisis.

The condition of the thrifts was concealed from the public, and Congress was apparently unconvinced of the seriousness of the problems confronting the industry. Regulators were either incompetent or indifferent, and the administration was too preoccupied with the budget deficit to entertain costly bailouts. Everyone appeared to be looking the other way and hoping that the industry, if left alone, would recover on its own—more of a case of wishful thinking than sound analysis.

So the banks began to attract funds to offset their losses from prior low-rate loans. They paid higher and higher interest rates, often by way of brokered accounts where large masses of funds were bundled and went seeking the highest returns in the country. Banks in Texas and California led the way. Having to pay higher interest rates meant more risky ventures, and more gambling. Once on this treadmill, getting off is nearly impossible; banks made poor loans as a result, either in areas in which they were unfamiliar or simply where the promised returns were higher. For a while, however, it appeared that the banks were recovering as their balance sheets looked healthy, or were made to look so through creative accounting practices.

Eventually, however, most of these loans went sour in 1986–88, but in 1983–85, these loans looked good on the books. Only a few highly publicized cases of failure finally alerted everyone that the industry was in trouble.[10] Edwin Gray, the new chairman of the FHLBB, after a long learning period, was one of the early warners, but he commanded little attention from an administration bent on following free-market principles. When he took office, 130 S&Ls were insolvent (even with liberal accounting practices), and half of these were merged or liquidated in 1983; by 1984 and 1985, more banks were becoming insolvent, and the FSLIC was rapidly losing its reserves to cover these institutions. The same story would be repeated in the next several years: more insolvent banks, with the FSLIC approaching bankruptcy. The granting of more authority to borrow funds to the FSLIC in 1987 (over $10 billion) merely prolonged the agony.[11]

Meanwhile, the amounts needed to solve the S&L crisis began to rise. They started at $15 billion in 1987 (with Danny Wall the new chairman), rose in just a few months in 1988 to up to $30 billion, then to $42 billion, and then to $50 billion. However, the crisis nature of the problem was concealed from the public in the election year of 1988, and the involvement of the future president's son in one of the failed S&Ls was not publicized.

Meanwhile, the FHLBB was merging failed banks, seeking new buyers for them, and subsidizing their acquisitions, all in an effort to rescue the industry.[12] In 1988, the FDIC disposed of 200 banks either through liquidation or by "sale," and the FSLIC disposed of 205 banks. (For comparison purposes, the same institutions disposed of 10 and 11 banks, respectively, in 1980.) Many complained of the sweetheart deals, aided by favorable tax provisions, that were deemed necessary to accomplish the restructuring of the industry. How many billions of dollars were lost in these deals remains problematic, but one informed estimate puts the total at over $32 billion.[13] By 1989, the RTC was controlling 275 institutions with assets of over $91 billion. How to dispose of these assets without depressing the markets for them was becoming a genuine concern.[14]

At least the problems of the S&Ls were becoming public knowledge; the Reagan administration, however, did not suffer any of the consequences of this debacle. The Council of Economic Advisors did not even trouble to address the issue in its annual reports. One would gather from the administration that there was nothing to be concerned about; its disregard of the crisis reflects its general approach of neglect in the face of nasty problems. Neither did Congress acknowledge its role as it delayed the authority of the insuring agencies to obtain funds to meet the problem and, thus, caused the waste of billions of dollars in additional costs. Of course, it was not a major issue in the issueless presidential campaign of 1988.

Finally, the major questions remain: What was the cause of the debacle, and how much will it cost to fix it? Although it is true that fraudulent activities were present in many cases of bank failure, fraud may not be the major culprit. Stories of lavish offices, wild parties, extravagant expense accounts, favoritism toward friends and relatives, extraordinary salaries, and the like correctly infuriated the public, and criminal proceedings against some of the bank officers have started but are not likely to satisfy the public because so many have already escaped. The indignation of the public is understandable, especially as the cost of rescuing the industry continues to climb. However, in the opinion of experts in the field, fraud was not the main problem. In the words of Lawrence White, a member of the FHLBB from 1986 to 1989:

The bulk of the insolvent thrifts' problems, however, did not stem from such fraudulent or criminal activities. These thrifts largely failed because of an amalgam of deliberately high-risk strategies, poor business judgments, foolish strategies, excessive optimism, and sloppy and careless underwriting, compounded by deteriorating real estate markets. [15]

One could add to this latter cause the Tax Reform Act of 1986 that made investments in real estate less profitable by removing some of the tax advantages to real estate investors. So the federal government was contributing to the collapse of the S&L industry at the same time that it was trying to solve its problems. In addition, the collapse of energy prices was a devastating blow to the thrifts that had loaned funds for energy exploration when prices were rising rapidly.

The estimated cost of remedying the problems varies considerably. Estimated costs have escalated from that original $15 billion to somewhere in the range of $300–500 billion (undiscounted) over a 30-year span. [16] The actual extent of the final cost of this debacle are still uncertain, but excessive quarreling over the numbers could obscure the more fundamental problems of its economic effects, and who was to pay the bill. In 1988, however, the public had not begun to feel the consequences of this sorry episode, and politicians were not affected as might have been expected.

NEW POLICY INITIATIVES

It was left to the Bush administration to propose new courses of action. Soon after taking office, the Bush administration began to formulate a plan for the thrift industry. In March, it submitted its bill to Congress which passed it in August 1989; the delay cost billions, but Congress was intent upon venting its anger. In fact, according to Lawrence White, a former member of the FHLBB, the entire Act that emerged, the Financial Institutions Reform, Recovery, and Enforcement Act (FIRREA) of 1989, was an Act of anger by the Bush administration and by Congress for having to spend large sums to bail out the thrift industry, now in disrepute. [17] The main provisions and assessments of FIRREA were as follows:

1. Authorized additional $50 billion to permit the disposal of the remaining troubled thrifts. The first $20 billion to be financed by the treasury before September 30 (too late to affect the Gramm–Rudman deficit ceilings); the remaining $30 billion to be financed "off budget," so as not to affect the budget deficit at all, through the newly created Resolution Finance Corporation (REF-

CORP). The Act also raised insured deposit premiums on the thrifts, eventually putting them on a par with commercial bank rates.

Clearly, the amounts authorized were insufficient as subsequent requests for additional funding totaling three times as much has demonstrated. Taking the funding out of the treasury's hands and putting it in the hands of a new agency not only raised the interest cost of borrowing, but once again provided evidence of the smoke and mirrors approach to the budget deficit. Misleading accounting tricks like these are surely disillusioning to the public and provided further evidence that politicians are untrustworthy.

2. Abolished the Bank Board and the FSLIC, giving the insurance function and other powers to the FDIC, while technically keeping two insurance funds and giving the disposal function to the Resolution Trust Corporation (RTC). The reminder of the FHLBB functions were transferred to other agencies.

The RTC was put into a difficult position; it lacked sufficient funds and was bound to accumulate more real estate than it could dispose of in a realistic manner. Keeping two insurance funds seemed at best unnecessary.

3. Raised net worth or capital requirements to bank standards (eliminating the goodwill provision), restricted loan activities, and increased penalties for illegal activities.

Together with the increased deposit insurance premiums, the increase in capital requirements might cause even more bank failures. In addition, profitable thrifts were penalized for the failed ones. Whatever the shortcomings of the Act, and there were many, the crisis in the thrift industry was being faced at last. It is not our purpose to continue the evaluation of FIRREA or to update it because that would take us beyond the scope of this chapter and beyond the assessment of the Reagan administration. The only purpose of introducing it at all was to enumerate one of the legacies of the Reagan years—the near collapse of the banking industry.

COMMERCIAL BANKING

The mess in the thrift industry is well known by now, and accordingly the foregoing account was sketchy by design. Less well known, but equally troubling, is the condition of the nation's commercial banks. R. Dan Brumbaugh, Jr., one of the first to predict the thrift problem, estimates that as of 1990, 976 middle-size banks were in trouble, and the FDIC would be broke if it closed all these insolvent banks. So once again the insuring agencies were permitting these banks to operate just as they did in the S&L case. Moreover, this does not include the big banks that are "too big to fail." The losses will only grow, as was painfully evident in the thrift industry. The GAO estimates that future losses will amount to $100–150 billion, or about half those of the thrift industry.[18]

The Bank Insurance Fund (BIF) which insures commercial banks has cash reserves of less than 1% of insured deposits; any failure of large commercial banks would deplete the fund quickly. In the commercial banking field, it is the large banks that are the weakest, and scenarios of their collapse, and the BIF along with them, are not difficult to imagine. Barth, Brumbaugh, and Litan, warn us against "gambling for resurrection" as was done in the thrift industry: "In sum, the federal government faces the risk of additional bank failure costs—if not now, then eventually—if the FDIC is forced by a shortage of cash and reserves to refrain from closing or reorganizing insolvent banks on a timely basis." [19] Increased competition from securitization of traditional bank loans and from other institutional changes in the financial field has forced banks to seek and make more risky loans in the hopes of capturing the needed spread between interest rates on deposits and loans. The authors offer reform proposals for the banking system including better regulatory practices, permitting banks to enter into new markets and allowing them to operate on a nationwide scale. Many others have offered solutions as well, including the banks themselves: Remove the restrictions imposed on commercial banks under the Glass–Steagall Act on investment banking; let banks sell insurance; permit banks to be affiliated with other types of organizations or corporations, and so on. Whatever the merit of these proposals, it should be noted that the financial community is alive with ideas of how to make the banks more profitable and less vulnerable to changing market forces. The difficulty has been how to erect enough safeguards so that the banks may explore new markets but are not gambling with insured deposits again.

These issues were raised, often acrimoniously, in the effort to produce legislation that would revitalize the banking industry. The result, the Federal Deposit Insurance Corporation (FDIC) Improvement Act of 1991, did little more than increase the borrowing power of the FDIC and provide for some deposit insurance reform. To increase the borrowing power of the FDIC, the Act required the setting of insurance premiums at a rate that would cover the additional borrowing and allowed the FDIC to borrow against the assets taken over from failed banks. The Act also required the FDIC to set new capital requirements. Experts in the field worry that the Act did not go far enough, and much was sacrificed in the heated debates over its provisions. Foregoing a detailed critique of the Act, we can easily summarize the feelings of these authors in their own words: "After twelve years of a seemingly endless banking crisis, the elements to solve it are clear, well understood, and ready to implement. But political interest groups so whittled down 1991 reform law that more Congressional bailouts and taxpayer exposure may still lie ahead." [20]

NOTES

1. Even the most monetaristic of the Federal Reserve Banks, the St. Louis Bank, was forced to admit the breakdown of the relationship between money and inflation and economic activity. In an article entitled, "Is Money Irrelevant", in the May/June issue of its *Review,* Gerald P. Dwyer, Jr., and R. W. Hafer concluded that "the short-run

linkages between the growth rates of money, income (both nominal and real) and prices are, as we have shown, quite loose. In any particular year, higher money growth is not associated with an equal increase in nominal income or inflation" (14). They, however, still maintain that over the long run, the relations are still important.

2. The Reagan administration, more interested in the goal of deregulation, paid little attention to these problems. The CEA in the Bush administration did address these issues in its *Economic Report of the President, 1990*, as it clearly stated "substantial movements in the velocities of the monetary aggregates in recent years have made rigid monetary targeting inappropriate. [But] . . . the Federal Reserve has not regressed to an undisciplined, ad hoc approach to policy. Rather, it has attempted to develop a more systematic, longer-run approach" (84).

3. Ibid. 88. The CEA in 1990 made this point very well: "Policy credibility is clearly useful to have, but achieving it may not be easy. Simply announcing a change in policy does not make it believable."

4. For a discussion of these issues, see Anthony S. Campagna, *The Economic Consequences of the Vietnam War* (New York: Praeger, 1991).

5. Martin Lowy, *High Rollers: Inside the Savings and Loan Debacle* (New York: Praeger, 1991), 35.

6. The changes in regulations were based on those listed in Stephen Pizzo, Mary Fricker, and Paul Muolo, *Inside Job: The Looting of America's Savings and Loans* (New York: McGraw-Hill, 1989), 12–13.

7. For an entertaining, if unsettling, account of these practices, see Pizzo, Fricker, and Muolo, *Inside Job*. See also, Martin Mayer, *The Greatest-Ever Bank Robbery* (New York: Charles Scribner's Sons, 1990).

8. See the excellent discussion of this period and the subsequent reactions to the view of the Treasury and OMB in Lowy, *High Rollers*, 20–54. The discussion in the text draws heavily on his clear analysis.

It is interesting that the two main administration figures in this episode, Donald Regan of Treasury and David Stockman of OMB, do not mention the S&L crisis in their otherwise detailed accounts of their years in the Reagan administrations.

9. In 1982, over 60% of the capital of the S&Ls was accounted for by goodwill; in 1985, over 50% was so accounted for. Lowy, *High Rollers*, 41.

10. See Irvine H. Sprague, *Bailout: An Insider's Account of Bank Failure and Rescues* (New York: Basic Books, 1986).

11. The data in this paragraph come from Lowy, *High Rollers*. For more comprehensive data as well as useful analysis on the S&L problem in the 1980s, see Lawrence J. White, *The S&L Debacle: Public Policy Lessons for Bank and Thrift Regulation* (New York: Oxford University Press, 1991).

12. White, *The S&L Debacle*, 108.

13. White, *The S&L Debacle*, 164.

14. Edward W. Hill, "The S&L Bailout: Some States Gain, Many More Lose," *Challenge* (May/June 1990): 38. Hill also attempted to measure the effect of the bailouts on each state and found that, in general, there will be a net transfer of funds to states in the southwest, whereas other states in the east and the rust belt will be losers.

15. Ibid. 117. Lowy, *High Rollers*, agrees with this general assessment stating "illegal conduct needs to be punished, but we have to understand that it didn't *cause* the S&Ls to fail. The interest sensitivity mismatch and imprudent lending decisions *caused* all but a relative few of the failures" (161).

16. Lowy, in *High Rollers,* estimates the total loss at between $150 billion and $200 billion discounted to January 1, 1991. No discount rate was supplied.

17. White, *The S&L Debacle,* 180. The provisions of the FIRREA are provided in the same place.

18. Quoted by Larry Martz, et al., "Bonfire of the S&Ls," *Newsweek,* 21 May 1990, 25.

19. James R. Barth, R. Dan Brumbaugh, Jr., and Robert E. Litan, "Bank Failures are Sinking the FDIC," *Challenge* (March/April 1991): 5. See also the following article in the same issue by Albert Gailord Hart, "How to Reform Banks—and How Not To," 16–24. Briefly, Hart proposes to:

subject *all* issuers of means-of-payment to banking controls . . . ; impose interest ceilings and standardized reserve requirements on all banks, so as to restore Federal Reserve control over the quantity of effective money; and terminate deposit insurance, access to Federal Reserve rediscount windows, and "too big to fail" protection except for banks which sign and fulfill "capital buildup contracts" . . . [avoiding financial fakery and flummery on bank capital]. (17)

20. R. Dan Brumbaugh, Jr., and Kenneth E. Scott, "A Political Logjam Still Blocks Banking Reform," *Challenge* (March/April 1992): 35.

Chapter 11

International Trade and the U.S. Position in the World Economy

The administration's grand plan for economic recovery, unveiled on February 18, 1981, did not have much to offer as far as conditions in the international trade area were concerned. Apparently, not much was required, for:

The administration's plan for national recovery will take a large step toward improving the international economic environment by *repairing domestic conditions*. [emphasis added]. Improving expectations and slowing inflation will enhance the dollar as an international store of value and contribute to greater stability in international financial markets. As interest rates come down and faster growth contributes to rising world trade, economic expansion in other countries will also accelerate.[1]

So much for the problems of international trade.

The only other elements in the administration's plans for international relations were the reduction of 12% from the Export-Import Bank's authority to make new direct loans and a 26% reduction in foreign development aid. It is obvious that the administration was focusing on domestic economic conditions and was not concerned about the long-standing problems in the international area.

In July 1981, this obvious omission was corrected in the administration's "Statement on U.S. Trade Policy." In this statement, five major policies were enumerated aimed at promoting "open trade and reducing trade distortions."[2]

1. Restoring strong noninflationary growth at home [To increase investment, reduce costs, and raise productivity, and to permit U.S. firms to respond better to changing economic conditions]

2. Reducing self-imposed trade disincentives [To remove needless regulations and complex laws that inhibit trade]

3. Effective and strict enforcement of U.S. trade laws and international agreements [To remove trade barriers]

4. A more effective approach to industrial adjustment problems [To remove government from efforts to respond to shifts in industrial fortunes and permit the free market to operate]

5. Reducing government barriers to the flow of trade and investment among nations [To expand and improve the free flow of trade, especially in services and investment]

These operating principles would appear to be in line with the administration's general thrust of promoting free markets by removing artificial restrictions and constraints wherever possible. In every subsequent *Economic Report,* the CEA showed its commitment to these aims, even if the rest of the administration did not. The CEA was anxious to explain the benefits of free trade, the evils of protectionism, and, indeed, the theory of international trade in general. It became increasingly difficult for the Council to maintain such principles over the years as the administration increasingly departed from them; the CEA apparently became isolated on these issues from the administration it was supposed to serve.[3]

While the CEA was ardently promoting free trade, the administration was only paying lip service to that principle; in fact, it was probably the most protectionist administration since the great depression. It was joined, of course, by Congress, eager to respond with protectionist legislation to the loss of jobs, to the claim of deindustrialization and, in general, to the clamors of trade unions and U.S. industries allegedly hurt by trade. The real difference between the White House and Congress was which clients would be served. The administration, proclaiming adherence to free and fair trade, responded to its clients in a manner that Niskanen suggests that ''a cynic might conclude that the administration wanted to maintain control of the distribution of protectionist favors and opposed only those trade restraints proposed by Congress.''[4]

PRINCIPLES VERSUS PRACTICE

Contrary to Niskanen, one need not be a cynic to conclude that the administration allowed political considerations to overrule its grandiose pronouncements on free trade. Responding to political pressures, it simply resorted to restrictions on free trade and called them something else, as if changing the name of trade restraints removed the arguments against them.

Hence, ''voluntary restraint agreements'' (VRAs) that imposed limitations on imports to the United States were instituted under the preposterous claim that these were voluntary actions by the exporting countries and did not constitute protectionist measures. That these agreements were contrary to U.S. trade laws and GATT did not seem to bother the administration.

There was a VRA in autos and another for steel. The auto agreement was with Japan that ''volunteered'' to limit its auto exports to the United States to 1.68 million per year for 3 years and to 2.3 million in 1984. The cost to the American consumer was estimated at over $1 billion per year or some $240,000 per job saved. The Japanese were delighted to comply with the administration's request as they promptly shipped only the higher priced cars, loaded with optional equipment. The Japanese profited handsomely; the U.S. consumer did not fare as well. In 1985, the VRA was dropped, now an apparent failure because the U.S. auto industry remained in serious trouble. The protection offered by the Reagan administration did not work any magic, and the industry has seen many plant closings since, with the loss of thousands of jobs.

By contrast, the administration imposed increased tariffs on the importation of motorcycles to save the Harley-Davidson Company. In this case, the anti-free trade worked as the company managed to survive the competition from abroad.

Another VRA was instituted in the case of steel. First, imports of specialty steel were restricted for 4 years; in 1984, VRAs were sought from all major steel-exporting nations, to offset minor subsidies available to them, to protect domestic steel companies. Again the cost would be on the order of $1 billion per year. The industry remained troubled until it learned how to produce specialty items, made to order for the customer by small, mini-mills that were flexible and able to adapt readily to changing demands.

Another example of trade restrictions contrary to the professed belief in free trade can be found in the textile and apparel industry. Already heavily protected by high tariffs, the industry sought further protection from competition from third world countries in the form of a Multi Fiber Agreement. This agreement imposed quotas and limited imports from about two dozen countries at a cost of millions for the American consumer.[5] It is interesting to note that these imports were those of low-cost commodities, largely consumed by low income people. So, to save the jobs of some relatively high-paid workers at an enormous cost, it became necessary to force the most disadvantaged consumers to bear the cost; low wage workers in third world countries were penalized as were low income consumers in advanced countries.

Not to belabor the point, trade restrictions of various kinds were followed in the case of footwear, shakes and shingles, and agricultural commodities. More barriers to free trade can be found in "buy American" or even "buy state" statutes, in laws that require shipping of goods in American ships, in the prohibition of sales of goods or services that might endanger national security, in building codes written to prohibit foreign goods, and in statutes that prohibit or limit ownership in U.S. firms. In 1950, 54% of all imports entered the U.S. duty free; in 1984, with all the rhetoric of free trade, only 32% were free of tariffs, and these percentages do not even cover the voluntary agreements mentioned earlier.[6]

The apparent hypocrisy of an administration proclaiming free trade while practicing protectionism was not lost on anyone, particularly on our trading partners, and the contradiction only fueled similar sentiments in Congress, members of which not only repeated the free trade rhetoric but insisted that America was being hurt by being too open while the rest of the world was protectionist. They called for a "level playing field," a slogan that played well with the public, if not with reality.

THEORY VERSUS POLICY

It was suggested above that the theoreticians in the administration were often divorced from the policy makers. This is certainly applicable in the case of international trade. Conflicts between abstract and practical reasoning, between the reflective and the pragmatic, are present in any administration, of course, and political compromises are commonplace. In this administration, however, where ideology played such an important role, the conflicts seem all the more striking. Given this background, we can proceed to analyze the source(s) of the trade problem according to the administration, and the policies proposed, versus those followed, as a consequence.

In its first *Economic Report of the President* (ERP) of 1982, the CEA clearly set out the administration's general approach to international issues: "The Administration's approach to international economic issues is based on the same principles which underlie its domestic programs: a belief in the superiority of market solutions to economic problems and an emphasis on private economic activity as the engine of noninflationary growth." [7] The CEA maintained that a strong dollar would benefit the United States as well as the rest of the world, and no intervention into exchange rate markets was warranted by government. Neither is the trade deficit by itself a major concern, and, in any case, the current account balance is a better indicator of the nation's trade position.

These are only highlights of the administration's approach, but they do indicate the tone of its trade beliefs. Accordingly, policy approaches could be expected to be minimal, letting the markets do the work—a policy called "benign neglect" by others. [8]

In its ERP of 1983, the CEA, now chaired by Martin Feldstein, began to worry over the growing strength of the dollar and the high real interest rates in the United States. There was no call to depart from the reliance on market forces in trade relations, but the CEA did begin to worry that the strong dollar's effects on exports might lead to policies it did not favor: protectionism, exchange market intervention, and changes in macroeconomic policies. On the latter, it was not willing to sanction a reversal of monetary policy to end inflation nor reverse fiscal policy to greater restraint that would lead to lower real interest rates and a lower dollar. [9]

In 1983, the adverse trade balances continued, and more concern was registered from those who were directly affected by them. The merchandise trade deficit ballooned to over $65 billion in the early estimate, double that of 1982, and expected to double again in 1984. The CEA, too, was becoming alarmed not only at the deficits themselves but, again, at the possible remedies that might be proposed that might do more harm than good. Table 11.1 provides some of the data on international transactions that clearly show why the administration began to worry. The merchandise trade balance had been negative since the mid-1970s, but the amount of the deficit really began to grow alarmingly in 1983 and continued to grow until 1988 when some improvement was evident. The same could be said for the current account balance, and it became obvious that the income from investments and services was no longer able to offset the merchandise trade deficit.

The CEA was confident that although the large and growing trade deficits were a cause for concern, they were easily explained and did not call for panic

Table 11.1

U.S. International Transactions (in billions)

Year	Merchandise			Investment Income			Other Items	Bal. on Current Account
	Exports	Imports	Net	Receipts	Payments	Net		
1977	120.8	−152.0	−31.1	32.2	−14.2	18.0	−1.4	−14.5
1978	142.1	−176.0	−33.9	42.2	−21.7	20.6	−2.1	−15.4
1979	184.5	−212.0	−27.5	64.1	−32.9	31.2	−4.7	−1.0
1980	224.2	−249.7	−25.5	72.5	−42.1	30.4	−3.4	1.5
1981	237.1	−265.1	−28.0	86.4	−52.3	34.1	2.1	8.2
1982	211.2	−247.6	−36.4	83.5	−54.9	28.7	0.7	−7.0
1983	201.8	−268.9	−67.1	77.3	−52.4	24.9	−2.1	−44.3
1984	219.9	−332.4	−112.5	85.9	−67.4	18.5	−10.2	−104.2
1985	215.9	−338.1	−122.1	88.8	−62.9	25.9	−16.5	−112.7
1986	223.4	−368.4	−145.1	88.6	−67.0	21.6	−9.7	−133.2
1987	250.3	−409.8	−159.5	104.7	−82.4	22.3	−6.5	−143.7
1988	319.3	−446.5	−127.2	107.8	−105.5	−4.6	5.3	−126.5

Source: Council of Economic Advisors, *Economic Report of the President, 1990*, 410.

reactions. It identified three areas that explained the increase in the trade deficit: (1) the appreciation of the dollar; (2) the loss of exports to countries now heavily in debt; and (3) the increase in income (and hence imports) in the United States exceeded those of Europe and Japan. Despite the rapid increase in the merchandise trade (or structural) deficit, the CEA was not overly concerned with it, claiming that service exports offset some of the deficit and, hence, the normal merchandise deficit, estimated at between $20 billion and $25 billion, "need not be a cause for special concern."

Of more concern to the CEA was the rise in the value of the dollar in both nominal and real terms vis-à-vis the price levels in other countries. Here, U.S. exports were clearly hurt and the loss of competitiveness of U.S. firms presented a real problem. Why did the dollar rise in value? The CEA identified three sources: reduced expectations of inflation in the United States; increased real interest rates in the United States; and the "safe haven" that the United States offered to foreigners. The first and last of these sources are not controversial, but the rise in real interest rates as a major cause of the strong dollar caused quite a stir.

Feldstein linked the rise in the dollar to the rise in the federal budget deficit, and that linkage brought him ridicule from the administration and eventual dismissal as chair of the CEA. The low rate of saving in the United States was not sufficient to finance the ballooning budget deficits, and interest rates began to rise; foreigners began to buy dollars to purchase U.S. bonds. Attracted by high real interest rates, they bid up the price of the dollar to buy the bonds that the American public was not. The American public was buying VCRs and foreign cars. In the process, the value of the dollar rose by some 50%, making it extremely difficult for American producers to sell abroad and making it more attractive for U.S. firms to relocate abroad. The consequences for the U.S. economy were enormous.

But the administration did not want to hear about this analysis, and it rejected the twin deficit linkage. Although crowding out was made less of a problem with the capital inflow, the administration wanted to hear that investment in the United States was made more attractive via the new tax laws and regulation relaxations, and the strong dollar was a sign of economic strength not weakness.

Again, some of the possible remedies were immediately rejected: protectionism, exchange rate intervention, credit controls, and a change in macroeconomic policy. Again, the latter was the only acceptable policy, but this suggestion cost Feldstein his job because he advocated a reduction in the federal budget deficit that would lower real interest rates and bring down the value of the dollar. Exporters would clearly benefit as a result, but import-competing firms would gain as well. The rest of the administration, particularly Treasury Secretary Donald Regan, was not pleased with the advice that the way to remedy the trade situation was to decrease government spending or raise taxes.

So the administration continued its policy of benign neglect, perhaps for ideological reasons, but in so doing it made a serious choice: It abandoned the export- and the import-competing sectors. It chose to let the manufacturing sector decline, and with it the jobs connected to it in favor of buying goods made abroad from our trading partners. It chose to sacrifice some of the industrial base, the agricultural sector involved in exports, the housing sector, and those firms struggling to compete with foreign competitors. It encouraged the consumption of foreign-made goods from television sets to automobiles at the expense of domestic investment; the twin deficits encouraged the buy now–pay later mentality that characterized the 1980s. William Greider quotes from a memo written by Feldstein on the subject:

The question of whether it would be desirable to have a lower-valued dollar is equivalent to asking whether it is better to allow the *temporary* [emphasis added] increase in the budget deficit to reduce domestic investment and interest-sensitive consumer spending or to reduce the production of goods for export and of goods that compete with imports from abroad. The answer to this question is clear in principle: it is better to reduce exports and increase imports.[10]

Clearly, Feldstein had more faith in the administration's pledge to reduce the budget deficit than did others outside the administration. Greider suggests that the strong dollar preserved low inflation as everyone acknowledged, one of the administration's accomplishments, and no one wanted to sacrifice this when an election was on the horizon.[11] Hence, they cynically wrote off some sectors of the economy—manufacturing, construction, agriculture—and permitted some sectors to benefit—computers, office buildings and retailing, and, in general, service sector areas. The long-run effects of this policy of benign neglect have proved to be anything but benign and to many, in fact, have been disastrous.

In 1985, the CEA reiterated its analysis of the trade problems of the United States, although lacking Feldstein, it began to move away from the twin deficit idea. Now it was the after-tax rate of return on investment that was attracting capital, not the high real interest rates resulting from the strong dollar. In its 1986 ERP, chaired by monetarist Beryl Sprinkel, the CEA barely acknowledged any real trade problems at all, and, ironically, after discussions of the examples of protectionism, it paid further lip service to the principles of free trade. In 1987, the CEA finally acknowledged that the dollar had begun to depreciate in early 1985 back to where it was at the start of the Reagan years. The Group of Five had agreed to force the dollar down and had succeeded in doing so. Presumably, a depreciated dollar should have improved the ability of the United States to export more of its output; still, the evidence of Table 11.1 shows little or no improvement in the merchandise trade deficit. The CEA attributed the lack of gains to the lag in the response of import prices to changes in the exchange rate. Foreign producers apparently chose to narrow their profit margins and maintain market shares.

The United States became a net debtor to the rest of the world in 1987, a fact acknowledged by the CEA but minimized when viewed in the context of the size of the U.S. GNP. The CEA warned, however, that the absolute size of the indebtedness could be a source of trouble, especially if foreigners suddenly stopped supplying the United States with their savings and stopped buying U.S. bonds. The CEA expected improvements in the U.S. external deficit and, thus, was not ready to panic. The depreciated dollar was expected to boost exports.

In general, the CEA saw improvements ahead and maintained that the loss of manufacturing jobs was due to the recession, not the trade imbalance. Nothing new was proposed to confront the trade problems because there were forces at work to do the job, as long as free trade was preserved. Cooperation among nations was necessary, of course, to insure that free and open trade practices continued. Otherwise, the problems of trade imbalances were largely macroeconomic in character, and once these macro causes were eliminated, conditions would improve.[12]

OTHER VIEWS ON TRADE

We have already seen the surrender of free trade principles to the favored clients of the administration. Clearly, the monetarists, supply-siders, and other economic conservatives who inhabited the administration could not have been happy with that development and must have felt in continuous conflict with the more pragmatic members of the administration. But at least in theory, if not in practice, the economic advisors were generally echoing the traditional trade theory.

The traditional trade theory model (Krugman calls it the Mass. Ave. Model) essentially attributes a trade deficit to macroeconomic forces. An excess demand for goods that cannot be satisfied by domestic production must lead, via a few simple algebraic equations, to a negative external balance. For the United States, the macroeconomic factors are easy to identify: An expansionary fiscal policy, not financed by domestic savings, led to huge budget deficits; as a consequence, the overstimulated economy led to increasing imports, especially because other nations did not stimulate their economies; to finance the budget deficits, the federal government resorted to borrowing. This pushed up real interest rates in the United States, attracting capital inflows from the rest of the world. In the process, the value of the dollar rose and that hurt U.S. exports. (An expansionary monetary policy would lower interest rates, increase domestic output, and lead to currency depreciation, if foreign interest rates did not fall or fall as far. Currency depreciation would lead to increases in exports, but the offsetting capital flows would lead to uncertain effects on the current account.)

In the traditional view, persistent trade deficits can be cured by fiscal constraint, bringing the budget into balance and discouraging imports; monetary policy could then be expansionary, bringing down the value of the dollar and encouraging exports. Of course, free trade is a necessary ingredient to the success of these macroeconomic policies. Also, a nation finding itself in the predicament of the United States in the 1980s could appeal to its major trading partners with trade surpluses to stimulate their economies to aid in the smooth realignment of trade flows.[13] It became quite popular then for economists, in and out of government, to advocate a large depreciation of the dollar if the trade deficits were to be reversed. Of course, the appropriate macroeconomic policies were necessary as well, particularly a more restrictive fiscal policy to reduce the budget deficit.

But the dollar did depreciate after 1985, and still the trade deficits persisted. Was the mainstream theory wrong that depreciation of the dollar was necessary? Many began to question whether changes in exchange rates could work, and some held that exchange rates did not matter. Defenders of exchange rate adjustments reminded critics that there were always lags in the adjustment process, and to some extent their predictions were verified.[14] Other economists conceded that exchange rate adjustments may work in the long run, but in the short run (that could be quite long), the necessary adjustment needed may simply be too large for the economy to manage, and a falling dollar, combined with rising interest rates, would lead to a recession.[15] The arguments for and against exchange rate adjustments as a factor in trade imbalances rapidly become theoretically complex and are better left to other sources for clarification.

Another view of the U.S. trade problem emerged to challenge the traditional view. The structuralist view (Krugman calls it secularist) emphasized the decline in U.S. competitiveness for the trade imbalance. The U.S. productivity growth had fallen behind our trading partners, the quality of U.S. goods had deteriorated, and the technological sophistication of the United States had slipped. These microeconomic factors are responsible for the trade woes, not the value of the dollar. Moreover, other nations with whom we compete are engaged in some form of aid to their industries—some form of an industrial policy—that supports their industries and puts U.S. industries at a disadvantage. Adhering to the free market ideology and the policy of benign neglect has led and will continue to lead to the deindustrialization of the United States, the loss of high-paying, skilled manufacturing jobs to be replaced by low-paying, service-type jobs. In this view, only a more realistic view of the problems can lead to solutions; an industrial policy is needed for U.S. industries to compete in the new global market.

Others have argued that the whole concept of trade has changed in the new global economy, and if we are to compete in it, U.S. firms need to adapt to changing economic conditions. Goods are and can be produced anywhere in the world, and interdependence among nations is the rule. The American corporation is no longer relying on large volume or large investments in the pursuit of profits; it produces goods with the inputs of foreign firms at all points in the production and distribution process. There is no unique domestic good in the global economy, and, in fact, what modern corporations provide best in this high value world is services: engineering, financial, and managerial. This requires a highly educated, skilled labor force able to identify opportunities and seize them.[16] Trade statistics are not very meaningful in a world that transcends national borders.

Still others hold trade restrictions of other nations responsible for the U.S. trade imbalances. If only the playing field were level, the U.S. firms would be able to compete. Japan, with its trade surplus, became an obvious target for this view. Japan bashing was politically popular and gave rise to calls for protectionism of all kinds. A less hysterical view held that once markets were lost, for instance, electronics to Japan, they were impossible to regain; or, quite simply, U.S. firms would abandon these lost markets altogether.

Clearly, these and other views not mentioned, analyses of the trade problems of the United States are quite diverse in their identification of the sources of the problem and of the policies necessary to solve them. With such confusion over theory, and such contrariness in the evidence of the 1980s, it is little wonder that uncertainty over what to do about the trade issue soon appeared. After reviewing the theoretical and policy controversies, Krugman concludes:

What we have thus come to realize, after a decade in which the confidence of economists in the conventional wisdom—and of the public in economists—was profoundly shaken, is that the conventional wisdom was sounder than it seemed. The international adjustment mechanism does indeed seem to work more or less as understood a decade ago, and the policy views that were based on that understanding are still tenable.[17]

Hooper and Mann also found that macroeconomic factors can account for the external deficit; the excessive growth of U.S. expenditures and the GNP and the rise in the value of the dollar account for about two-thirds of the external deficit, with the low savings rate in the United States, the debt position of developing countries, and adverse agricultural policies accounting for the remainder.[18] They warn, however, that the external deficit is likely to persist as long as the federal budget deficit and the low saving rate continue. Helkie and Hooper, in their empirical analysis of the external deficit, also find the same variables responsible for the deficit with, however, different emphases. They find relative price competitiveness to be the dominant force for the widening of the deficit and the fiscal expansion in the United States—growth of U.S. GNP versus that of other nations—to account for half of the rise in the deficit in the first place. One important difference in their work is their finding of a greater income elasticity of exports.[19] These endorsements of the traditional view will be hailed by many, but there are just as many who continue to debate both the theoretical foundation for them, and the policies that emanate from them.

LESS ORTHODOX VIEWS

In this brief summary of the trade situation in the 1980s, we have seen that the administration did not follow the advice of its traditional advisors, nor did it heed the criticisms of its dissenters. It did not reduce the federal budget deficit, nor did it establish an industrial policy. That is not to infer that the administration did nothing at all about the trade deficit, but what it did do satisfied neither camp. It preached free trade, threatened and cajoled its trading partners over trade matters, negotiated trade agreements, participated in international organizations' efforts to promote free and open trade, instigated a free trade agreement with Canada, and finally intervened to drive down the value of the dollar with the cooperation of the Group of Five. Still, because the trade balance did not improve significantly, its policies were seen as weak and ineffective. More was expected from such ardent free traders, particularly using the presidential powers to penalize other nations that resorted to trade restrictions.[20] The result was anger in Congress that was all too willing to harp on the trade deficit and blame everyone for it but the United States. Protectionism, Japan bashing, and chauvinism became popular positions to exploit for eager politicians.

As if to confound the experts, the trade balance did improve in 1988–91. The current account balance went from −$106.3 billion in 1989 to −$92.1 in 1990 and to −$8.6 billion in 1991. Exports increased more rapidly than imports so that the merchandise balance showed steady improvement; income from services and investments showed gains as well.

Without dissecting the balances for details, it would appear that the traditionalists were correct: The external balance would improve once the lag in the exchange rate adjustment was considered. Yet, the budget deficit continued to grow while monetary policy was not particularly expansionary. Whether the external imbalance would have been corrected by the usual means has been clouded for now because the recession of 1990–92 has intervened. Imports began to fall, not due to relative price changes but due to the recession; the macroeconomic equations have always related (inversely) imports to the state of the domestic economy. Krugman shows a median income elasticity of 1.8 for imports (and 1.2 for exports), so we should expect imports to be quite sensitive in a period of recession.

It remains to be determined how the elements of trade balances behaved in this recession. The traditionalists' view can explain part of the trends in the external balance, but the value of the dollar remained constant and interest rates dropped. Still, exports grew and capital continued to flow into the United States. There are apparent contradictions in these trends that will have to be explained before verification of the traditional model is achieved.

Not so for the dissenters from the Mass. Ave. model. They have maintained that international trade statistics are meaningless anyway. Reich, for instance, argues that half of the imports of goods into the United States represented not just finished goods but embodied services in the form of engineering, design, advertising, management services that are often just transfers within global corporations. They are the result of complex arrangements, employment contracts, long-term contracts, profit-sharing agreements, and so on that are difficult to interpret with the usual trade data because they are not market determined in the same way as other goods. Thus, he argues:

Trade statistics are notoriously imprecise, subject to wide swings and seemingly inexplicable corrections. The truth is that these days no one knows exactly, at any given time, whether America's (or any other nation's) international trade is in or out of balance, by how much it is out of balance, or what the significance of such an imbalance might be.[21]

The world of trade has changed in the global economy, in other words, but the trade statistics have not recognized it. Making policy on the basis of faulty or misleading data is likely to be ineffectual, if not useless, and could do more harm than good. In the global economy, nations cannot manage their fiscal and monetary policies in isolation; interdependence is demanded, cooperation is necessary. In the global economy, wealth and influence will flow to those who have the skills and talents to participate in this new world. Others, who do not or cannot acquire these skills—the production workers, the semi-skilled—will lose out. A gap between the skilled and the unskilled will develop and must be addressed.

It follows that education will play a key role in the global economy. A nation must be willing to provide the proper education for those who are able to utilize it and job training for those who are not. To prevent a vastly unequal distribution of income and wealth from developing, the tax code must be structured to prohibit this unhealthy development. Progressive taxes should be reintroduced.

Compare the needs of this world with the public policy in recent years.

Taxes have been reduced for the skilled and talented (symbolic analysts, Reich calls them), spending on the infrastructure has fallen, expenditures on education have been reduced, channeled in the wrong directions, and training for the unskilled has nearly disappeared. These are the wrong directions if the nation is to compete in the global economy. The United States, using the traditional view of trade, worry about foreign investment in the United States; instead, it should worry that its citizens are not acquiring the skills necessary to compete. Foreign investment may actually improve the chances of acquiring those skills. The trade data show imports and exports, but in the global economy, these may be misleading statistics; an automobile may be manufactured in one country with parts made in other countries, marketed by specialists in another country, financed by banks in a third country, designed by the residents in still another country, and so on.

What is the meaning of an import or export? What is the meaning of an "American" corporation engaged in some or all of these transactions? Protecting "American" corporations would seem absurd under these conditions. Not only would the activities of such a corporation be difficult to identify—what proportion was American-made—but the corporation itself has no particular allegiance to any country but will move and locate its activities where it is most advantageous to do so. "Buy American," a form of protectionism, is equally ludicrous, as has been repeatedly shown in the case of automobiles, but it would apply to other goods as well.

Clearly then, Reich has a view of the world of trade that is far different from the usual perception. In his global economy, trade imbalances would be deceptive and lead toward incorrect analysis of the problems and inappropriate policy responses. It is equally evident that the Reagan and Bush administrations were not addressing the real problems of the twenty-first century. Their tax policies, their education policies, their job training programs, their neglect of the infrastructure, their failure to recognize the need for international cooperation in economic matters, not just in lip service to the idea but real integration, and so on have been disastrous for the United States. In fact, their policies are the exact opposite of what was required. Hence, the United States will fall farther behind the rest of the world which apparently recognizes the new reality while the United States clings to the old.

Another area of concern to those who are more critical of traditional analysis of trade problems is that of direct investment: investment of foreigners in the United States and the investment of U.S. firms abroad. What are the effects, particularly on employment, of such direct investments?

Foreign direct investment in the United States has raised many fears that the United States is losing its industrial base to foreigners, that foreigners will be making the production decisions, taking home the profits, and dominating the economy. For Reich, such fears are mistaken in the global economy; foreign firms invest or take over American firms because they can make a profit here. They employ American workers who can benefit from learning the skills necessary to compete in the global economy and becoming more productive. Who owns the firm becomes less meaningful in this world.

Still, chauvinism is a powerful force in the United States, and the fears are not overcome by these more reasoned analyses. Was the depreciated dollar responsible for the observed increase in direct foreign investment? Was it the increase in protectionism by the administration or talk of more of it in Congress that prompted foreigners to produce in the United States rather than try to sell in the United States? Neither of these frequently heard arguments appears to have much explanatory power. Whether the dollar was relatively high or low, whether the products involved were subject to trade restrictions or not, foreign investment proceeded unabated.[22]

Much of the hysteria over foreign investment in the United States has subsided, now that jobs are being created by these firms. But the reverse side of the coin, direct investment of U.S. corporations in other countries, continues to aggravate in the stagnant U.S. economy. At bottom is the fear of exporting jobs, as well as capital. Jobs are lost to low-paid Mexican workers just over the border, and to third world countries all over the globe. Early in the decade, Bluestone and Harrison warned in *The Deindustrialization of America* that U.S. corporations moving abroad in search of lower costs, lower taxes, or other reasons left behind many displaced workers; former employees lost high paying jobs and were forced to take lower paying ones; they lost their pensions and benefits; and most important, they lost or in the future would lose the skills necessary to command higher wages.[23] Unions, often a convenient scapegoat, came in for their share of the blame for the trend to move abroad.

Bennett and Harrison concluded:

Whether it is "what they deserve," when deindustrialization occurs, the overwhelming weight of the evidence suggests that workers receive a heavy blow, only part of which can be systematically quantified. A large majority of those directly affected endure at least temporary income loss, while a significant minority suffer long-term damage to their standards of living and to their physical and emotional well-being.[24]

Workers cannot win: Capital is mobile, labor is not. The old lose more than the young, minorities more than whites, women more than men, but all lose.

The immediate effects of deindustrialization on the U.S. economy are evident, but they must be integrated into a broader picture of the structural changes that occurred in the 1980s. Therefore, elaboration of these structural changes in the U.S. economy are left to the next chapter. The topic was introduced here only to review whether and to what extent deindustrialization occurred as a result of the strong dollar or external deficits. It is clear that other factors played important roles in location decisions, and they were responsible for plant movements and investment decisions regardless of the value of the dollar or of external deficits.

LEGACY

In the early years of the administration, the policy of benign neglect saw the value of the dollar rise and the resultant decline in the ability of the United States to export. While the administration boasted of a strong dollar in a symbolic sense, the demise of export industries or import competing industries proceeded in a real sense. Manufacturing industries were left to compete as best they could, and too many could not. Agricultural products lost markets, and farmers, who had been promised growth in export markets and who had expanded their operations accordingly, now found these markets shrinking. So the administration consciously abandoned these sectors of the economy while they chanted the benefits of free trade.

Favoring domestic investment over exporting ones, the administration hoped to observe the increase in investment as a consequence of its tax and regulation policies. The investment they got was in office buildings, shopping malls, home computers, and in other service areas. They sacrificed the wealth-creating areas for the nonwealth ones, the high-paying jobs for the low-paying ones, the skilled ones for the unskilled ones. In a global economy, this trade-off was more than unfortunate, it was devastating. For after the banking deregulation, it was in those areas of domestic investment that the S&Ls found it profitable to speculate. They invested in shopping malls and office complexes, not in manufacturing industries where the payoff was much more uncertain.

Hence, the administration created a climate where investment was channeled into the wrong areas if its aim of long-term growth was to be achieved. If people like Reich are correct, the administration pursued the wrong policies if the United States was to compete in the global economy. It failed to solve the budget crisis to stabilize the dollar, but, more importantly, it failed to provide its citizens with the necessary means to compete in this new world: education, training, skills, and scientific knowledge to meet new technological challenges.

By its policies, it fostered a recrudescence of protectionism and chauvinism. The accusation that other nations were the cause of our problems found ready acceptance for those looking for excuses. When it reversed its policy of non-interference into exchange rate matters and the dollar fell, it not only indicated its earlier failures, but the reversal was too late. The damage had already been done and markets lost.

After some time, the external deficit fell but not sufficiently to remove the doubt that exchange rate changes were not enough to correct the imbalance. Other factors must be involved in the explanation of the trade deficit. U.S. goods were failing the quality tests; American managers were too interested in short-run profits to invest for long-term growth; labor productivity growth fell; technological superiority had passed to other nations; and, in general, U.S. firms had lost their competitiveness, as they failed to adapt to rapidly changing economic conditions.

Meanwhile, the administration was looking the other way as the merger and acquisition movement proceeded unabated by public policy (Chapter 12). Instead of new investment, corporations were grabbing each other up; instead of new industries and technology, firms were merging to make short-term profits on stock prices. All this amid the cry that funds for investment were in short supply and that the American public did not save enough. Yet funds for mergers and acquisitions seemed to be readily available.

In the end, the administration's trade policies, such as they were, were a failure. Their policies either did not address the problems at all, or addressed the wrong ones. They were simply not adequate or appropriate for an international economy that was changing too rapidly for strict adherence to the traditional view of international trade relations.

U.S. firms have begun to learn how to compete in the new world of trade, but the costs in the learning process have been enormous. Whatever costs have been incurred have been borne by painful bankruptcies, unemployment or underemployment, plant shutdowns and downsizing of industries, relocations and capital movements, and devastated communities. To these problems, the Reagan and Bush administrations have been unresponsive and, in fact, appear to have been unknowing.

NOTES

1. *A Program for Economic Recovery,* a message to Congress dated February 18, 1981, 25.

2. Council of Economic Advisors, *Economic Report of the President, 1982,* 176–177.

3. William A. Niskanen in *Reaganomics* (New York: Oxford University Press, 1988) reflects on his frustration at the failure of the administration to heed the advice of the CEA on matters of international trade or to understand the nature of trade imbalances, for example, the lack of understanding or appreciation of the fundamental equations of saving and investment (page 150).

4. Ibid. 147.

5. Ibid. 145.

6. Murray Weidenbaum, *Rendezvous with Reality* (New York: Basic Books, 1988), 123.

7. *Economic Report of the President, 1982,* 167.

8. There is, however, this warning paragraph:

Concern with the country's international payments position is appropriate when the basis of that concern is that the country is simultaneously experiencing a sustained deficit in its current account and a persistent depreciation of its currency in the exchange markets. The joint occurrence of these two events should alert economic policymakers to the possibility that the country may be losing competitiveness. (*Economic Report of the President, 1982,* 179).

9. *Economic Report of the President, 1983,* 61–70.

10. Quoted in William Greider, *Secrets of the Temple* (New York: Touchstone, 1987), 598. A little later in the memo Feldstein adds:

The fall in exports and the rise in imports that result from the stronger dollar are clearly causing unemployment and threatening individual firms with possible bankruptcy. Perhaps these adverse effects are more severe than those that would result from an equal decrease in the demand for plant and equipment, housing and other interest-sensitive goods . . . but at present the burden of proof lies with those who would claim that the industries involved in international trade are more vulnerable. . . .

11. Ibid. 599.

12. I have refrained from quoting the *Economic Reports* extensively because much of the analysis would be repetitive. Picking out highlights, however, could be unfair and too simplistic, and a more thorough discussion would better represent the views of the authors. Perhaps the shortcomings of the decision to select only limited points to cover can be offset by an extended quote that nicely summarizes the position of the CEA on the causes of the trade problems of the United States. It is taken from the *Economic Report of the President, 1988*, 90.

Instead, the growth of the U.S. trade deficit in the 1980s primarily reflects the influence of several interrelated macroeconomic developments. Rapid growth of spending (domestic demand) in the United States relative to both growth of spending in other countries and to growth of production (gross national product, or GNP) in the United States spurred U.S. demand for foreign imports and restrained foreign demand for U.S. exports. The need for many heavily indebted developing countries to reduce their international borrowing and improve their trade balances also cut into U.S. markets. Growth of U.S. spending relative to production and income implied a deterioration in the national saving-investment balance, which, in turn, owed much to the persistence of a large Federal deficit late into the current expansion. An increasing net inflow of foreign capital offset a declining national saving rate and helped to finance reasonably robust U.S. investment. This capital inflow, which was partly motivated by high prospective after-tax returns on U.S. investment, was one among several important factors that contributed to the strong appreciation of the U.S. dollar between 1980 and early 1985. Dollar appreciation, in turn, was the critical proximate cause of much of the deterioration in the U.S. trade balance, because it made U.S. exports more expensive in foreign markets and foreign imports less expensive in U.S. markets.

13. For a summary of the competing theories, see Paul R. Krugman, *Has the Adjustment Process Worked?* (Washington, DC: Institute for International Economics, 1991). Also see Chris C. Carvounis, *The United States Trade Deficit of the 1980s: Origins, Meanings, and Policy Responses* (Westport, CT: Greenwood Press, 1987).

14. Krugman, *Has the Adjustment Process Worked?*, 13–22.

15. Stephen Marris, *Deficits and the Dollar: The World Economy at Risk* (Washington, DC: Institute for International Economics, 1985). Also see his update, *Deficits and the Dollar Revisited* (Washington, DC: Institute for International Economics, 1987).

16. Robert B. Reich, *The Work of Nations: Preparing Ourselves for the 21st Century Capitalism* (New York: Alfred A. Knopf, 1991). Perhaps one paragraph can indicate what Reich means:

In the high-value enterprise, profits derive not from scale and volume but from continuous discovery of new linkages between solutions and needs. The distinction that used to be drawn between "goods" and "services" is meaningless, because so much of the value provided by the successful enterprise—in fact, the only value that cannot easily be replicated worldwide—entails services: the specialized research engineering, and design services necessary to solve problems; the specialized sales, marketing, and consulting services necessary to identify problems; and the specialized strategic, financial, and management services for brokering the first two. (85)

17. Krugman, *Has the Adjustment Process Worked?*, 50.

18. Peter Hooper and Catherine L. Mann, *The Emergence and Persistence of the U.S. External Imbalance, 1980–87,* Princeton Studies in International Finance, 65, Princeton, NJ: International Finance Section, Dept. of Economics, Princeton Univ., 1989, 92–93.

19. William L. Helkie and Peter Hooper, "An Empirical Analysis of the External Deficit, 1980–96," in *External Deficits and the Dollar: The Pit and the Pendulum,* eds. Ralph C. Bryant, Gerald Holtham, and Peter Hooper (Washington, DC: The Brookings Institution, 1988), 10–56.

20. For an examination of the policy responses of the administration in terms of theoretical advice, see Carvounis, *The United States Trade Deficit of the 1980s,* 123–166.

21. Reich, *The Work of Nations,* 114.

22. Ibid. 136–153.

23. Barry Bluestone and Bennett Harrison, *The Deindustrialization of America* (New York: Basic Books, 1982), 49–81.

24. Ibid. 80.

Chapter 12

The Structure of the Economy and Society

When it came to expressing its philosophy, the Reagan administrations were anything but subtle. Very early in his first administration, Reagan sent out rather clear messages that this would be a probusiness, hands-off administration. When he fired the striking air traffic controllers (PATCO), he not only established himself as a strong and decisive leader, but as antilabor as well. Moreover, constant referrals to the virtues of free markets, minimum regulations, low business taxes, and the like were not lost on the business and financial communities. The signals would have been difficult to misinterpret.

It is not surprising, therefore, to observe the great variety of actions of all those who could take advantage of the favorable atmosphere. Once the restraints were lifted, economic agents felt free to experiment and test the limits of the administration's tolerance; once their actions were ignored, excesses were bound to develop. The purpose of this chapter is to sketch some of these actions and trace their consequences for the economy and society.

MERGERS AND ACQUISITIONS

There have been several periods of serious merger–acquisition (M&A) activity in the United States. In the post-WWII period, a major upsurge in M&As occurred from the mid-1950s to well into the 1960s. These were conglomerate mergers where firms, mainly small and medium-sized ones, were acquiring other similar sized firms in unrelated industries. The aim was to diversify risk by entering into fields different from the main one of the acquiring firm, and by so doing provide some protection from the business cycle. Economic conditions in the early 1970s were not conducive to a merger movement, and the activity fell off; from the mid-1970s through the 1980s, however, the M&As witnessed another burst in activity.

This time the movement was characterized by takeovers, both hostile and friendly, of large public corporations, and numerous divestitures of unprofitable operations. In the 1980s, huge amounts were spent on megadeals involving very large corporations and requiring huge sums provided by the sale of junk bonds (or ''high yield'' bonds) by specialty brokerage houses, banks, and private sources. The era was characterized by the enormous accumulation of debt to finance these megamergers because many of the takeovers were heavily leveraged with the debt-to-equity ratio being very high. These leveraged buyouts

(LBOs) made fortunes for the few who engineered them, but the question is Did they benefit the economy as well? A closer look is required to answer this important question.

First some data are needed. For a quick impression of the M&A activity that took place in the 1980s, of the 100 largest transactions in history, 91 of them took place in the 1980s, and most of the remainder were probably in the works in that period![1] Over $393 billion was involved in these transactions with the largest being the takeover by Kohlberg Kravis Roberts of RJR Nabisco for over $24.5 billion in 1988. Clearly, these sums are impressive, and they were obtained at a time when people were decrying the lack of funds for real investment purposes. Altogether, from 1981 to 1988, 22,810 mergers took place with a total dollar value paid of $1.1 trillion.

Over the latter part of the 1980s, six industries led the parade of M&As: banking and finance; miscellaneous services; wholesale and distribution; computer software; supplies and services; and retail. Without pausing to discuss the matter, it should be noted that the service industries dominated the M&A activity in the 1980s. Similarly, data on the means of payment are also interesting but will just be mentioned here with more comments later. Of the number of mergers from 1981 to 1988 where the means of payment was indicated (9515), 43% were cash transactions, 29.4% were stock, 26.7% were some combination, and 0.9% were debt.

Looking further into the means of payment, of the acquisitions of publicly traded companies in the latter half of the 1980s, about 64% used cash, 23% stock, and 14% used some combination. Cash was apparently used in these cases because less disclosure is required of the buyer.[2] For the acquisition of privately held companies, the reverse was observed: cash 26%, stock 48%, and combination 27%. Stock is preferred in these cases to avoid paying capital gains taxes. In all cases, debt played a minor role in the M&As tabulated.

Without question, what aroused the public's interest was the acquisition of publicly traded firms and those publicly traded firms that went private. In both cases, the availability of junk bonds facilitated the activity; the assets of the acquired company furnish the collateral and the earnings are supposed to take care of the debt incurred. As indicated earlier, huge amounts of funds were involved in these deals, and the brokerage houses, lawyers, and accountants made large profits from them. In addition, banks, insurance companies, and pension funds participated in these deals, and in the case of banks threatened to upset the conflict of interest laws.

News reports of hostile takeover fights, of raiders and greenmail, white knights, and the like made the 1980s appear as go-go years, where greed was elevated to a national virtue. MBAs were popular and business courses flourished; everyone wanted in. The names of brokers Ivan Boesky and Michael Milken became synonymous with the excesses of the 1980s, but other brokerage houses, banks, and S&Ls were also involved. Insider trading and other fraudulent practices were common but, once discovered, helped spell the end of the go-go eighties.

Also emphasized in the press were the cases where publicly traded firms were taken over and made into private ones. In the mid-1980s, about 22% of all public takeovers were characterized as "going private." In these cases, the current management or replacement management acquired the firm; in other instances an investment group did so; and in some cases, the employees banded together to acquire their former company. In the latter case, the motivation is obvious—to save their jobs—but in other cases, the justification is not readily apparent. However, if one considers that a great deal of money was made in the initial transaction and that most of these acquisitions reverted to public ownership in a few years at highly profitable stock prices, the rationale for "going private" is quickly understood. What bothered everybody was the fact that very little of their own money was put up by these investors, and their rate of return was phenomenal. These leveraged buyouts rewarded their investors handsomely, but did they benefit the economy in the same way?

It is not at all obvious why mergers and acquisitions should benefit the economy. Exchanges of pieces of paper do not improve the productivity of the firms involved, nor will efficiency be necessarily improved. Moreover, such activity might rob the economy of funds that might have been spent on real investment that would increase the productive capacity of the nation and provide jobs and opportunities for its citizens. Perhaps the examination of the arguments made on both sides might help clarify this important issue.

Hailing the decline of the public corporation, Michael Jensen presents a strong case for LBOs. The classic struggle between owners and managers would finally be resolved; firms will be made more efficient, especially with regard to the debt incurred—they must be more efficient in effect; management becomes more flexible and can respond to changing situations faster than the old public corporation; management will not have the incentive to accumulate cash, not needed for expansion, that often goes into unfamiliar areas of production instead of being paid out to stockholders. In the latter case: "Debt is in effect a substitute for dividends—a mechanism to force managers to disgorge cash rather than spend it on empire building projects with low or negative returns, bloated staffs, indulgent perquisites, and organizational inefficiencies."[3] To the extent that the old public corporations hoarded cash, they prevented their stockholders (and the financial community) from investing in other promising industries that needed the funds to develop.

Others have argued that takeovers were needed to correct the past conglomerate activity. Unwise acquisitions in the past require divestiture of some operations and restructuring of the firm to improve efficiency; managers simply cannot run conglomerates that include vastly different operations and product markets. Most of the arguments in favor of LBOs concern efficiency—higher profits, greater productivity growth, lower operating costs, and, in general, more tightly run firms.[4]

Critics of LBOs are quick to point out that the highly successful ones are balanced on the other side by cases of failure. Instances of success may well have been insured by the time period in which they occurred—the atmosphere of the 1980s. The picture is not as rosy or clear as proponents would suggest. Instead of being an incentive for efficiency as Jensen suggested, the weight of debt has proved to be overwhelming and, instead of forcing efficiency, has made the corporations cut back on research and development (R&D) and cut back on investment. Preoccupied with debt, management has closed plants, reduced employment, forced the sale of assets, hampered the ability to pursue long-range goals, and forced concentration to the short run. (Potential targets of LBOs are forced to pursue short-run goals to avert takeovers—a side effect of M&A activity.) Finally, the 1980s witnessed the dramatic accumulation of debt from all sources, so much so that there may be cause for alarm, prompting many to suggest that the tax laws be revised to remove the advantage of interest deductibility.

These are only the main arguments in the M&A issue, particularly on the LBO option. Unfortunately, empirical evidence may not resolve the issue of effects on the economy of the LBO activity that mushroomed in the 1980s. There are many who refuse to acknowledge the available evidence that indicates the failure of mergers, both present and past ones. After examining numerous studies, Adams and Brock find ". . . the weight of empirical evidence suggests that merger mania and corporate bigness do *not* enhance economic performance. Instead, the evidence suggests that more often than not they *undermine* efficiency in production, *sabotage* innovation and technological advance, and *compound* rather than cure, America's competitiveness problem." [5] They go on to cite some data on the failure rate of M&As: from *Business Week*—"A half to two-thirds of all mergers don't work; one in three is later undone. In 1985, for every seven acquisitions, there were three divestitures"; from a study by Mckinsey & Co.—"The merger record of 56 large U.S. firms over the period 1972–83 . . . most (39 of 56) of the firms that embark on diversification programs fail"; from Peter Drucker—"Two mergers out of five are outright disasters, two neither live or die, and one 'works,' " and so on; there is no need to repeat similar findings from other sources—the record is, in the words of another study, "dismal."

Also, if the past is any guide, the mergers of the 1960s and early 1970s were not very successful; the profitability of the acquired unit fell, many were subsequently sold, and takeovers by the LBO route did not always succeed due to the heavy debt burden.[6] Some comments, however, can be ventured on the likelihood of future problems.

The issue of efficiency, central to the controversy, is a microeconomic matter that can only be settled on a case-by-case basis. The focus of this book is a macroeconomic perspective, and so the issue must be set aside. On the macroeconomic side, it is disturbing to observe that R&D expenditures may be reduced in the face of debt problems. The evidence is mixed on this score, but the possibility is troubling for an economy struggling to compete in the global economy.[7]

Equally important is the evidence that suggests that real investment may also be a casualty of debt problems. To sacrifice investment is to hinder economic growth and economic opportunity for an economy that badly needs both. Furthermore, what happens to these highly leveraged firms in a recession? When their revenues fall, how will they meet debt payments? It is likely that many, as many as 10% of public corporations, will go bankrupt.[8] If interest rates are allowed to rise for macroeconomic reasons, the debt burden of the leveraged firms will be enormous. There is no industrial policy to come to the rescue of these firms, and recent administrations appear unwilling to consider any institutional innovations that might operate in such situations.

It should be noted that the Reagan administration, as in so many other cases, was willing to make judgments on matters on which others were more cautious. While acknowledging that takeovers could be harmful to the economy by increasing concentration, by fostering tax-motivated deals, by crowding out productive projects from capital markets, and by encouraging management to forego long-term investment for short-term profits, the CEA found:

The available evidence, however, is that mergers and acquisitions increase national wealth. They improve efficiency, transfer scarce resources to higher valued uses, and stimulate effective corporate management. They also help recapitalize firms so that their financial structures are more in line with prevailing market conditions. In addition, there is no evidence that mergers and acquisitions have, on any systematic basis, caused anticompetitive price increases.[9]

In short, there was nothing to worry about, and, of course, the marketplace could take care of itself. There was no need for public policy at least at the federal level; state regulation should take care of the types of abuses that might be found. The possible macroeconomic instability or reduced growth rates did not concern the CEA, and, in fact, it ignored the issue as if it were settled by their preliminary announcements.

According to Adams and Brock, the Reagan administration followed the simplistic and circular reasoning of free-market ideologues in its antitrust policies and in its sanctioning of and justification of mergers. "The Reagan administration's most conspicuous antitrust achievement was its emasculation of the nation's merger policy . . . [and] created a hospitable environment for one of the most voracious feeding frenzies and mass 'corpocide' movements in American history."[10]

The administration's devotion to the free market meant that it was also unconcerned with the possibility of an increase in the concentration of industry. Nor was it anxious to apply its antitrust weapons in these, as well as other, instances. Perhaps it was less interested in M&As because some of them were undertaken to escape the antitrust laws that prohibited some mergers but permitted others where competition was threatened. If the administrations were correct that benefits of M&As outweigh the costs, their reluctance to condemn them would be understandable; but how could they weigh benefits against costs without undertaking the painstaking task of performing the necessary empirical work?

The U.S. economy, however, needs neither an increase in instability nor threats to economic growth. Real investment, as suggested earlier, has been faltering. One reason often given by economic conservatives and others is the lack of funds available for that purpose due to the lack of savings, and so on. But if funds were lacking for real investment, how is it they were available to finance the M&As and LBOs? Did the high interest rates on junk bonds prevent real investment but encourage financial investment? Were the banks, including the S&Ls, so ready to invest in high-risk securities but unwilling to invest in less risky productive investment. Indeed, when the merger mania took off, expenditures on M&As began to exceed by far the amounts spent on real investment and R&D spending. To ask these questions is to call attention to some serious problems with respect to the vulnerability of the U.S. economy created by the new kind of speculation that flourished in the 1980s.

The atmosphere created by the Reagan administrations helped financial entrepreneurs to extend the boundaries of acceptable financial ventures; in the name of efficiency, they justified their practices and reaped the rewards. In the process, they changed the structure of the economy, making it more unstable and less able to respond to global challenges. Economic growth and technical superiority are threatened by the insecurities of debt and short-term management. In looking the other way, the Reagan administrations fostered changes in the economy that ran counter to what they hoped to achieve.

As might be expected, the possible adverse effects on labor were not seriously considered. In fact, the success of these M&As was often measured by the effect on before and after stock prices and price earnings ratios of the transaction, clearly focusing on the benefits to stockholders. But in many cases, M&As resulted in divestitures of parts of the new entity. In the period 1981–88, 7715 divestitures took place, about 33% of all M&A activity.[11] Either firms were streamlining their new operations or, equally likely, selling off parts of the corporation to help pay interest on junk bonds in the 1980s or retire junk bonds in the 1990s. In the process, many people lost their jobs.

Unfortunately, there are no records of just how many jobs were lost or how many workers were "displaced" by the restructuring of American corporations. The data show that between 1979 and 1989, some 9,417,000 workers, 20 years and older, lost their jobs because of plant closings or moves, slack work, or the abolishment of their positions or shifts.[12] Clearly, this category is much too broad to identify lost jobs due to M&A activity. As a consequence, we are forced to report anecdotal evidence to illustrate the extent of the problem.

In House hearings on the impact on workers of M&A activity, various witnesses provided the following cases.[13] In the Goodyear case, 1700 workers lost their jobs; in the Owens-Cornings Fiberglass case, 1000 jobs were cut with the possibility of 14,000 more; in the Safeway Stores case, between 3000 and 4000 jobs were eliminated; in the Lucky Stores case, 14,000 lost their jobs; in the Diamond Bathhurst case, 3800 became unemployed; in the Gimbels case, 3500 lost jobs; in the airlines industry, hundreds more were displaced. These are but a few of the examples of displaced workers due to M&A activity; they are not meant to be complete estimates, and, of course, many were reemployed.

The employment loss and the total effects of corporate restructuring are probably understated anyway. In the attempt to forestall takeovers, for instance, many corporations undertook to make their firms less susceptible. They attempted to ward off takeovers by increasing profits and stock prices by reducing costs, variable costs in the short run, meaning, of course, human resources. Thus, they downsized their work force due to the threat of takeovers much as firms in the past increased benefits to ward off unions. These cases are even more difficult to quantify, and, thus, the total jobs lost due to M&As may never be known.[14]

In addition, there is evidence to suggest that the labor markets have moved from "rigid labor markets" to more "flexible labor markets." The former are characterized by institutional forces wherein labor and management could reach understandings that both sides could view as fair arrangements on contracts, wages, terms of employment, and so on that did not change rapidly. In flexible labor markets, firms respond more readily to market forces, creating more insecurity for workers who face the specter of unemployment, wage concessions, benefit cutbacks, and the like. Many factors could be responsible for the shift in labor market forces such as foreign competition, deregulation, the decline of unionism, the shift to a service economy, the changing composition of the labor force, and the not-so-subtle changes from past macroeconomic policies where employers could count on the federal government to ensure the proper level of aggregate demand to enable the firms to assume production amounts that would enable them to grant wage demands, assume price stability, and so on. Still, the link between labor and financial markets suggested in the corporations' reactions to possible takeovers (its willingness to reduce its labor force) may have been underestimated as a major factor in recent years.

Finally, we might ask what happens in the case of foreign takeovers: Do they create or destroy jobs? Recall the argument that U.S. workers gain employment, knowledge, and skills from foreign investment and, therefore, should not be unalterably opposed to foreign ownership. Again, data problems abound, but one estimate puts the additions to jobs by the establishment of new facilities at 45,151 from 1982 to 1986, and the job gains due to expansions at 341,281; however, the loss of jobs due to cutbacks was estimated at 442,295, for a net loss of jobs of some 55,863 jobs. After justifying their estimating procedures, the authors conclude: "Anyway you look at these numbers, you reach the one startling conclusion: *employment from new plants and expansions is less than employment cutbacks* during the period [emphasis in original]."[15] The absolute numbers may be incorrect, but the conclusion does warrant some reflection about the job-creating effects of foreign takeovers.

But the devastation to workers and to the community in which they were formerly employed is incalculable. The point is that in the calculations of the success of corporate restructuring and in arguments over the increase in efficiency, one group is frequently overlooked—those who are most vulnerable, the workers. Moreover, the total effect on a community of the plant closings goes far beyond the loss of jobs; many communities found themselves depressed, and through a "multiplier" effect, the devastation spread over a wide region.

In the early 1990s, M&A activity has declined considerably. Whether due to the lack of profitable opportunities or to the lengthy recession, some of the obsession of the 1980s has dimmed. The pressure to do something about the perceived problem has also subsided, but while the M&A activity was at its height, some legislative proposals were entertained. A listing of these might be instructive, if only to witness the degree of concern that M&As were beginning to engender. First and foremost, proposals were made to reduce or limit the deductibility of interest expense in the cases of hostile takeovers (and other types too); second, to prohibit takeovers by foreigners when financed by debt; third, to establish schedules of acceptable debt to equity ratios and eliminate interest deductibility in cases where the ratios were outside the standards set by industry. More regulations were suggested in areas where pension funds were used in M&As, where other tax benefits were available, and where the rights of bondholders and shareholders were threatened.[16] In the 1990s, the legislative agenda does not include much to alter the conditions of M&A activity, although interest deductibility remains a topic on the fringes of concern.

THE DEBT ECONOMY

The 1980s were characterized by the enormous growth of debt—both private and public. Indeed, the boom of the period owes its origin to the use of debt by all economic agents. The nation appeared to live and prosper by the use of the credit card. The Reagan administrations accomplished what no ardent Keynesian dared to attempt—a large deficit-driven boom. They outdid the Keynesians while attributing the upswing to supply-side economics, an exercise in doublespeak that would have delighted George Orwell. However, the real question, not asked then except by spoilsports, is what would be the effects on the economy over the longer run? The economy boomed in the short run, and the Reagan administrations basked in light of the economic recovery, but would there be a hangover in the long run? Would our grandchildren be burdened by the excesses of those who had a party in the 1980s?

Table 12.1 provides some summary data. The growth of the federal debt, nearly 80% in the recovery period and over 125% since 1980, is by now no

Table 12.1
The Growth of Debt in the Economy, 1983–88 (in billions)

	1983	1988	% Change
Public Debt:			
Federal	$ 1,177.9	$ 2,117.8	79.7
State and Local	357.7	604.5	68.7
Corporate	1,022.9	1,899.5	85.7
Nonfarm noncorp.	645.8	1,145.1	77.3
Household	1,811.6	3,191.5	76.2
Farm	188.4	137.6	-27.0
Total Credit Market debt owed by domestic nonfin. sectors:	$ 5,204.3	$ 9,096.0	74.8

Source: Board of Governors, Federal Reserve System, Federal
Reserve Bulletins.

longer a surprise. Earlier, it was suggested that the debt was the result of the tax cuts not accompanied by spending cuts, but essentially it reveals the failure of supply-side economics. In the postmortem of the Reagan administrations, one can only marvel at campaign rhetoric of the evils of budget deficits, and the hypocrisy following the record deficits actually produced.

Less familiar is the record of the states and localities. In the 1983–88 period, states and localities were also accumulating record deficits as their debt increased by 69% (125% since 1980). This is due, in part, to the cutbacks by the Reagan administrations anxious as always to transfer programs back to the states or localities. Similarly, revenue sharing programs were eliminated, forcing local governments to assume the expenditure burden formerly shared with the federal government. In addition, it must be recalled that states had adopted tax limitation laws of their own in the attempt to put a ceiling on property taxation. Now they were forced to maintain spending on popular programs without the tax revenue to fund them. Limited also by reliance on tax structures that do not respond so quickly to changing economic conditions, they found it difficult to maintain the same level of expenditures without resorting to borrowing.

Corporations also found it advantageous to borrow both for reasons of tax deductibility and for all those corporate maneuverings in stock values, stock repurchase programs, and in M&As. Corporate borrowing increased by over 85%, and corporate bonds alone rose by over 101% in the recovery period 1983–88. Similar increases can be found in the noncorporate business sector where indebtedness rose by over 77%.

Households, too, increased their reliance on debt. With real wages falling or stagnant, they maintained their living standards by borrowing. Their debt outstanding reached $3 trillion, representing an increase of over 76% from 1983 to 1988 (over 108% since 1980). Total installment credit rose by over 80% from 1983 to 1988 (123% from 1980); and automobile paper alone rose by 98% (154% from 1980). Consumers were busy buying the latest products so heavily touted by advertisers and, in addition, were fascinated by foreign made goods from VCRs to autos, borrowing to acquire them, and adding to the balance of payments problem. Whatever the reason for going into debt, these are huge amounts, and it does not take much economic sophistication to realize that such rates of increase could not continue, particularly if and when a recession occurred. Indeed, in 1990, when a recession did hit, consumers were in no position to help in the turnaround—they were too burdened with debt to spend—and because consumption spending is a large portion of the GDP, one major sector was not contributing to the recovery.

Of course, neither was the business sector. The Federal Reserve, in the effort to stimulate borrowing, reduced interest rates many times over the course of the recession but to no avail. Firms were too heavily indebted to borrow more no matter how low the interest rate fell. For example, in a series of reductions, the discount rate fell from 6.98 in 1990 to 3.0 in mid-August 1992, and the prime rate fell from over 10% to 6% in the same period without providing the necessary incentive for firms to borrow. To be sure, real interest rates appeared too high by historical standards, and this accounted for some of the reluctance to borrow. Still, monetary policy was made impotent under these conditions, although the monetary authorities seemed not to be aware of the loss of their influence. Add to the debt burden problem the normal uncertainty found in investment spending during a recession, and no help could be found for a recovery from the business sector either.

Only the farm sector managed to reduce its indebtedness, but not really by choice. Many farms went bankrupt in the 1980s, and many more had their bank financing discontinued. Still others were loaned up to their limits. Farmers were encouraged to borrow by the federal government in the 1970s, and banks were happy to oblige, as farmers were promised a booming export market. Many farmers borrowed to enlarge their farms or to acquire new equipment. But that export market did not develop, and, in fact, the United States lost markets in the USSR food embargo fiasco. This left farmers overextended and unable to meet their loan obligations. Forced farm sales and auctions of farm equipment were the result.

TOO MUCH DEBT?

It is clear that the debt economy of the 1980s made it vulnerable to any disturbance in economic conditions. When the recession started in 1990, the extent of the reliance on debt of the 1980s soon was apparent. The go-go years were over, and the boom was seen as artificial; the credit card mentality simply could not continue. Parties are fun, but someone must pay the bill.

Too much debt, therefore, added to the instability of the economy. Moreover, when economic problems develop, monetary and fiscal policies cannot be employed as they were intended to by countercyclical means. Monetary policy can push down the rate of interest, but if no one wants to borrow, the policy is impotent: You cannot push on a string, as the saying goes. Fiscal policy is also powerless when policy makers refrain from actions that might stimulate the economy but lead to increases in the budget deficit.

But what is too much debt? There is no magic answer, for instance, as to the proper debt/equity ratio for corporations, and economists disagree over whether there is any danger in the present experience. Have lower inflation rates in the 1980s encouraged firms to take more risks with their capital and shift their horizons to the short run? Perhaps there is some justification for borrowing more on a short-term basis and altering the debt/equity ratios more in line with the ratios found in other countries. [17]

Still, in a macroeconomic sense, there should be more concern with the concentration on the short run. Again, long-term real investment may well be sacrificed to the detriment of economic growth and technological advances. Too much concern for the short run—for short-run profits, for quick results—could result in too much "paper entrepreneurialism" that focuses on financial rewards and subordinates production matters.

These are familiar concerns voiced in the 1980s, but now, in the early 1990s, they are no longer possibilities but experience. Many of the fears expressed are now reality: Debt is a large problem. Consider this fact: In the boom period of 1983–88, the U.S. economy (nominal GNP) increased by 4.4% while total debt increased by 75%! Potential trouble was seen by many, including the cautious Paul Volcker, Federal Reserve Chairman:

The strongly rising stock market and lower interest rates had the effect of greatly increasing consumer wealth, measured by current market values, and lowering the cost of capital to business. Nonetheless, the trend of debt creation, with its implications for greater leveraging and potential financial fragility, remains disquieting. . . . Indeed, . . . there is already ample evidence in the financial area of the consequences for individual institutions of extended financial positions and unduly loose credit standards. [18]

The financial fragility is easily demonstrated in the case of commercial banks and S&Ls. The S&Ls sought high returns and invested in junk bonds, and the consequences are well known. Commercial banks also lent huge sums for LBOs, exposing themselves to potential disaster. For example, here are some of the ratios of highly leveraged loans to bank equity for some large banks: Continental 127%, Bank of N.Y., 127%, Wells Fargo 119%, Bank of Boston 103%, and Manufactures Hanover 107%. [19] Clearly these, and other, banks were courting danger and diverting funds to LBOs that might have been available for more productive purposes. Furthermore, when the value of many junk bonds plummeted in the 1990s, the banking system was forced to retrench and become more restrictive in their lending practices. Their caution may be commendable but they were refusing loans that might have proved fruitful for economic development and have helped turn the economy around from the recession.

BANKRUPTCIES

It would not be surprising to find that in a period of financial excesses and risk taking that the bankruptcy rate would exhibit the same trend. We have already witnessed the failure of hundreds of banks in the 1980s and the collapse of the banking industry. The record for the rest of the economy is not much better.

For nonbusiness bankruptcies, 312,914 petitions were filed in 1981; in 1988, the number had risen to 526,066, an increase of 68%. For businesses, 47,415 petitions were filed; in 1988, 68,501 were, an increase of 44%.[20] The business failure rate (failure rate per 10,000 listed enterprises) rose from 42.1 in 1980 to 110 in the first year of the "boom," then to 120 in 1986 during the merger mania, before falling slowly to 98 in 1988. Interestingly, in the early 1980s, the number of larger firms (over $100,000 liability class) that failed exceeded the smaller ones, but for the rest of the 1980s, the reverse was true.[21] Were these divestitures of smaller parts of the merged firm, or were smaller firms simply overreaching themselves in the attempt to grow?

Of course, this question cannot be answered by summary data such as these. Nor can much be inferred about the causes of the failures without a great deal of microeconomic analysis. This would take us too far afield and require extensive study in itself. So we are forced to leave the data on bankruptcies in the suggestive stage, without adequate explanation except to note that the data are consistent with the claim that the 1980s were characterized by excesses of all kinds and that the number of bankruptcies increased across the board.

Before leaving the topic of business failures, it might be instructive to look, very briefly, at business formation. Looking at the index of net business formation, it appears that the rate was greater during the Carter years than in the probusiness Reagan administration. With 1967 = 100, the Carter years show indexes of 131, 138, 138, and 130; in no single year did the Reagan administrations come close to these data. The highest index occurred in 1981 at 125 and fell, thereafter averaging about 120 until reaching 124 in 1988. Again, no confirmation of supply-side economics can be found here.[22]

Looking at just small business in the 1980s, the net growth rate (birth rate minus death rate) of small industries was not impressive as the rate averaged about 1.0; construction industries averaged 0.5; manufacturing, 0.9; wholesale trade, 1.3; retail trade; −0.6; and services, 2.7. Again, the growth of the service industry is verified along with the probability of low-paying jobs that accompany it.[23]

SUMMARY AND CONCLUSIONS

The Reagan administrations did not set out to alter the structure of the economy. True, some changes might have been predicted from their probusiness, antilabor biases. Yet, profound changes were made to the economic structure due to their policy of benign neglect and avowed and unquestioning belief in free markets unfettered by government. They simply looked away as the developments that altered the economy were taking place; they either ignored these developments or declared them beneficial. Whatever problems were acknowledged were admitted in a theoretical sense—bad things could happen—but not likely to occur in practice.

So the administrations watched the unprecedented merger movement in the 1980s and saw possible dangers but then concluded that there was no cause for concern. The free market would take care of whatever problems arose. In this atmosphere created by the Reagan administrations, greed was justified, and its acceptance created a get-rich-quick society. Hostile takeovers, leveraged buyouts, greenmail, and white knights became the bywords for this frenzied period. The M&A activity was justified by the desire for efficiency, found more in the justification than in reality. In the game, some won—lawyers, accountants, brokers—and some lost—workers and consumers.

Also, in the process, the economic structure was changed: The concentration of industry proceeded unchallenged, and the antitrust laws were deemed obsolete and ineffective. There was no need to oversee the primarily beneficial effects of free-market players. The results are somewhat less satisfactory. The economy suffered as real investment was postponed, and economic growth stalled along with it; technological advances were sacrificed as unaffordable; foreign competition crippled many industries and domestic firms fell behind; thousands of jobs were lost; and many communities were devastated. These are the products of benign neglect.

Meanwhile, the Reagan administrations looked on and prematurely pronounced the observed changes as beneficial to the economy. No need to worry; let the unknowing critics do that. The administrations were too busy glorifying the boom of the eighties, seemingly unaware of, or disinterested in, the debt accumulation that fueled the recovery. Given the peculiar fiscal and monetary mix, the public sector was forced to borrow to finance its operations. Unwilling or unable to rectify the situation, huge budget deficits resulted that prevented the macroeconomic policies of the past; fiscal policy was constrained and monetary policy was made impotent.

Corporations borrowed to finance their M&A activities, using junk bonds for the job, or borrowed to retire those junk bonds when interest payments became a burden. Not much borrowing was undertaken to finance real investment that would have encouraged economic growth. Households borrowed to buy the goods and services that falling real incomes prevented them from buying with current income. Households, too, were deceived into seeing the surface prosperity and were persuaded easily to buy now rather than wait.

The recovery was indeed fueled by debt, but the burden of the debt was to make the economy more unstable and less amenable to correction. Of course, many bankruptcies ensued and many banks felt the problem all too acutely. When the era ended, firms stopped borrowing, banks stopped lending, and consumers attempted to restore their finances. Only the public sector continued to borrow, but feeling the weight of huge deficits, now made worse in recession, began to cut back on expenditures on education and health programs and other programs that will sacrifice long-run economic development.

Monetary policy was made helpless by the accumulated debt and the burden it presented. No matter how far interest rates were pushed down, they provided no inducement to overextended firms and households. Where were the borrowers now?

So the policy of benign neglect did not live up to its promise. Instead, the economy has become more concentrated, banks more shaky, and economic growth made more difficult as real investment stalled. In the face of all this, the federal government would not or could not remedy problems that were emanating from the changing economic structure that it failed to recognize.

NOTES

1. These and other data in this section were taken from Merrill Lynch, *Mergerstat Review* (Chicago, IL: W. T. Grim & Co.), 1990. Data on the largest 100 transactions can be found on pages 27–33. It should be noted that these data are not corrected for inflation, and although that does not do serious harm to the conclusions reached here, it should be kept in mind for other purposes.

2. Lynch, *Mergerstat Review,* 36.

3. Michael C. Jensen, "Eclipse of the Public Corporation," in *Harvard Business Review* (September–October 1989): 32. Reprinted in Joint Economic Committee, *Corporate Time Horizons,* Hearings. 101st Cong., 1st sess., 1989 (Washington, DC: Government Printing Office, 1990), 26–39.

4. Many of the arguments on the issue can be found in Congressional Research Service, *Leveraged Buyouts and the Pot of Gold: Trends, Public Policy, and Case Studies,* a report for the Committee on Energy and Commerce, House, 100th Cong., 1st sess., 1987 (Washington, DC: Government Printing Office, 1987). See also Alan J. Auerbach, ed., *Mergers and Acquisitions* (Chicago: University of Chicago Press, 1988); and David J. Ravenscraft and F. M. Scherer, *Mergers, Sell-Offs, and Economic Efficiency,* (Washington, DC: The Brookings Institution, 1987).

5. Walter Adams and James W. Brock, "Reaganomics and the Transmogrification of Merger Policy," *The Antitrust Bulletin* (Summer 1988): 338. Reprinted in *Leveraged Buyouts and Bankruptcy,* Hearings of the House Committee on the Judiciary, 101st Cong., 2nd sess., May 17, 1990, 258–309.

6. Ravenscraft and Scherer, *Mergers, Sell-Offs, and Economic Efficiency,* 192–215.

7. Jensen provided some evidence to suggest no decline in R&D expenditures, but

the aggregative nature of the data hide more than they reveal—the years chosen and the influence of defense R&D cloud the conclusions of the study. Other studies related by Scherer suggests that the results are very mixed indeed and that more study is required to answer the question. See Jensen in JEC *Corporate Time Horizons,* 9; and Scherer's testimony in the same place, 40–41.

8. See Ben Bernanke and John Campbell, *Brookings Papers on Economic Activity* 1(1988): 121.

9. *Economic Report of the President, 1985,* 196.

10. Adams and Brock, "Reaganomics and the Transmogrification of Merger Policy," 309–310.

11. *Mergerstat Review,* 59.

12. U.S. Department of Labor, *Displaced Workers, 1985–89,* BLS, Bulletin 2282, June 1991, 5.

13. U.S. Congress, House Committee on Government Operations, *Impact on Workers of Takeovers, Leveraged Buyouts, Corporate Restructuring, and Greenmail,* 100th Cong., 1st sess., 1987, various pages.

14. See the paper presented by Richard S. Belous, "The Impact of Mergers and Acquisitions on Labor Markets," Ibid. 79–97.

15. Norman J. Glickman and Douglas P. Woodward, *The New Competitors: How Foreign Investors are Changing the U.S. Economy* (New York: Basic Books, 1989), 316.

16. Congressional Research Service, *Leveraged Buyouts and the Pot of Gold,* xvii.

17. Ibid. 33–35.

18. Ibid. Quoted from testimony before the Committee on Banking, Finance, and Urban affairs in February 1986.

19. Statement of Walter Adams and James Brock before the Committee on the Judiciary, House, *Leveraged Buyouts and Bankruptcy,* 101st Cong., 2nd sess., 1990, 31.

20. Bureau of the Census *Statistical Abstract of the United States, 1992,* 538.

21. *Economic Report of the President, 1991,* 394.

22. Ibid. 394.

23. Bureau of the Census *Statistical Abstract of the United States, 1992,* 538.

Chapter 13

The Social Structure

In the *Program for Economic Recovery* of 1981, there was no mention of poverty, and the only notice given to the issue was in the promise to provide a "safety net" for the "truly needy." The safety net was designed to protect the incomes of Social Security recipients, the unemployed, the chronically poor, and veterans, while eliminating entitlements for the unintended. We have already seen that the safety net had many holes in it, and expenditure reductions went far beyond eliminating the benefits of the undeserving. (See Chapter 9.) Beyond entitlements, the Reagan administrations also attacked other social programs—housing, urban development, education, social service programs—as part of their efforts to control spending.

Inevitably, these cuts led to the charge that the Reagan administrations pitted the haves against the have-nots. In their tax and spending policies, they favored those who needed no help, and turned aside from those who did. In effect, they polarized the society and began the policy of societal division in many ways. Many reached the conclusion that this was class warfare.

Their opposition to public housing and welfare (benefiting mostly inner city blacks) along with their opposition to civil rights legislation and South African sanctions was seen as racist and fueled the black versus white chasm. Their ideas of federalism pitted states against localities, urban dwellers against suburban. Their opposition to the Equal Rights Amendment and their disregard for the needs of women, such as day care centers that accompanied their changing family roles, subordinated women in society; when they claimed discrimination, women were dismissed, and when they clamored for equal pay for equal work, they were ignored. As a consequence, the division between males and females was reignited.[1] In general, their continuous harping on welfare recipients, on the long-term unemployed receiving compensation, on the disabled receiving disability benefits, and on all other undeserving beneficiaries of federal largess created an atmosphere of distrust (hatred?) and suspicion about the nonworking population from those who were employed, especially the working poor.

It is possible to overstate the case here, but there is little doubt that deep divisions were either created or exacerbated in the Reagan years. After all, the Reagan men were out to challenge the prevailing sentiment about the role of government in the society, and it should, therefore, come as no surprise that they upset traditional habits of thinking and alienated the affected groups.

These alterations and movements in the social structure are interesting and important in a complete evaluation of the effects of the Reagan revolution, but they would take us too far afield to pursue them. In what follows, however, the movements in the economic structure will illuminate and help explain the strains and stresses revealed in the social structure.

ECONOMIC SHIFTS

In the end, who won and who lost in the economic game has a great deal to do with how various groups feel about the Reagan years. This is not to denigrate the political and social aspects that influence the decision but only to emphasize the power of economic outcomes to ameliorate the perceived losses in other areas. So the question for us shifts to how to determine who won and who lost.

So many indicators of winners and losers have been presented to the American public, some claiming this group won, and others claiming the opposite, that it is not surprising that some confusion remains. The fault lies with investigators using different concepts of income, different definitions of households, different time periods, and different methodologies. In some cases, the investigator may be biased and choose the variables to obtain the results hoped for in the beginning; in other cases, the choices made may merely reflect the preference of the researcher, the availability of data, and so on. In any case, the necessary care to interpret these data can hardly be expected of the general public, and so the field is open for all kinds of misleading ''scientific results.'' To correct this (considering space limitations), we will present several different types of evidence, discuss the shortcomings, and compare them with other studies.[2]

Table 13.1 provides the data for one of the most common means of assessing the inequality of income. The share of aggregate income received by fifths of income recipients reveals how the income was distributed by groups, and the Gini ratio reveals the degree of inequality. Using either the household or family as the unit, it is clear that inequality increased in the 1980s.

Using either unit, there is a great deal of stability in the income shares received by fifths. There is very little change in the distributions up to the 1980s, and most observers of these data noted the constancy over the years, although the reasons for the stability were not always evident. Beginning in 1982, however, there are observable shifts in the distribution toward greater inequality. For example, using the household unit, *all fifths except the highest fifth lost ground from 1979 to 1989* (two peak business cycle years for comparison purposes). The highest fifth gained 5.9%, the top 5% gained 11.8%, and the lowest fifth *lost* 7.3%. From 1981 to 1989, the numbers are similar with the highest fifth gaining 5.6%, the top 5% gaining 14.5%, and the lowest fifth again losing 7.3%. So in terms of households, the bottom 80% of households lost ground in either the 1979–89 or 1981–89 periods.

Table 13.1

Share of Aggregate Income Received by Each Fifth and Top 5% of Households and Families in Selected Years

Unit and Year	Percent Distribution of Aggregate Income						Gini Ratio
	Lowest fifth	Second fifth	Third fifth	Fourth fifth	Highest fifth	Top 5%	
Households							
1989	3.8	9.5	15.8	24.0	46.8	18.9	.431
1988	3.8	9.6	16.0	24.3	46.3	18.3	.427
1981	4.1	10.1	16.7	24.8	44.4	16.5	.403
1979	4.1	10.2	16.8	24.7	44.2	16.9	.404
1969	4.1	10.9	17.5	24.5	43.0	16.6	.391
Families							
1989	4.6	10.6	16.5	23.7	44.6	17.9	.401
1988	4.6	10.7	16.7	24.0	44.0	17.2	.395
1981	5.1	11.3	17.4	24.4	41.8	15.3	.369
1979	5.3	11.6	17.5	24.0	41.7	15.8	.365
1969	5.6	12.4	17.7	23.7	40.6	15.6	.349

Source: U.S. Bureau of the Census, Current Population Reports, Series P-60, No. 172, Money Income of Households, Families, and Persons in the United States: 1988 and 1989, 371.

Using the family as the unit, the same general conclusions emerge, only the numbers are higher. For example, the highest fifth gained 7.0% from 1979 to 1989 and 6.7% from 1981 to 1989; the top 5% gained 13.3% and 17.0% during the same periods; meanwhile, the lowest fifth again *lost* 9.8% and 13.2%. As before, the bottom 80% of the distribution lost ground in either period.

The trend toward inequality is clearly seen in the Gini ratio designed to measure it. The Gini coefficient ranges from 1 (indicating perfect inequality) to 0 (indicating perfect equality).[3] Note in Table 13.1 that in either unit of reference, the Gini coefficient is increasing, meaning that inequality is increasing. In the case of households, inequality increased 6.7% from 1979 to 1989, and for families, 9.9%. Observe also that inequalities in both series accelerated from 1981 to 1989.

If one looks at the Gini coefficient from the post-WWII period, a significant U-turn appears in the data. The ratio reached its lowest values (greater equality) in the 1967–68 period, and then gradually crept upward to its post-war peak in 1989. When plotted, the 1980s clearly show a dramatic increase in inequality.[4]

Although frequently quoted, these data can be misleading. First, the CPI used to correct for inflation was changed for the housing component of the index in 1983. Historical trends that do not correct for the changes in inflation can be misleading. Second, these data do not correct for family size. In effect, a family of four with $15,000 income is treated as equivalent to a single individual with the same income. Clearly, the needs of a family increase with the numbers of individuals in it, although there are economies of scale to consider as well. Third, only gross cash income in included in the analysis, thus ignoring income in kind, such as government transfers of food stamps, housing allowances, and so on, as well as taxes paid by families. Because transfer payments have increased over the post-WWII period, and taxes have fluctuated, these omissions can potentially distort the conclusions. In brief, as measures of family welfare, the Census data are simply deficient and conclusions based on them should be interpreted with caution.[5]

ADJUSTED MEASURES OF INEQUALITY

Correcting for the shortcomings of the Census data is easily accomplished for an updated CPI series. Correcting for family size is more controversial. Per capita data could be used to adjust for family size, but this would not account for the age structure of the family nor adjust for economies of scale with additional members. An equivalency scale is needed to adjust family size into a measure of equivalent persons. The scale most convenient but not ideal is the poverty thresholds used in the measurement of poverty. This scale, for instance, assumes that a family of four needs two times the income of a single individual, and a family of nine needs four times that of an individual. Thus, family income is adjusted by dividing income by the poverty threshold for the appropriate family size to arrive at adjusted family income (AFI).

In the AFI, each family receives equal weight in the income distribution. Perhaps a better measure of inequality is to weigh the income distribution by individuals. Here, each person rather than each family receives equal weight, and large families receive greater weight than smaller ones. For example, a family of four receives four times the weight of a family of one. Each member of the family is credited with the income of the family. Moreover, when using quintiles to measure inequality with the individual distribution, each quintile contains exactly 20% of the population, not 20% of the families.

Table 13.2 gives the results of the adjustments on the shares of income received by quintiles for selected years. By any measure, income inequality increased from 1979 to 1987. The lowest quintiles lost the most ground, having seen their cash income measure decrease by 13.3%, their adjusted family income weighted by families fall by 8.3%, and when weighted by individuals, fall by 17.3%. In fact, the bottom 60% of the distribution saw their shares diminished; only the top 5% experienced any increases in their share of the national income. Looking at the distribution by persons, in some ways the superior view for inequality measures, the lowest 5% lost 17.3% whereas the top 5% gained 5.8%. There seems little objection to the conclusion that inequality increased over the period.

The same general conclusions were reached by Lynn A. Karoly in a study published by the Rand Corporation. Using a similar methodology, she found, using the individual measure, that the bottom 10th percentile of individuals lost

Table 13.2
Shares of Family Income by Income Quintile and Change over Time, for All Families

Quintile	1973	1979	1987	Percent Change 1979-87
A. Shares of Mean Cash Family Income:				
Lowest	4.0	4.5	3.9	-13.3
Second	10.2	11.2	10.2	-8.9
Middle	17.1	17.9	17.1	-4.4
Fourth	25.0	25.2	24.9	-1.2
Highest	43.7	41.2	43.9	6.5
B. Shares of Adjusted Family Income[1] Weighted by Families				
Lowest	5.0	4.8	4.1	-8.3
Second	11.1	11.1	10.2	-8.1
Middle	16.9	17.1	16.4	-4.1
Fourth	24.1	24.4	24.4	-
Highest	42.9	42.7	44.9	5.2
C. Shares of Adjusted Family Income[1], Weighted by Persons				
Lowest	5.6	5.2	4.3	-17.3
Second	11.9	11.7	10.7	- 8.5
Middle	17.2	17.4	16.8	- 3.4
Fourth	23.8	24.3	24.3	-
Highest	41.4	41.5	43.9	5.8

[1] Income as a fraction of poverty.
Source: Committee on Ways and Means, House of Representatives, <u>Background Material and Data Within the Jurisdiction of the Committee on Ways and Means</u>, March 1989, 987.

10.2% and the top 10% gained 15.0% in the period 1979–87. Together with the examination of other data, she concluded: "The data . . . leave little room for doubt that the distribution of income among families and individuals has become less equal. . . . Thus while the rich have been getting richer, the poor have become even poorer."[6]

In terms of understanding the changes in the structure of society, it would be instructive to break down the distributions even further to examine different family types. Dividing the AFI for each family type by the appropriate poverty index, it is possible to see how each family type fared in the period. For example, the lowest quintile for all families received 92% of poverty income in 1979 and only 83% in 1987, for a loss of 9.8%. In the same period, the highest quintile gained 15.6%. Using only the bottom and top quintiles to illustrate the trends in the same period, we can observe the following: For all families with children, the lowest quintile lost 16.5% and the highest gained 16.7%; for married couples with children, the numbers are 7.5% loss against a 19.1% gain; for single mothers with children, the lowest fifth lost 21.2% while the highest fifth gained 9.8%; for nonelderly childless families, the loss at the bottom was 7.6% and the gain at the top was 12.1%; for nonelderly unrelated individuals, the data are −10% and 16.9%; only the elderly family types gained in all ranges on the order of 12–16%. The record is clear, the top fifth of the income distribution by family types gained over the period along with the elderly in all quintiles. However, the most disadvantaged groups were losing and particularly single mothers with children.[7]

Before leaving these studies, it is important to note that both the Karoly and Ways and Means studies show a peculiar U-shape in the distributions (except for the elderly), meaning the lower tails were losing and the upper tails of the distribution were gaining. This lends support to the thesis that the middle class was shrinking in the period covered. We will postpone discussion of this phenomenon until later.

Critics of the foregoing studies might object to the exclusion of in-kind benefits to disadvantaged groups and to the omission of taxes. To measure economic well-being, both noncash income and taxes should be considered. The Ways and Means study added to cash income the in-kind transfers such as food stamps, school lunches, and housing benefits, but omitted health insurance (both private and government provided) and pension plans. Data by family or individual are lacking for the latter. Also, *federal* income taxes and payroll taxes were included for an indicator of taxes paid. Thus, there is some attempt to include noncash income and taxes in the measurement of well-being; although not perfect, the resulting measure should better serve to indicate trends in the income distribution.

In general, the previously observed trends are continued in this methodology. Table 13.3 shows only the summary for all families. The most striking observation is how similar the results are when comparing the posttax, included benefits distribution with just the cash distribution (last column). The bottom fifth lost 9.2% when taxes and benefits are included, and 9.8% when they are not; similarly, the top gained 18.7% after taxes, but gained 15.6% before taxes and benefits.

Some other results of the study are not included in detail here but are revealing: Income losses were concentrated among young families—families where the head was under age 35; inequality among nonwhite families grew more than inequalities among white families; income taxes were probably more responsible for reducing inequalities than were transfer payments; and the progressivity of taxes was reduced by the 1981 tax law and increased slightly by the subsequent revisions, which confirms the analysis of the tax burden discussed in an earlier chapter.

These results are interesting by themselves but are presented here in partial

Table 13.3

Posttax Income, Including Noncash Benefits for All Families, 1979 and 1987 (as a fraction of poverty and in 1987 dollars)

	Avg. Post tax Income		% Change	Avg Pre tax, Pre- Benefit % Change 1979-1987
	1979	1987		
All Families:				
Lowest	0.98	0.89	-9.2	-9.8
Second	1.91	1.90	- .5	- .5
Middle	2.69	2.84	5.6	5.2
Fourth	3.62	4.01	10.8	9.3
Highest	5.84	6.93	18.7	15.6
Average	3.01	3.31	10.0	9.3

Source: Committee and Ways and Means, House, *Background Material and Data on Programs Within the Jurisdiction of the Committee on Ways and Means,* March 1989, Table 35, 1004.

support of the thesis that the structure of society was indeed altered by the economic events of the 1980s. The society was being fragmented by changes wrought by the Reagan administrations, with those at the bottom, the least advantaged, being the losers.

Another measure of inequality designed to facilitate comparisons over time is the relative income measure. The relative income measure is designed to provide some information about the shape of the distribution that is lacking in the use of median income measures or in the Gini index. "The relative income measure . . . shows the extent to which the income of a person (or group of persons) diverges from the middle income of the universe."[8] Thus, over time it is possible to determine whether income inequality is increasing or decreasing. Operationally, it is necessary to take money incomes and assign values to individuals and then adjust incomes for differences in family size according to equivalence scales that take account of different family needs. After calculating the median levels of equivalence-adjusted incomes, it is an easy matter to assign each individual a value equal to his adjusted income to median adjusted income. In terms of Table 13.4 therefore, a person with a value of 0.25 has only one-fourth the income of a person in the middle of the distribution, and a person with a value of 2.0 has twice the relative income of a person in the middle.

From Table 13.4, it is again evident that inequality has increased over the period covered. Inequality decreased from 1964 to 1969, increased slightly in 1974 (not shown), then began to increase more in 1979, still more in 1984 (not shown) until 1989 when the series stops. For example, persons with less than 0.50 of the median, increased from 19.2% in 1964 to 20.0% in 1979, an in-

Table 13.4
Percent Distribution of Persons, by Relative Income, Selected Years

Relative Income	1964	1969	1979	1989
Less than .50	19.2	17.9	20.0	22.1
Less than .25	6.7	5.5	6.7	8.3
.25 to .49	12.6	12.4	13.3	13.7
.50 to .74	14.5	15.0	14.5	14.1
.75 to .99	16.3	16.9	15.5	13.9
1.00 to 1.24	14.3	15.0	13.8	12.7
1.25 to 1.99	23.9	24.2	24.3	22.6
2.00 and over	11.7	10.9	11.9	14.7
2.00 to 2.99	8.7	8.1	8.6	9.9
3.00 and over	3.1	2.8	3.3	4.8
Less than .50 or 2.00 and over	31.0	28.8	32.0	36.7

Source: Adapted from Bureau of the Census, Current Population Reports, Trends in Relative Income:1964 to 1989, P-60, No.177, December 1991, 8.

crease of 4.2%; from 1979 to 1989, the increase was 10.5%. For those with less than one-fourth of the median, the increase was even more pronounced: from 1979 to 1989 their number increased by 24%! Those persons with more than two times the median saw their numbers remain relatively constant from 1964 to 1979, but their numbers rose from 11.9% to 14.7% from 1979 to 1989, an increase of 23.5%.

Clearly, the upper tail was increasing and the lower tail was increasing, meaning the dispersion of incomes was increasing. This can also be seen in the last line of Table 13.4 where those with relative incomes of less than 0.50 or over 2.0 are represented. Their numbers increased from 31% in 1964 to 32% in 1979 and to 36.7% in 1989, an increase of 14.7% in the latter decade alone.

Another interesting feature of the data is the apparent decline in the middle ranges of relative incomes. For example, in the ranges of 0.50 to 0.74% and from 1.0 to 1.24% of the median, the numbers of people in these categories were falling. Thus, there is further evidence of the decline in the middle of the distribution—the middle class. This is but another piece of evidence to support the hypothesis to be discussed later that the middle class is disappearing.

Space limitations prohibit the elaboration of detailed results of this study, but a few outstanding features should be discussed. As far as age groups were concerned, persons under 18 and persons 18 to 64 years old, increased dramatically in the lower income ranges. For those with less than 0.50 of the median, among 18 year olds, the number increased from 21.2% in 1964 to 24.5% in 1979 and to 29.1% in 1989, an increase of 18.8% in the last decade; For the 18–64 age group, the increase from 1979 to 1989 was 14.6%. On the opposite end, those with 2.0 or greater than the median increased by 27% for the under-18 group, and by 19% for the 18–64 group for the decade 1979–89. Persons over 65 saw their numbers fall at the lower end of the distribution and rise at the top end; at the low end there were 13% fewer people, and at the top end, there were 47% more. Although elderly people were doing better, the young were not thriving, setting up another split in the society, the generational one where the young feel deprived as the problems of the elderly were being addressed. The young worried that the high payroll taxes they were paying now, and forecasted to increase in the future, to finance Social Security for the old would not be available to them when the system collapsed.

Among whites, inequalities increased dramatically. Those with less than 0.50 of relative income rose from 15.5% in 1964 to 16.7% in 1979 to 18.9% in 1989 (a 13% increase from 1979); those with 2.0 or more of relative income rose from 12.9% in 1964 to 13.1% in 1979 to 16% in 1989 (a 22% increase over 1979). Among blacks, inequality decreased over the period. The number of people at the lower end fell from 48.5% in 1964 to 44.1% in 1979 to 43.9% in 1989; those at the top end rose from 2.3% to 3.2% to 5% in 1989 for the same periods.

Finally, the benefits of education are once again confirmed in this study. For those who did not finish high school, those at the 0.50 relative income found themselves increasing rapidly; in 1964 there were 22.6% at this bottom level, in 1979 there were 29%, and in 1989 there were 38.4%, (a 32% increase over 1979)! Their numbers also fell by 20% in the top ranges—a rather dismal performance for those who lacked a high school education. But the same is true for those with a high school education. Their numbers rose from 7.7% in 1964 for the under 0.50 group to 11% in 1979 to 15.7% in 1989 (a 43% increase over 1979); their numbers at the high range also decreased by 4% from 1979 to 1989. Only those with some college training were able to reduce the proportion at the 0.50 level and to increase the proportion at the higher levels. Those with 1 to 3 years of college were able to reduce their numbers at the lower end by 15% from 1979 to 1989, and those who completed college decreased theirs by 10%. This latter group was able to increase its numbers at the higher end by 19% from 1979 to 1989. The lesson is again clear: Education was rewarded in the period covered, and although this may not be startling news, it does furnish the evidence for another split in the society—the educated versus the uneducated.

INEQUALITY IN LABOR INCOME

The trends in inequality are again confirmed if labor income alone is considered. Karoly concludes that the trends "confirm the well-documented stagnation in the level of the wage distribution as measured by real median labor income."[9] Table 13.5 provides some of the data to support that conclusion. It is clear that for all workers, wages increased up to the early seventies and then

Table 13.5
Percentage Change in Real Absolute Percentiles of Wage and Salary Income

Period	Weekly Income			
	Percentile			
	10th	25th	75th	90th
All Workers:				
1967–1974	12.5	2.0	2.2	8.7
1975–1979	6.8	6.1	-0.6	4.1
1979–1987	-6.4	-5.5	2.2	0.7
Men:				
1967–1974	-1.1	1.7	7.8	10.5
1975–1979	3.3	-0.5	1.5	6.0
1979–1987	-12.8	-10.0	-3.5	1.2
Women:				
1967–1974	18.9	12.2	10.1	6.5
1975–1979	12.0	10.9	8.4	4.5
1979–1987	-1.3	1.2	6.8	17.9

Source: Adapted from Lynn A. Karoly, *The Trend in Inequality Among Families, Individuals, and Workers in the United States* (Santa Monica, CA: Rand Corporation, 1992), 37.

began to decline into the early eighties; they picked up again from 1983 but were still below the peak of 1973 (not shown). Over the period 1979–87, real wages fell for those at the bottom and the top of the wage distribution. For men alone, the real wage declines were experienced almost entirely by those at the bottom—in the 10th and 25th percentile. Moreover, the greatest declines occurred in the 1979–87 period, while those at the top saw their incomes increase. Clearly, the gap (by 35%) between the lowest and highest percentiles increased since 1967.

For women, real wages increased faster at the bottom of the distribution than at the top, narrowing the gap between them; in the 1979–87 period, the reverse took place and real wages fell for the bottom 10th and rose dramatically for the 90th percentile, thereby increasing the gap between them once again (by 20%).

The data indicate that not only has the gap between workers at the bottom and at the top increased, but that the shape of the distribution has changed as well. Without exhibiting all the data series, we can state the conclusions of the Karoly study. For men, "inequality among men has been increasing since the early 1960s," with the upper tails increasing faster since 1975, and the lower tail dropping steadily, particularly since 1978–79.

For women, wage income was becoming more equal with wage growth at the bottom, rising faster than those at the top. However, about 1979 the inequality began to increase again as the top of the distribution increased rapidly. In terms of race and gender, the data reveal that "the gains in median weekly wages among black men and women were higher compared to those among white men and women, thereby increasing the black : white earnings ratio." [10] Only Hispanic men had declines in income between 1979 and 1987.

Finally, there was no decline in inequality when the economy recovered in the 1980s. Contrary to what normally occurs in the upswing when inequality lessens, there was no reversal, and the recovery did not benefit those at the bottom.

OTHER OBSERVATIONS

Numerous studies have tended to confirm the analysis of Bluestone and Harrison that the inequality among workers exhibits a U-turn with the inequality decreasing from the 1960s to the mid-1970s and then increasing thereafter. [11] Karoly finds similar trends in her study. There appears to be an increase in inequality among all workers which Bluestone and Harrison attribute primarily to "the increasing dispersion of hourly wage rates" and not to such other factors usually cited—the baby boom effect, the entrance of women into the labor force, the shift to the service sector, and differences in education and training. [12] In other words, there has been an uneven growth in jobs with the low-paying jobs growing and the middle levels declining, and the higher-paying ones increasing after 1979.

As might be expected, other researchers were quick to conduct their own studies on these matters. They are too numerous to recite in detail, so only the conclusions will be mentioned. The U-turn hypothesis seems to be confirmed for men, but not for women. For women, there was no trend in equality until 1980 when their inequality began. Inequality has increased between the educated and noneducated, between more experienced and less experienced, and among workers in particular industries. All of these inequalities increased since 1979. There also appears to be an increasing inequality within groups as well as between groups. [13]

The relevant concerns here are not the accuracy of these studies about inequality, but the strains and stresses that such growing inequalities induce in the society. In any economy, at any time, there are winners and losers, and participants in the economy are well aware of the game. When inequalities grow, *and become evident* over a period of time, resentments are likely to be aroused. These resentments can and do manifest themselves in group reactions: the haves against the have-nots, the blacks and minorities against the whites, males against females, educated against the noneducated, young against the old, and so on. It does not matter whether these academic studies are correct or not, it is the perception of inequalities that is operative. In the end, the society is divided along various lines, dictated largely by economic fortunes. The cohesiveness dissolves as each group blames the other for its misfortunes, and only calls to patriotism, really chauvinism, can rally the society, as occurred in the rescuing of Kuwait. Otherwise, the divisiveness is evident in the frustrations of everyone, particularly as they see their concerns unexplained and unaddressed.

Of course, not all of these problems can be attributed to the Reagan administrations. The problems began before Reagan took office. Yet they increased during his years in office, and the divisions were exploited for political reasons. The indifference of these administrations to the developing problems only served to remind those who were injured that government served the favored and ignored the rest; their open hostility to the pleas of those at the bottom served to differentiate the society into haves and have-nots, the deserving and the undeserving.

Poverty data also show the continuation of past divisions. Although poverty statistics are suspect, and hence controversial, the data show no significant change in the Reagan years. When Reagan took office, the overall rate was 13%; it rose during the depression of 1981–82 to 15.4% before falling back to 13% in 1988. Sharp differences can be found, however, among groups: black and Hispanic poverty rates are three times that of whites; the rate for children has risen to near 20% while declining for persons 65 or older to 12%; and female-headed families register a rate of 37% (52% for blacks) compared to the rate for all families of 11%. These trends preceded the Reagan administrations, of course, but they exacerbated all the problems associated with societal divisions that emanated from other sources. The perception was that the poor were getting poorer, and although that might have been true, the poverty measures only reflect that reality during the depression years. Again, however, it must be remembered that the measurement of poverty is imprecise. Recent attempts to correct the data for taxes and transfers will be an improvement, but the data are not available to make any observations about long-term trends or the 1980s in general.[14]

Another observation that has received a great deal of attention has been the assertion that the middle class has declined. The origin of the concern can again be found in the work of Bluestone and Harrison. They found that good jobs, the jobs that were responsible for a middle class, were disappearing, and poor jobs were increasing in what they referred to as the deindustrialization of America. Others soon took up the issue as it appeared to be an explosive one for the nation.[15]

The results of the studies depend on the definition of middle class, the family unit, the inflation index used, and the general methodology used. Early studies found that the middle class was shrinking, and that the lower class was increasing; Thurow found that both the upper and lower classes were increasing. The specifications of these studies varies considerably, however, and later works disclosed flaws in them. Horrigan and Haugen finally undertook to clarify the results, and although the last word on the issue is far from being heard, we

Table 13.6
Distribution of Families into Classes, Selected Years (in percent)

Year	Classes		
	Lower	Middle[1]	Upper
1969	33.7	58.8	7.5
1973	32.1	57.6	10.3
1979	31.8	56.0	12.3
1981	34.4	54.2	11.4
1985	33.3	52.7	14.0
1986	31.7	53.0	15.3

1. Middle class defined as between $20,000 and $55,999 in 1986.
Source: Monthly Labor Review, May 1988, 9.

will use their research as definitive for now.[16] Table 13.6 shows some of their results.

In interpreting these results, it is necessary to compare years that are at the same stage in the business cycle, and even then the results are confusing. Still, the trend is clear, and according to Horrigan and Haugen, "this study suggests that the consensus view of a declining middle class is correct. However, unlike some studies, this one finds that most of the decline in the proportion of families in the middle has gone to the upper class, not the lower."[17] For example, comparing 1973 and 1986, both years of recovery, finds that the lower class fell by 1.2%, the middle class fell by 8%, and the upper class increased by 49%. These amounts will vary depending on initial and ending years chosen. Yet the fact remains that there has been some shrinkage in the middle, and some growth at the top. The Karoly study, using a different methodology, also confirms that the lower and upper classes have been increasing at the expense of the middle class.

Assuming the shrinkage of the middle class is real, what is the significance of that reality? Clearly, the middle class has always acted as a buffer between the classes. Many people aspired to become a typical American family in the middle class and share the visions of the good life with those who defined it. Now these aspirations are foiled for those at the bottom, as more families are falling out of the middle class; at the same time, more families were moving out of the middle class into the upper class. Those who could have benefited from the Reagan years, the educated, the skilled, did so, but for those striving to enter the middle class, the possibility was dimming. The ideal American family seems to have been the loser in an administration that presumably promoted that very image in its characterization of the American society—the Norman Rockwell image.

Fears developed that the current generation could not count on having a standard of living higher than their parents, as previous generations were able to assume. The point is that another area of strain developed in the society that pitted one class against another and dashed the hopes of many for advancement, forestalling the American dream of upward mobility. The data show that if the 1980s were a party, some were invited and others were snubbed.

THE DISTRIBUTION OF WEALTH

The distribution of income has always received more attention than the distribution of wealth. That fact in itself reveals a great deal about the success of wealthholders in concealing the extent of the maldistribution of wealth by their ability to shift the focus of concern to income. Yet, the distribution of wealth is far more unequal than income and much more difficult to remedy. In the United States, wealth is easily passed on from generation to generation, relatively untaxed, and the perpetuation of inequalities is guaranteed, and again relatively unnoticed. There seems to be an acquiescence to the disparity in wealth accumulation stemming from the wistful dream of many that someday they could somehow be in that favorable situation, and they would not want their holdings disturbed by policies that would redistribute them. That few realize that dream does not seem to deter the dreamers.

Reflecting the lack of attention, relatively few studies have been done about the distribution of wealth, and the corresponding lack of data also hinders the analysis of the problem. In recent years, the Federal Reserve Board has conducted some research on the topic, and some of its findings are startling and worth reporting.[18] The survey found that the top 10% of families ranked by income owned 51% of all liquid assets, and the top 2% owned 30%. These same groups owned 72% and 50% of stock, 70% and 38% of bonds, 86% and 71% of nontaxable holdings. The top 10% of families owned 50% of property and 78% of business, whereas the top 2% owned 20% and 33% of these forms of wealth.[19]

These data show an enormous concentration of wealth at the top of the income scales. The Reagan administration tax cuts of 1981 further guaranteed this concentration by reducing the taxes on inherited wealth. Confirming the relative inattention given to the question of wealth, this part of the tax actions of 1981 received little notice.

More recently, the Bureau of the Census has undertaken the analysis of household wealth.[20] Some of its findings for 1988 are equally startling. Table 13.7 displays some of its findings. The inequalities in the distribution of wealth are readily apparent. The lowest quintile possessed 7% of the wealth, whereas the highest quintile had 44.4%, over six times the lowest. In terms of dollars, the highest 20% had over 25 times as much wealth as the lowest, $111,770 versus $4324. Furthermore, these proportions have not changed very much in the 1980s.

In terms of race, the median wealth of whites was $43,279 while that of blacks was only $4169, one-tenth that of whites. The wealth disparity among whites mirrored that of the overall distribution, but the disparity among blacks

Table 13.7
Median Net Worth, by Monthly Household Income, Quintile, and Race, 1988

Quintiles	Median Net Worth	Percent	White	Black
All Households:				
Median net Worth	$35,752		$43,279	$4,169
Net Worth by				
Income Quintile:				
Lowest	4,324	7.0	8,839	0
Second	19,694	12.3	26,229	2,408
Third	28,044	15.7	32,802	8,461
Fourth	46,253	20.6	50,372	20,215
Highest	111,770	44.4	119,057	47,160

Note: Hispanic households are omitted from this table to save space. Their experience is similar to that of black households.

Source: Adapted from Judith Eargle, U.S. Bureau of the Census, Household Wealth and Asset Ownership: 1988, *Current population reports,* Ser. P-70, no. 22, Tables B and H.

was even greater. The bottom fifth of black households had virtually no wealth at all, whereas the top fifth had $47,160. In fact, 60% of black households owned less wealth than the bottom 20% of white households!

As might be expected, the data reveal that wealth holdings were similar to those found earlier with low income groups holding more of their wealth in durable goods (autos, housing) and less in financial assets and businesses. This is particularly so among blacks. Wealth holdings increased with age as well, with the elderly owning nearly twice as much wealth as those less than 35 years.

There is no need to belabor the point: The distribution of wealth in extremely unequal, more so than is the distribution of income. The society is becoming one of haves versus have-nots, creating divisions that foster alienation and potential unrest. Occasionally, it manifests itself directly as in the rioting and looting that took place in the 1960s and more recently in Los Angeles in 1992. Television and advertisements show the world what goods and services are available, but not to all. Envy apart, how much does it take to convince those who do without that the society is somehow unjust?

Again the Reagan administrations cannot be held responsible for the inequalities of wealth. This condition has been observed whenever studies of the distribution have been undertaken. Yet, the Reagan administrations were oblivious to the problems developing out of the maldistribution and probably helped to exacerbate them with its policies. They tended to favor those who already had accumulated wealth through their tax policies, their indifference to inner city problems, their opposition to civil rights laws, their cutbacks in housing funds, and so on, and, in general, their lack of sympathy for the more disadvantaged in the society. America offered the opportunities, they seemed to say, and if those at the bottom failed to take advantage of them, it was basically their own fault.

Yet, divisions caused by the unequal distributions of income and wealth are not likely to recede and disappear with economic progress. A rising tide lifts all boats is the cliché used by more fortunate, but it should be noted, not if the boats have holes in them, or not if the rowboats that the poor own have been tossed ashore. In the 1980s, economic growth did not benefit all groups, and many came to challenge the belief that economic growth provides for increased opportunities, and a way out of economic deprivation. Many began to lose faith in the American dream—the dream of continued progress.

OTHER SOCIETAL DIVISIONS

As previously noted, when Reagan campaigned, he appealed to and brought into the political process groups that had previously been alienated from the mainstream—the political far right, the religious fundamentalists, the anti-abortionists, and others. With each group, there was one or more overriding cause which they pursued vigorously. In the process, they managed to split the society in varied and essentially uncalled-for divisions. These divisions often reinforced those that were created by economic conditions.

The abortion issue created sharp divisions among the free-choice advocates and the right-to-life proponents. These were acrimonious and sometimes violent confrontations. As in so many other instances, answers to moral questions were asked of the law, and the courts were asked to settle the issue, and once they did so, neither side was satisfied. Attacks were made on planned parenthood clinics, and despite the attacks on free speech, restrictions on their activities became law.

Prayers in the schools was another issue that followed the same kind of scenario. Elevated to a national political issue, this controversial activity created a great deal of heat without resolution. Again, groups lined up behind this trivial concern, creating needless divisions. Public support of religious schools was still another allied issue that accompanied the prayers in school controversy.

These issues occupied much of the public's attention in the 1980s, as the voices were loud and insistent. Once given a voice, these former alienated groups made themselves heard and, in the process, fostered more intolerance than enlightenment, more anger than understanding. While many of the serious problems of the 1980s were evolving, too many minds were focused on these relatively inconsequential concerns.

Some of these more important issues, other than strictly economic, can only be mentioned here. The Reagan administration's neglect of environmental

problems is one such issue. Environmental groups fought to keep business interests out of public land, to protect resources from exploitation from commercial interests, and to keep the existing laws in effect and enforced by lacka-
daisical public servants. In the process, more conflicts among groups—
environmentalists versus commercial interests and affected workers—was assured.

The Reagan administration's attempt to reformulate existing views on federalism created more friction among other groups. The federal government was
pitted against the states, which, in turn, were pitted against localities, and cities
against rural areas. Attempts to transform the responsibility for various functions, for example, AFDC and medicaid, were sharply opposed by the states,
and the transformation of the types of grants from the federal government created squabbles over which unit of government should administer the funds and
for which purposes. The future of federalism in the United States was left
clouded by the attempts to recast it.

Finally, the remaking of the Supreme Court in the conservative image may,
in the end, be Reagan's most lasting legacy. What could not be achieved by
persuasion and through the legislative process could now be achieved through
the courts. Again, lacking any such mandate for reinterpretation of the law or
societal preferences, more factions were inevitable. In the 1990s, these trends
became even more pronounced and aggravated with the appointment of inferior
judges, some of whom were rejected. The Clarence Thomas case in the Bush
administration stands as an example of the blatant use of the court for political
and ideological purposes, both of which could tarnish the court's image and
could even encourage the opposite of the conservative cause—disrespect for
the law. Once again, groups surfaced to split the society: feminists versus the
male-dominated Senate, whites versus blacks, blacks versus blacks, and, of
course, conservatives versus liberals.

In the end, these societal divisions did not create the coalition necessary to
perpetuate the conservative domination of national politics. As such, they were
unnecessarily harmful—they did not accomplish the purpose for which they
were tolerated by the more thoughtful, and they created divisions that were to
linger long beyond their creators. Reagan was too old, or too lazy, or too
indifferent, or too detached to mold these dissenting groups into a coalition that
would survive beyond his tenure. His successor, George Bush, did not command the allegiance of these factions, and the political influence of these groups
diminished, but their causes and their one-issue concerns remained to partition
the society.

One must be concerned over whether the attempt at political realignment was
worth the turmoil in society. The politics of division not only caused national
unity to deteriorate but it may have contributed to the disenchantment of the
political process and to the increasing disrespect for politicians in general.[21]
The irony here is that the president who helped restore faith in the presidency
may well have helped destroy the faith in the political process.

CONCLUSIONS

Many have been all too ready to blame the Reagan administrations for the inequalities and internal strife that characterize the nation in the 1990s. But the inequalities in income and wealth did not start with the Reagan years nor will they end anytime soon. It is fair to state, however, that his administrations were unconcerned with these inequalities and failed even to acknowledge them seriously, and that his policies helped to prolong them during his tenure and will help to extend them into the future. According to conservative dogma, the government should not be concerned with these market-determined outcomes anyway—equality of outcomes—and should only help to ensure equality of opportunity. That it failed to address the former has been demonstrated; that it failed to provide the latter must be inferred from its actions, not its rhetoric. Frankly, there is not much evidence to support the claim that it at least attempted to provide for greater opportunities for those in need. Whatever policies could do the job—educational, training, enlightened welfare and community programs, and the like—were treated with benign neglect. Only the rhetoric soared.

Moreover, in so many ways, the society was rent into a variety of factions. Economic conditions split the nation into contentious groups—the old versus the young, the educated versus the noneducated, women versus men, black versus white, the employed versus the unemployed, and the welfare recipient versus the taxpayer. Added to or supplementing these, the society was also stratified by social issues—abortion, prayers in schools, feminists issues, environmental matters, anticommunist hysteria, and strident ideology.

Thus, the structure of society underwent some wrenching changes, with all manner of factions taking sides on a variety of issues. The economic structure of society changed in ways that can be observed. They manifest themselves in the distribution of rewards, and although the measurements may be flawed, the trends are not. It was a period of the haves against the have-nots in a kind of class warfare. The Reagan administrations threw a party but failed to invite everyone.

The social issues were equally disrupting as they turned one group against another, dividing the nation into true believers against everyone else. There were crusades, led by over zealous leaders, to twist the nation to its particular cause; there was no room for compromise, and rational thought was often sacrificed to simplistic slogans. In this atmosphere, created in large part by Reagan's political ambitions, hostility overtook civility, and the national mood turned surly. Meanwhile, those who did not take part in these divisive debates, some unknown number, looked on with dismay at this contentious society.

In summary, without following up on these areas, it is only possible to suggest that the society was indeed altered both by economic and noneconomic matters. In the 1990s, it is still possible to discern the same divisions, the same factions, and, in many cases, the same issues that divided the nation in the

1980s. Whatever alterations that society suffered in the 1980s appear not so easy to reverse, even as the political landscape may be changing.

NOTES

1. Of all the Reagan critics, Robert Lekachman emphasizes this aspect, in *Visions and Nightmares: America after Reagan,* (New York: Macmillan, 1987).

2. For those interested, a good source that discusses and compares various studies on inequality is Lynn A. Karoly, *The Trend in Inequality Among Families, Individuals, and Workers in the United States: A Twenty-Five-Year Perspective* (Santa Monica, CA: The Rand Corporation, 1992).

3. The Gini ratio is obtained from the Lorenz curve. In the Lorenz curve, households are arrayed from lowest to highest income. The Lorenz curve plots the cumulative percentage of households against the cumulative percentage of income received by these households. A 45 degree line would, therefore, measure perfect equality. The Gini coefficient measures the area below the 45 degree line (the Lorenz curve) as a proportion of the total area, that is, the difference between the Lorenz curve and the 45 degree line.

4. Karoly, *The Trend in Inequality Among Families, Individuals, and Workers in the United States,* 11.

5. In addition to these shortcomings, there are a number of other weaknesses not commonly known. The data are obtained from surveys of some 60,000 households, and these households report only 72% of aggregate money income as determined from other sources. Both the lower and higher income groups tend to understate their incomes—the former in underestimated transfer payments, and the latter in nonwage earnings and uncooperative responses. The Census Bureau adds back some of these income sources, but only 90% of aggregate income is accounted for. Another problem, called "top coding," is the lumping together of incomes exceeding some maximum, for example, everyone earning more than $99,999 is put into one group of "$99,999 or greater." This distorts the upper ranges on income. Finally, the Census data assume that the composition of the family unit surveyed did not change even though the data are collected only in March for the previous year. In recent years, family composition can change rapidly from one year to the next. For more on these issues, see The Congressional Budget Office (CBO), *Trends in Family Income: 1970–1986,* February 1988; see also U.S. Congress. House Committee on Ways and Means, "Trends in Family Income and Income Inequality," in *Background Material and Data on Programs Within the Jurisdiction of the Committee on Ways and Means,* 101st Cong., 1st sess., 1989.

6. Karoly, *The Trend in Inequality Among Families, Individuals, and Workers in the United States,* 19–20.

7. Data from the Committee on Ways and Means, "Trends in Family Income and Income Inequality," Table 29. Similar conclusions with respect to single mothers and the elderly were found in the CBO study, *Trends in Family Income: 1970–1986.*

8. U.S. Department of Commerce, BLS, Current Population Reports, *Trends in Relative Income: 1964 to 1989,* P-60, no. 177, 1991, 1.

9. Karoly, *The Trends in Inequality Among Families, Individuals, and Workers in the United States,* 35.

10. Ibid. 43.

11. Barry Bluestone and Bennett Harrison, "The Great American Job Machine: The Proliferation of Low-wage Employment in the U.S. Economy," A study prepared for the Joint Economic Committee, 1986; and *The Great U-Turn* (New York: Basic Books, 1988).

12. Bluestone and Harrison, *The Great U-Turn,* 119–120.

13. See Karoly, *The Trend in Inequality Among Families, Individuals, and Workers in the United States;* McKinley L. Blackburn and David E. Bloom, "Earnings and Inequality in the United States," in *Population and Development Review,* 13 (3) (December 1987): 575–609; Gary Burtless, "Earnings Inequality over the Business and Demographic Cycle," in *A Future of Lousy Jobs,* ed. Gary Burtless (Washington DC: The Brookings Institution, 1990), 77–122; and in general the bibliographies of these works should direct the reader to other sources too numerous to include here.

14. The data for 1989 indicate that when the numbers are adjusted for taxes, transfers, and noncash items, the distribution of income is made more equal: the bottom quintile increased its share from 3.9% to 5.1% and the top quintile's share decreased from 46.7% to 44.3%. One of the more significant conclusions of these estimates is that contrary to popular opinion: The effect of government transfers is much more significant than taxes in redistributing income." U.S. Bureau of the Census, Measuring the effect of benefits and taxes on income and poverty: 1989, *Current population reports,* ser. P-60, no. 169-RD 1990.

15. Barry Bluestone and Bennett Harrison, *The Deindustrialization of America* (New York: Basic Books, 1982); see also Lester Thurow, "The Disappearance of the Middle Class," in The *New York Times,* 5 February 1984, E2; and "A Surge in Inequality," in *Scientific American* 256(May 1987): 30–37; Robert Z. Lawrence, "Sectoral Shifts and the Size of the Middle Class," in *Brookings Review* (Fall 1985): 3–10; Neal H. Rosenthal, "The Shrinking Middle Class: Myth or Reality?" in *Monthly Labor Review* (March 1985): 3–10.

16. Michael W. Horrigan and Steven E. Haugen, "The Declining Middle-Class Thesis: A Sensitivity Analysis," *Monthly Labor Review* (May 1988): 3–13.

17. Ibid. 9.

18. See Dorothy S. Projector and Gertrude Weiss, *Survey of Financial Characteristics of Consumers* (August 1966); and "Survey of Consumer Finances, 1983," *Federal Reserve Bulletin* (September 1984): 679–692, and subsequent reports based on this survey in March 1986 and 1989.

19. "Survey of Consumer Finances, 1983," 689.

20. U.S. Bureau of the Census, Household wealth and asset ownership: 1988, *Current population reports,* ser. P-70, no. 22.

21. For more on this, see E. J. Dionne, *Why Americans Hate Politics* (New York: Simon & Schuster, 1991).

Chapter 14

What If Reagan Had Been Allowed to Be Reagan?

After the apparent shortcomings of Reaganomics was revealed to everyone, it became fashionable among Reaganites to blame the failures on whatever institutions came to mind: Congress, foreigners, liberal Keynesians, the bureaucracy, and any other convenient scapegoat. It was, therefore, an easy transition to the next inference: If Reagan had been allowed to be Reagan, everything would have worked out as planned. Apparently, the real Reaganomics was not permitted to operate, and the program was thwarted before it had a chance to develop. Or the White House staff members did not permit many of Reagan's ideas to be given a chance and, in fact, "protected" the president from his more unorthodox initiatives. But Reagan was fond of delegating responsibility among his trusted aides and only wished to set the agenda; this was his management style. This contradiction is ignored by followers who claim that Reagan was thwarted by non-Reaganite appointees.

Of course, much of the complaining can be attributed to defensive tactics and to apologia, but many people actually believed that the program was not given a chance and that the real principles that guided Reagan were not fully reflected in the ordinary tussle of political compromise.

I do not believe that this charge is correct. No economic program of any president has been enacted in full without some concessions to political and economic realities. No president has seen blind acceptance of his views without compromise. Nevertheless, Mr. Reagan got most of what he sought; he was much more successful than his predecessors in getting his economic program through without major sacrifices. That he did not get all of it, and therefore failure was inevitable, seems unwarranted and contentious.

Recall that the major innovations occurred in the first term and that the fresh administration wanted to "hit the ground running" before too many objections to the economic program could be raised. We have seen that the administration knew that parts of the plan did not fit together and that there were contradictions inherent in the overall plan. It would, however, not be deterred and, with religious zeal, pursued its objectives despite the reservations expressed by critics.

It follows that no amount of evidence to the contrary would have convinced these true believers who will maintain forever that if only Reagan had been allowed to be Reagan. . . . So the question remains: What would Reagan have done if he were left alone? What did he hope to accomplish?

THE REAGAN VISION

An examination of Reagan's speeches and his autobiography reveals little of any intended revolution on his part. His mission was to reduce the role and importance of government in the economy. Before he was elected, he identified government as the major problem and vowed to get it off the backs of the American people. When his terms ended, he expressed pride in his success in reducing taxes and in reducing the rate of growth of government spending.[1] This was no visionary bent on restructuring the society and the economy; this was no revolutionary sworn to overthrow the existing order.

On the contrary, here was a man who developed a set of biases over the years, who had made some value judgments about the functioning of the economic system, and who simply wanted to halt, not reverse, the direction of change. In short, what we observed was the real Reagan; there never was a Reagan who was somehow prohibited from revealing himself. Here was a man who spoke in parables and analogies about moralism, patriotism, and nationalism, and who was very successful at convincing an audience that there was depth and substance to his remarks.

But parables and analogies cannot be made operational. They can only serve as illustrations to reveal some hidden truths. For Reagan, they were the means used to communicate deeply felt prejudices, but they did not lead to plans to make them commitments. Those expecting a revolutionary zeal to accompany the strong rhetoric were in for a letdown. In the following section, some well-respected conservatives assess the Reagan administrations and express their disappointment.

CONSERVATIVE DISAPPOINTMENT

With the election of Ronald Reagan, conservatives raised their hopes, unquestionably too high, that the welfare state erected by FDR would be reversed. They, indeed, hoped for a true revolution. They did not get one.

George Will maintains that Reagan was not recognizably conservative, not a Keynesian either, but a Panglossian, who gave us a narcotic of cheerfulness.[2] Irving Kristol recognized the conservative disappointment in Reagan, claiming that there was no revolution because Reagan did not push hard for the conservative agenda.[3] Even more pointedly, John Fund, a *Wall Street Journal* editorial writer, wrote: "Ultimately, the fact that Ronald Reagan left office as the most popular president in modern history means that he settled for less change than either he or his supporters wanted or could have gotten. . . . On controversial issues, he let his followers eat rhetoric."[4]

These are but a few samples of the assessment by conservatives of the Reagan achievements. Reagan drew back from controversial and divisive issues and did not push the issues so dear to conservative thinkers. Was he not truly a conservative or was he, and particularly his staff, overly concerned with his popularity and what would play in the press? Was he so obsessed with popularity that he failed to use his power for conservative causes, or was he held back by an overprotective White House staff who would not let him risk his political capital on risky proposals? Why did Donald Regan insist that Reagan should follow his gut instincts and ignore his staff?[5] What these and other critics have done is mistake rhetoric for commitment. It is not at all clear that Reagan ever repudiated the New Deal. True, he did attack liberals and Democrats for their practices and policies that overextended the New Deal goals, but he did not advocate the complete dismissal of those goals. In the words of William Niskanen, "In retrospect, there was little reason to expect a Reagan revolution. As candidate and president, Reagan endorsed the major surviving programmes of the New Deal and the post-war consensus on foreign policy and defense."[6] Finally, Nobel Laureate James Buchanan, of public choice fame and a constitutionalist, also considers the Reagan years a failure:

I assess the Reagan presidency as one of failed opportunity to secure the structural changes that might have been within the realms of the politically possible. The result is that, after Reagan, the institutions in place will remain roughly the same as those existing in 1980. . . . It [the Reagan presidency] seems to have been too interested in playing the policy-within-politics game, too interested in pushing its policy agenda within a relatively short time perspective.[7]

CONCLUSION

An analysis of his prepresidential, and preobstructionist staff, rhetoric reveals that Reagan basically wanted to return America to original values—family, work, neighborhood, peace, and freedom—and away from those the Democrats had constructed out of New Deal principles. In the end, Reagan added freedom from government to FDR's four freedoms.[8]

Thus, the Great Communicator was able to convince whatever audience he was addressing that he was on their side and was going to move America presumably in the direction the audience favored. The vision of the American dream that he espoused permitted the audience to remember when times were better and America was strong.

This vision is supported by metaphoric language, a tendency to divide the world into clear heroes and villains, simplification, cinematic language, themes involving community, and the tendency to treat criticism of himself as criticism of the United States. In addition, Reagan has the gift of presenting his beliefs in simple, emotionally evocative symbolic slogans, delivered in a warm, comforting manner.[9]

But what were those beliefs? As far as economics is concerned, Martin Anderson tells us that he had studied economic issues over time and took many positions on them. He developed his ideas over time, one at a time, but did not propose any overall economic plan.[10] Because Anderson was the original architect of the initial economic plan, his appraisal is worth noting. Apparently, Reagan's set of loose ideas, slogans, prejudices, and concerns was molded by others into a whole economic plan that would pass the respectability test. We also know that once the plan was formulated, Reagan became an instant cheerleader for it; we also know that once the plan was in place, he was able to distance himself from it and its consequences. His reliance on others, in economic as well as all other matters confronting his presidency, allowed him to claim that his principles were being followed, and at the same time permitted him to distance himself from whatever adverse consequences followed from their implementation.[11]

NOTES

1. Ronald Reagan, *An American Life* (New York: Simon and Schuster, 1990), 52–53.

2. George F. Will, "How Reagan Changed America," *Newsweek,* 9 January 1989, 13–17.

3. Irving Kristol, "The Reagan Revolution that Never Was" The *Wall Street Journal,* 19 April 1988, editorial.

4. John H. Ford, "The Secret of Reagan's 'Success,' " The *Wall Street Journal,* 23 January 1989, A14.

5. David Boaz put the disenchantment with Reagan succinctly when he wrote

A president who appoints cabinet officers that are on record as opposing his professional goals, who never bothers to tell his secretary of the treasury what his economic policy goals are, who avoids making tough decisions on spending programs, whose aides are so concerned with photo opportunities and spin control that they lose sight of substance—such a president will soon find himself rolled by the Washington establishment.

Assessing the Reagan Years (Washington, DC: Cato Institute, 1988), 5.

6. William Niskanen, "Reaganomics: A Balanced Assessment," in *Reaganomics and After* (London: Institute of Public Affairs, 1989), 21.

7. James M. Buchanan, "Post-Reagan Political Economy," in *Reaganomics and After,* 1, 14.

8. Mary E. Stuckey, *Getting into the Game: The Pre-Presidential Rhetoric of Ronald Reagan* (New York: Praeger, 1989), 74. See also Paul D. Erickson, *Reagan Speaks: The Making of an American Myth* (New York: New York University Press, 1985).

9. Mary E. Stuckey, *Playing the Game: The Presidential Rhetoric of Ronald Reagan* (New York: Praeger, 1990), 4.

10. Martin Anderson, *Revolution* (Stanford: Hoover Institution Press, 1990), 112–113.

11. As George Wills states, he was not a great communicator because he could not deliver bad news. ". . . a great communicator will communicate complicated ideas, hard choices and bad news. Reagan has had little aptitude and less appetite for those tasks." *Newsweek,* 9 January 1989, 17.

Chapter 15

Conclusion

The judgments of the conservatives are now recorded: The Reagan revolution never occurred. True believers and those who staked their professional reputations on the Reagan administrations' policies will never be persuaded otherwise, but thoughtful conservatives are not blinded by ideology nor convoluted reasoning. To the serious conservative, the Reagan years are seen as only a temporary slowing, just a diversion, of the trend toward growing involvement in the economy.

On the other side, many liberal economists would agree with James Tobin that "the awful truth is that Reaganomics was a fraud from the beginning. The moral of its failures and of its legacies is that a nation pays a heavy price when it entrusts its government and economy to simplistic ideologues—however smooth their performance on television." [1] This harsh indictment by a liberal economist might have been expected, according to Reagan advisors who knew they were going to alienate the Keynesian economists. After all, they were creating a revolution, and Keynesians were the enemy.

Yet, what emerges from these assessments (and others not cited) is that only the framers of the Reagan economic plan are willing to defend it and justify the results. Most outsiders have serious doubts and reservations about the plan itself and certainly over the results and long-term consequences. The controversies are likely to continue for some time, and perhaps some consensus may be possible. In the meantime, enough results are in to make some judgments now. Accordingly, I turn to mine.

CONCLUSIONS

Government Spending

Measuring success or failure of economic policies is never an easy—one cannot know what would have happened in the absence of those policies. All that one can do, which is the approach followed in this book, is to attempt to measure the results against what was promised. If the goals of the policies were clearly established at the outset, it is a straightforward task to observe how closely the goals were met. Fortunately, and to its credit, Reagan's economic plan, at least for the first term, was well defined. Careful and thoughtful assessments of intentions versus accomplishments are at least made possible.

As indicated in the last chapter, the primary, and perhaps the only, goal of Ronald Reagan was to reduce the role of government in the affairs of society, be they economic or social. In this endeavor, he was not very successful. In the area of government spending, he only rearranged the expenditures of government while leaving the institutional structure in place. In this regard, conservatives were correct to brand him a failure and a failed revolutionary.[2] He did not dismantle the bureaucracy nor sever the myriad of programs they administer. Government expenditures as a percent of GNP, for example, were higher when he left office than when he entered.

However, he did manage to alter the composition of spending mainly by increasing expenditures on national defense. Spending changes in other areas were much more difficult to achieve simply because he did not have a mandate to do so. Where he was able to limit the growth of government spending, it was at the expense of those at the bottom of society. The powerless and least vocal groups became the focus of economy in government earning his policies the unfair and inequitable label. As someone said, it was insensitivity passing for toughmindedness, to which we could add, it was spite passing for waste cutting.

Even here, reductions in social programs were made, but the basic structure of social welfare spending remained. Reductions in the growth of government spending may please some, but this hardly passes for the promised dramatic reversals of social thought.

In any case, these reductions were matched by increases in spending on interest payments to cover the additional costs brought on by the growing budget deficits. It is likely that budget deficits did forestall the introduction of new programs, and, to this extent, the administration's success at limiting government intervention may be understated. But because no fundamental changes were made in government operations (i.e., balanced budget amendment, line item veto, etc.), future occupants of the Oval Office may not feel constrained by past deterrents. The blockage of new or expanded programs may not last far beyond the Reagan administrations. Witness, for instance, the criticisms of his successor for failing to do more to fight the recession of the early 1990s and to alleviate the suffering of the public, and the promise by the Democrats to respond to such pleas.

Finally, he failed to convince the nation that government is the problem; instead, he helped restore faith in government. What he failed to see was that Americans really wanted those programs he railed against, so that all he could do was to stir up discontent against paying for them; he was unable to convince the nation that the programs were unneeded, unnecessary, and wasteful.

Taxation

No one likes to pay taxes, so rallying the public behind the ongoing tax revolt movement was an easy task that fit in well with the overall philosophy of limiting government involvement in the economy. By limiting revenue, government spending is made more difficult; by cutting taxes, more power is returned to the private sector. Thus, any movement toward either of these directions is a measure of success for a conservative administration.

As previously shown, of course, these tax reductions (particularly those of 1981) were somewhat unfair and inequitable because higher income groups received most of the benefits. This was probably the intent anyway, as Stockman suggested, and it satisfied conservative philosophy at the same time. In this sense, supply-side nostrums and Laffer curve drawings were smoke screens to convince the unwary of the scientific nature of the tax proposals. Andrew Mellon and Calvin Coolidge argued the same trickle-down effects in the 1920s without the elaborate 1980s justifications and equally without any empirical evidence that these policies work. In the 1920s as well as the 1980s, taxes were deemed too high, encouraged unproductive investment, and hindered private incentives. Without proof of these assertions, it was necessary to concoct rationales and repeat them loudly and often. Repetition would eventually pass for analysis, proclamation for evidence.

Yet, to put into practice tax policies that were unconfirmed by evidence, uncriticized by professional debate, and unrefined by analysis is basically unacceptable as a route to public policy. That such policies resulted in the redistribution of income and power from the bottom to the top that created greater inequalities in the name of some untested ideas of a few arrogant individuals seems to me to be reprehensible.

The tax reform bill of 1986 did have some reform elements in it, but the goal of simplicity was sacrificed. Only the rate structure was simplified, not a remarkable feat, while leaving the basic structure intact. Progressivity suffered in these tax measures in the name of simplicity. Lower income groups received some benefits, but those in the middle were left to wonder about the justice of tax reform, and many became disenchanted with the claims made for success in the tax area. In the campaign of 1992, the taxation of the middle class became a standard issue, showing the strong possibility of future changes in the tax code to reflect these concerns.

Although tax cuts pleased everyone, the Reagan tax policies failed as far as conservatives were concerned. There were no major reversals to the familiar tax code. Many conservatives wanted a new tax code based on consumption rather than income as the taxable base. They either wanted the tax code slanted to favor saving over consumption or a direct consumption tax such as the value added tax (VAT). Other conservatives wanted a drastically simplified tax code and a single rate of taxation. The Reagan administrations shied away from confrontation and ignored these conservative principles in favor of some marginal changes in the existing code, some that satisfied liberals and some that appealed to conservatives. The result was that there was no revolution in tax matters either, and none was even proposed. Again, even the tax changes that were made may not survive for very long; the presidential campaign of 1992 revealed a strong push for tinkering with the tax code again with initiatives aimed at capital gains taxes, imposing new rates on higher income groups, new incentives for investment, health and education, and so on.

The repercussions of such cavalier fiscal policies were disastrous. Budget deficits soared, and the nation was forced to borrow, much of it from foreigners, to keep operating. Saddled with such huge deficits, fiscal policy was paralyzed and monetary policy was constrained. The economy was allowed to operate without constraints or guidance; macroeconomic policies were suspended. Free markets and competition, always part of conservative dogma, became a mantra for all in the administration. Individualism was once more elevated to the top, and greed, passing for progress, was championed and sanctioned.

The result, of course, was a debt-fueled expansion, one that outdid the most ardent Keynesian proposal. Consumption, not investment, led the boom, as households were eager to join the public sector in their reliance on debt. The stock market boomed, even in the recession, as funds released from taxation flowed to it. But the illusions of the 1980s had to end sometime, and the first sign was the stock market crash of 1987. The market recovered, but the economy did not. The economy slowed and eventually stagnated in the recession of 1990, the natural outcome of the excesses of the 1980s.

Deregulation

It is the area of deregulation that conservatives found the Reagan administrations most wanting of all. Deregulation, started in the Carter administration, was essentially abandoned in the Reagan years, and no changes to the economic structure were even attempted. Again, despite the rhetoric, the Reagan administrations preferred not to push this element of their program. What changes to the economic structure that did occur in these years were initiated by the private sector that sensed the indifference of the Reagan administrations; as indicated earlier, many of these structural changes were undesirable (the mergers and acquisitions, LBOs), but the administrations looked the other way. Neither the frenzy of the merger movement nor the dismantling of those presumably burdensome regulations occupied the attention of the administration officials.

The failure to continue the battle against government regulations disturbed the conservatives who saw it as a lost opportunity and a surrender to complacency. Liberals too were unhappy with the regulatory policies of the administrations but for different reasons. They objected to the channeling of all regulatory changes through the Office of Budget and Management (OMB). Ostensibly for the purpose of examining them for cost-effectiveness, OMB really forestalled many regulatory changes, discouraged others, and, in general, was a powerful obstacle to the entire regulatory process.

Because neither conservatives nor liberals were pleased at the administrations' efforts in the regulatory area, the question is: Who was? The answer must be those who were interested in maintaining the status quo and who stood to benefit from inaction. These could be the political interests, often unrelated to economic interests, who saw little to be gained by pushing ahead with controversial issues that lacked political appeal. Regulatory issues may be popular with conservatives, but they did not excite the public, and not worth spending political capital on.

So again, the Reagan administrations retreated from one of its most cherished beliefs: that government was on the backs of industry causing it to flounder in the face of foreign competition and lose out in the global economic race. They failed to address the issue and resorted, in this as in so many other instances, to tough rhetoric as a substitute for action.

Inflation

The reduction in inflation was applauded by all sides. Conservatives always place a high value on price stability, and liberals too, although grudgingly, were pleased at the results. Everyone was surprised at the speed with which inflation was brought under control, and the price stability that followed. The trouble with claiming this as a victory is that most of the credit goes to the Federal Reserve and Paul Volcker. The administration could only stand on the sidelines and rely on Volcker's determination to battle inflation.

Another difficulty with the claim of victory over inflation is to convince those who lost that the triumph was laudable. To achieve this success, the economy had first to be put through a wringer, incurring a devastating recession to squeeze out the inflationary tendencies as well as reverse the inflationary expectations that had developed. Those who proposed this drastic solution did not suffer unduly and probably had the ability and the means to protect themselves. The inflation fighters were those at the bottom of the society who paid with unemployment, bankruptcies, and family disruptions. The price to achieve price stability via this cold bath technique was simply too high, and the costs fell on the wrong groups.

Whatever success, then, that can be accorded the lowering of the inflation rate must be tempered by the human costs necessary to achieve it. Viewed in these terms, the success story is unprincipled because the pain was not shared equally and because similar results probably could have been achieved over a longer time span.

These are the main elements of the Reagan economic program. It is not surprising that all the promises made were not kept; they were, after all, contradictory and irreconcilable. What is more interesting is that he disappointed conservatives so much while alienating liberals at the same time. There is no great success story here for anyone, and there certainly is no revolution to report. In terms of the costs involved, it is doubtful whether the marginal changes he made were worth it. Particularly so when the changes did not materially affect the structure of the economy or its functioning and are not likely to last far beyond his tenure in office.

Other Parts of the Reagan Plan

Before any final summation, it might be useful to look at some other goals of the administrations that were ''subsidiary'' to the main elements. The promise to balance the budget appears pathetic in retrospect. No amount of hiding behind a constitutional amendment or line item veto can divert attention from this basic failure. Many of the half-hearted conservatives who inhabited the Reagan administrations now had to speak in Alice in Wonderland language. Their previous fears of budget deficits suddenly were found harmless, whereas the true conservative found that borrow and spend is not much different from tax and spend.

The public sector led the way to the building of an unstable debt economy, and everyone else followed suit as the nation began using a credit card to finance its excesses of consumption over production. When the economy could not produce what it wanted to consume, it imported. Trade balances suffered, and many domestic firms were damaged as the dollar soared and exports tumbled. High real interest rates attracted funds from abroad, but hampered domestic investment. When these trends were reversed, it was too late. U.S. firms were either too far in trouble or had relocated abroad.

So the twin deficits continued as another goal—trade imbalance reversals—of the Reagan presidency was easily sacrificed and, together with the budget deficit, was cavalierly dismissed as unimportant or the fault of others.

The promised increase in saving did not occur nor did the investment increases that were to follow. Consumption rose instead and led the way to recovery. Investment remained flat, and any new investment was confined to areas that do not promote long-term growth or supply worthwhile jobs. Jobs were created in the period, millions of them, but they were in the service industries where the pay is low and working conditions inferior. The high-paying jobs in wealth-creating industries went somewhere else. Family incomes fell generally and standards of living deteriorated even as the recovery continued.

In brief, the supply-side miracle failed to materialize, but the administrations appeared oblivious to the economic conditions that were slowly becoming evident to all. Their indifference to the growing problems was deplorable, but they seemed content to relegate them to the next generation of policy makers. It would not do to upset the Reagan record, nor take any of the shine out of his lustre. In an administration devoted to public relations, what else would be expected? So they hailed the tenuous recovery and chanted the wonders of the free market. They either just did not care to acknowledge any unpleasant information or their capacity for self-deception was remarkable; the former would be unprincipled and the latter pathetic.

These highlights of the Reagan record were not intended as a complete summary but meant only to pull together some of the main elements of the economic plan to review promises with results. A similar review of the legacy of the Reagan administrations and the likely repercussions on future generations is in order before attempting any final assessments.

THE REAGAN LEGACY

Administrations come and go, some leaving an indelible mark on the nation, and others barely making a scratch. The Reagan administrations' legacy will last far beyond his tenure in office. Not because he created a revolution and fundamentally altered the structure and functioning of the economy, as his supporters expected, but because he left the economy in shambles. In the wake of the Reagan administrations, the record shows a few modest successes and a string of failures, failures that others would have to remedy. In the end, it is not a proud legacy but a disenchanting one for loyal followers and a frustrating one for critics.

In summary form, here are the *main* elements that justify that conclusion. The details can be found in Chapters 9–14.

1. Macroeconomic policy making has been paralyzed. An active fiscal policy has been disregarded due variously to the huge budget deficits, budget gridlock, and the paucity of ideas in Washington. The Reagan and Bush administrations have been unable to reconcile the public's desire for new or improved government programs with their ideological views, and the result was a policy of inaction—better to do nothing at all, even when, as in the 1990–91 recession, some action could have been justified. On the taxation side, the nation is now subject to taxophobia. Increases in taxes are anathema; decreases are normal. For a nation to sacrifice its fiscal policies, its ability to influence the economy, is to surrender helplessly to the vagaries of economic fluctuations.

Monetary policy, expected to take up the slack, is also not in any condition to do the job of stabilization. The banking system was left in disarray at the end of the Reagan administrations, and the Bush administration was left with the cleanup job at enormous cost. With the twin deficits, monetary policy was also constrained by the prospect of capital flight when interest rates fell below those elsewhere, and the loss of domestic real investment when they rose too high. Moreover, the huge debt overhang from the 1980s made monetary policy ineffective anyway, for no matter how low interest rates were driven, no one wanted to borrow anyway.

So both monetary and fiscal policies were made inefficient or ineffective by actions taken or not taken in the 1980s. This is quite a legacy to leave to combat the first recession to follow in the 1990s. The economy was allowed to drift and stagnate because ready solutions were either absent or rejected.

2. The problems of functioning in a global economy remained. Balance of payments problems were only symptomatic of many underlying structural con-

ditions. U.S. industries lost in the global economy as recognition of the problem in this area was not forthcoming and as little was done to correct the trends. Industrial policies were ignored (and derided) in the United States because reliance on the free market was the hallmark of the Reagan/Bush administrations. Our competitors had no such ideological blinders, and the results were predictable: the loss of our manufacturing base along with the primary jobs in it. Along with the lost jobs went the power of organized labor, and the ability of labor to protect itself from abuses and exploitation.

Deindustrialization proceeded even as the nation was involved in shifting paper around in the game of paper entrepreneurialism. The merger and acquisition movement wrecked many firms, cost jobs, and accomplished little except to divert attention away from the making of goods to the making of money. The structure of the economy and the degree of concentration were changed by the shifting of economic activity from manufacturing to services in a move that will have repercussions for many years to come.

3. Finally, the American dream, so identified with the narcotic years of Ronald Reagan, has been shattered. Living standards deteriorated, and the hope of doing better than the previous generations evaporated, leaving a confused and disturbed public. It is not the type of mood that the nation needs to compete in the global economy being formulated. It is one of silent despair, not the optimism and energy necessary to meet whatever challenges emerge in the future.

Finally, there is the issue of fairness. The Reagan/Bush policies were viewed as helping those who did not need help and neglecting those who did. One result is that the nation was polarized in various ways: haves against the have-nots, blacks and minorities versus whites, and generation versus generation to name a few. Those who got left behind in the go-go years of the eighties are not going to disappear but will be around to haunt our social policies for years. The lack of innovation in social matters and the lack of ideas fostered by years of blaming the victim will disturb the domestic tranquillity until the problems are faced.

This legacy has already affected the Bush administration as it failed to respond to the recession of 1990–91, failed to seriously address social problems in areas of education, health, and crime, and failed to recognize the malaise of the population longing for some semblance of hope that the next century will find the next generation with better prospects.

Whether some elements of this legacy can or will be reversed is problematic. Only time will reveal how much is permanent and how much temporary, how much is salvageable and how much is irreversible.

FINAL ASSESSMENT

There was no Reagan revolution except in the eyes of some die-hard true believers with a marvelous capacity for self-deception, a familiar trait in the

Reagan administrations. Some, no doubt, were more cynical or had other motives for joining in the chorus, but essentially what developed was a small group of arrogant people who managed to push a social experiment onto the nation. Despite sufficient warnings that the economic program was contradictory and inconsistent, they forged ahead, promising too much, too soon, and too painlessly.

All politicians promise more than they can deliver, but they usually leave some room for maneuver when the results come in. In the Reagan case, the economic program was so well defined, so clearly set out, that the promises took on a different perspective from the normal. So disdainful of existing economic thought were the Reagan planners that they confidently predicted economic outcomes and haughtily ignored any adverse criticisms. The trouble is they knew the pieces of their economic program did not fit together, yet they cynically went ahead anyway. Thus, the program was basically fraudulent.

Social experimentation is often a useful exercise to revitalize a community. Social experimentation that is known to be flawed at the outset is unscrupulous and unconscionable, the more so when the effects last over many generations. The economic program was bound to fail, and as shown in this book, it not only failed, but whatever successes were achieved came about despite the economic policies rather than because of them. It did not fail because of Congress, or because of any other factor or institution other than its own internal contradictions. Blaming others simply will not suffice and will not stand as an explanation for the lack of success.

The dreadful legacy just outlined is evidence enough that the Reagan administrations not only failed to solve contemporaneous problems and may have made them worse but also managed to pass on a number of problems for future generations to solve without the necessary tools or attitudes to solve them.

With hindsight, we can observe that the effects were not long in becoming manifest. Reagan left office just in time, as the economy was already slowing down. Soon a significant recession and a period of economic stagnation would follow. The policy paralysis also was soon apparent as the Bush administration failed to address this economic stagnation, preferring to let the economy drift and somehow recover without help. Clearly, the obsession with free-market nostrums, expounded by Reagan and adopted by Bush, resulted in the do-nothing philosophy and eventually revealed the bankruptcy of the conservative ideology. Mr. Bush lost the election of 1992 to proponents of change. The American public was no longer willing to settle for rhetoric over action, for ideology over reality.

To conclude, the economic program of the Reagan years failed. It failed conservative tests, failed liberal tests, failed to achieve the goals it set for itself, and failed the American public that invested such hope and trust in it. In its failure, it left the economy with many more serious problems to solve than might have been the case if this unwarranted and deceptive program had not been adopted. Those who steadfastly maintain that the Reagan economic policies were a success had better ponder how the nation would ever deal with a failure.

NOTES

1. James Tobin, "Reaganomics in Retrospect," in *The Reagan Revolution,* eds. B. B. Kymlicka and Jean V. Matthews (Chicago: The Dorsey Press, 1988), 103.

2. I am not an economic conservative and do not want to appear to speak for them. The interested reader should consult their opinions directly. A good place to start is with David Boaz, ed., *Assessing the Reagan Years* (Washington, DC: Cato Institute, 1988); and *Reaganomics and After* (London: Institute of Economic Affairs, 1989).

Select Bibliography

Aaron, Henry J., and Joseph A. Pechman, eds. *How Taxes Affect Economic Behavior.* Washington, DC: The Brookings Institution, 1981.

Ackerman, Frank. *Reaganomics.* Boston: South End Press, 1982.

Anderson, Martin. *Revolution.* New York: Harcourt Brace Jovanovich, 1988.

Auerbach, Alan J., ed. *Mergers and Acquisitions.* Chicago: University of Chicago Press, 1988.

Blinder, Alan S. *Economic Policy and the Great Stagflation.* New York: Academic Press, 1979.

Bluestone, Barry, and Bennett Harrison. *The Deindustrialization of America.* New York: Basic Books, 1982.

————. *The Great U-Turn.* New York: Basic Books, 1988.

Boaz, David. *Assessing the Reagan Years.* Washington, DC: Cato Institute, 1988.

Boskin, Michael J. *Reagan and the Economy.* San Francisco: Institute for Contemporary Studies, 1987.

Buchanan, James M. "Post-Reagan Political Economy." In *Reaganomics and After.* London: Institute of Public Affairs, 1989.

Burtless, Gary, ed. *A Future of Lousy Jobs?: The Changing Structure of U.S. Wages.* Washington, DC: The Brookings Institution, 1990.

Cain, Glen G., and Harold W. Watts. *Income Maintenance and Labor Supply.* New York: Academic Press, 1973.

Campagna, Anthony S. *U.S. National Economic Policy, 1917–1985.* New York: Praeger, 1987.

————. *The Economic Consequences of the Vietnam War.* New York: Praeger, 1991.

Cannon, Lou. *Reagan.* New York: G. P. Putnam's Sons, 1982.

————. *President Reagan: The Role of a Lifetime.* New York: Simon and Schuster, 1991.

Canto, Victor A., Douglas H. Joines, and Arthur B. Laffer. *Foundations of Supply-Side Economics.* New York: Academic Press, 1983.

Carvounis, Chris C. *The United States Trade Deficit of the 1980s: Origins, Meanings, and Policy Responses.* Westport, CT: Greenwood Press, 1987.

Congressional Budget Office. *An Analysis of the Roth-Kemp Tax Cut Proposal.* Washington, DC: Government Printing Office, 1978.

————. *How Changes in Fiscal Policy Affect the Budget: The Feedback Issue.* Washington, DC: Government Printing Office, 1982.

————. *The Changing Distribution of Federal Taxes: 1975–1990.* Washington, DC: Government Printing Office, 1987.

DeFina, Robert, and Murray Weidenbaum. *The Taxpayer and Government Regulation*. St. Louis, MO: Center for the Study of American Business, Washington University, 1978.

Dionne, E. J., Jr. *Why Americans Hate Politics*. New York: Simon and Schuster, 1991.

Eads, George C., and Michael Fix, eds. *The Reagan Regulatory Strategy*. Washington DC: The Urban Institute Press, 1984.

Eisner, Robert. *How Real is the Federal Deficit*. New York: Free Press, 1986.

Feldstein, Martin, ed. *Behavioral Simulation Methods in Tax Policy Analysis*. Chicago: University of Chicago Press, 1983.

Friedman, Benjamin M. *Day of Reckoning*. New York: Random House, 1988.

Gerston, Larry N., Cynthia Fraleigh, and Robert Schwab. *The Deregulated Society*. Pacific Grove, CA.: Brooks/Cole, 1988.

Gilder, George. *Wealth and Poverty*. New York: Basic Books, 1981.

Goodman, Marshall R., and Margaret T. Wrightson. *Managing Regulatory Reform: The Reagan Strategy and Its Impact*. New York: Praeger, 1987.

Greider, William. *Secrets of the Temple*. New York: Touchstone, 1987.

Harberger, Arnold C., and Martin Bailey, eds. *The Taxation of Income from Capital*. Washington, DC: The Brookings Institution, 1969.

Heilbroner, Robert, and Peter Berstein. *The Debt and the Deficit*. New York: W. W. Norton, 1989.

Hibbs, Douglas A. *The American Political Economy: Macroeconomics and Electoral Politics*. Cambridge, MA: Harvard University Press, 1987.

Hulten, Charles R., and Isabel V. Sawhill. *The Legacy of Reagonomics*. Washington DC: The Urban Institute Press, 1984.

Johnson, Haynes. *Sleepwalking Through History*. New York: W. W. Norton, 1991.

Jones, Charles O., ed. *The Reagan Legacy*. Chatham, NJ: Chatham House Publishers, 1988.

Karoly, Lynn A. *The Trend in Inequality Among Families, Individuals, and Workers in the United States: A Twenty-Five-Year Perspective*. Santa Monica, CA: The Rand Corporation, 1992.

Krugman, Paul R. *Has the Adjustment Process Worked?* Washington, DC: Institute for International Economics, 1991.

Kymlicka, B. B., and Jean V. Mathews, eds. *The Reagan Revolution*. Chicago: The Dorsey Press, 1988.

Lekachman, Robert. *Greed is not Enough*. New York: Pantheon, 1982.

———. *Visions and Nightmares: America after Reagan*. New York: Macmillan, 1987.

Lindsey, Lawrence. *The Growth Experiment*. New York: Basic Books, 1990.

Litan, Robert E., and William D. Nordhaus. *Reforming Federal Regulation*. New Haven, CT: Yale University Press, 1983.

Lowy, Martin. *High Rollers: Inside the Savings and Loan Debacle*. New York: Praeger, 1991.

Marris, Stephen. *Deficits and the Dollar: The World Economy at Risk*. Washington, DC: Institute for International Economics, 1985.

Meiners, Roger E., and Bruce Yandle. *Regulation and the Reagan Era*. New York: Holmes and Meier, 1989.

Niskanen, William A. *Reaganomics*. New York: Oxford University Press, 1988.

———. "Reaganomics: A Balanced Assessment." In *Reaganomics and After*. London: Institute of Public Affairs, 1989.

Noll, Roger G., and Bruce M. Owen. *The Political Economy of Deregulation: Interest Groups in the Regulatory Process:* Washington, DC: American Enterprise Institute, 1983.

Okun, Arthur M. *The Political Economy of Prosperity.* New York: W. W. Norton, 1970.

O'Neill, Tip. *Man of the House.* New York: St. Martin's Press, 1987.

Palmer, John L., and Isabel V. Sawhill, eds. *The Reagan Experiment.* Washington, DC: The Urban Institute Press, 1982.

———. *The Reagan Record.* Cambridge, MA: Ballinger, 1984.

Phillips, Kevin. *The Politics of Rich and Poor.* New York: Random House, 1990.

Pizzo, Stephen, Mary Fricker, and Paul Muolo. *Inside Job.* New York: McGraw-Hill, 1989.

Ravenscraft, David J., and F. M. Scherer. *Mergers and Economic Efficiency.* Washington, DC: The Brookings Institution, 1987.

Reagan, Ronald. *An American Life.* New York: Simon and Schuster, 1990.

Regan, Donald T. *For the Record.* New York: Harcourt Brace Jovanovich, 1988.

Reich, Robert B. *The Work of Nations: Preparing Ourselves for the 21st Century Capitalism.* New York: Alfred A. Knopf, 1991.

Reichley, A. James. *Conservatives of Change: The Nixon and Ford Administrations.* Washington, DC: The Brookings Institution, 1981.

Roberts, Paul Craig. *The Supply Side Revolution.* Cambridge, MA: Harvard University Press, 1984.

Sahu, Anandi P., and Ronald L. Tracy. *The Economic Legacy of the Reagan Years.* New York: Praeger, 1991.

Sprague, Irvine H. *Bailout: An Insider's Account of Bank Failure and Rescues.* New York: Basic Books, 1986.

Stein, Herbert. *Presidential Economics.* New York: Simon and Schuster, 1984.

Stockman, David A. *The Triumph of Politics.* New York: Harper & Row, 1986.

Stone, Charles F., and Isabel V. Sawhill. *Economic Policy in the Reagan Years.* Washington, DC: The Urban Institute Press, 1984.

Tolchin, Susan J., and Martin Tolchin. *Dismantling America: The Rush to Deregulate.* New York: Oxford University Press, 1983.

U.S. Congress. Joint Economic Committee. *Corporate Time Horizons,* 101st Cong., 1st sess., 1989.

———. House. Committee on Energy and Commerce. *Leveraged Buyouts and the Pot of Gold: Trends, Public Policy and Case Studies,* 100th Cong., 1st sess., 1987.

———. House. Committee on Government Operations. *Impact on Workers of Takeovers, Leveraged Buyouts, Corporate Restructuring, and Greenmail.* 100th Cong., 1st sess., 1987.

U.S. Bureau of the Census. Trends in relative income: 1963 to 1989. *Current population reports,* ser. P-60, no. 177, Washington DC, December 1991.

———. Measuring the Effect of Benefits and Taxes on Income and Poverty: 1989. *Current population reports,* ser. P-60, no. 169-RD, Washington, DC, 1990.

———. Household Wealth and Asset Ownership: 1988. *Current population reports,* ser. P-70, no. 22. Prepared by Judith Eargle. 1990.

Wanniski, Jude. *The Way the World Works.* New York: Simon & Schuster, 1978.

Weidenbaum, Murray. *Rendezvous with Reality.* New York: Basic Books, 1988.

White, Lawrence J. *The S&L Debacle: Public Policy Lessons for Bank and Thrift Regulation.* New York: Oxford University Press, 1991.

Index

About the Author

ANTHONY S. CAMPAGNA is Professor of Economics at the University of Vermont. His interests include macroeconomic theory and policy. He is the author of five books and is presently planning and researching a book on the Carter administration.